The Ontology of Death

Also Available from Bloomsbury

Another Finitude: Messianic Vitalism and Philosophy, Agata Bielik-Robson
Heidegger and the Emergence of the Question of Being, Jesús Adrián Escudero, trans. Juan Pablo Hernandez Betancur
Epicurus and the Singularity of Death: Defending Radical Epicureanism, David B. Suits
Vibrant Death: A Posthuman Phenomenology of Mourning, Nina Lykke
The Ethical Imagination in Shakespeare and Heidegger, Andy Amato

The Ontology of Death

The Philosophy of the Death Penalty in Literature

Aaron Aquilina

BLOOMSBURY ACADEMIC
LONDON • NEW YORK • OXFORD • NEW DELHI • SYDNEY

BLOOMSBURY ACADEMIC
Bloomsbury Publishing Plc
50 Bedford Square, London, WC1B 3DP, UK
1385 Broadway, New York, NY 10018, USA
29 Earlsfort Terrace, Dublin 2, Ireland

BLOOMSBURY, BLOOMSBURY ACADEMIC and the Diana logo are trademarks of Bloomsbury Publishing Plc

First published in Great Britain 2023
This paperback edition published in 2024

Copyright © Aaron Aquilina, 2023

Aaron Aquilina has asserted his right under the Copyright, Designs and Patents Act, 1988, to be identified as Author of this work.

For legal purposes the Acknowledgements on p. ix constitute an extension of this copyright page.

Series design by Charlotte Daniels
Cover image: *The Dance of Death*. Artist: Anonymous, German, 16th century; Date: 16th century; Medium: Pen and brown ink, brush and brown ink, watercolor, gouache.
(© agefotostock / Alamy Stock Photo)

All rights reserved. No part of this publication may be reproduced or transmitted in any form or by any means, electronic or mechanical, including photocopying, recording, or any information storage or retrieval system, without prior permission in writing from the publishers.

Bloomsbury Publishing Plc does not have any control over, or responsibility for, any third-party websites referred to or in this book. All internet addresses given in this book were correct at the time of going to press. The author and publisher regret any inconvenience caused if addresses have changed or sites have ceased to exist, but can accept no responsibility for any such changes.

A catalogue record for this book is available from the British Library.

A catalog record for this book is available from the Library of Congress.

Library of Congress Control Number: 2023937586.

ISBN: HB: 978-1-3503-3948-4
PB: 978-1-3503-3952-1
ePDF: 978-1-3503-3949-1
eBook: 978-1-3503-3950-7

Typeset by Deanta Global Publishing Services, Chennai, India

To find out more about our authors and books visit www.bloomsbury.com and sign up for our newsletters.

For John, who survives with me.

Contents

Preface	viii
Acknowledgements	ix
List of Abbreviations	xi
Introduction: Literature, questions, death	1
Dead politics	3
Literature's sword	10
1 *The Instant of My Death*	19
2 Death penalties	37
Horses	37
For whom the bell tolls	38
The impossibility of my death	48
3 Missing death	63
Station: Limbo	63
Living corpses	66
Acknowledgement *contra* recognition	80
4 After death, anonymity	95
Angels and demons	95
The unbecoming subject	97
The human thing	110
5 The death of no one	125
Who? What?	125
Anonymous voices	126
Sovereign (without) subjects	136
Conclusion: The death of me	151
Notes	159
Bibliography	201
Index	218

Preface

This book examines several literary works of fiction that present us with a protagonist condemned to death. The implicit question that runs throughout this project may be phrased as follows: Why would such a varied group of authors, from Sophocles to Blanchot, from Dickens to Nabokov, among others, be concerned with what is seemingly such a niche corner of human experience? The exceptional situation of these condemned individuals is made more complex in light of the fact that these same narratives offer their protagonists an escape – through the action of an Other – from the sovereign decision that decrees their demise. With such an interruption of the death penalty, we have before us, then, the problematic concept of the dead man walking... away from their own death.

Here, these narratives are read as shedding new light on the death penalty in two key ways. Through their universalization of the experience of condemnation, the reader is led to comprehend the death penalty as the very foundation of political society and human existence, and so even we who live on outside of death row are nonetheless fundamentally implicated within the fatal and multifaceted matrices of the penalty. Second, in subverting the supposed certainty of death through the protagonists' survival of their own sentence, these narratives gesture beyond the sovereign–subject relation and lead us to conceive the human subject otherwise, both on ontological and political grounds.

To carry out this reading, this book takes on a particularly anti-Heideggerian examination of that instant when 'death' and 'self' collide and contests the idea that 'my death' is an irreplaceable possession, thus condemning to death Heideggerian 'Being-towards-death'. In a sustained engagement with Blanchot's thought, which also encompasses the work of Hegel, Levinas, Derrida and Agamben, this work concludes by re-evaluating the human, less as a named and recognizable 'being' than as an anonymous living corpse or 'thing', residing beyond names and concepts.

Acknowledgements

From the moment I began writing this book in October 2015, I have found myself lucky enough to be the recipient of exceptionally kind and generous support. I would first like to thank the Faculty of Arts and Social Science, at Lancaster University, who fully funded the version of this project that was my doctoral thesis. Without their financial aid, I would not even have been able to begin this work. At the same time, I must thank all the staff of the Department of English and Creative Writing at Lancaster who have helped me along the way – special gratitude must be expressed to Dr Michael Greaney (for his enthusiastic reading), Prof. Mark Knight (for his solid guidance) and Prof. John Schad (for the many meandering conversations). Of course, my PhD supervisor, Prof. Arthur Bradley, has been the cornerstone of the development of this book; without his constant interest, vital advice, understanding and humour, this would have been a much poorer work. I cannot overstate my debt to him for his support of my ideas – both when I was a student researcher and subsequently.

I would also wish to thank Professor Alison Stone (for her openness), and especially Professor Laurence Hemming (for his friendship), from Lancaster's Department of Politics, Philosophy and Religion, and both for their thought-provoking conversations. Similarly, all the staff members at the University of Malta are thanked here – who instilled in me an unwavering love of literature, a passion for rigorous research and a joy in forging my own readings, even when erroneous – especially Dr Mario Aquilina (for his unwavering belief in me), Professor Ivan Callus (for the steady inspiration), Professor James Corby (for the company in battle) and Dr Omar N'Shea (for all the coffees shared about the Ancient Near East).

Thanks are also due to Bloomsbury Academic and its editors for their guidance throughout the process. Furthermore, I would like to thank Faber & Faber Ltd for their permission to quote Seamus Heaney, and W. W. Norton for their permission to quote Charles Martin's translation of *Metamorphosis*.

No work is ever purely academic – hidden in this book, visible only to me, are multiple instances where I incorporate the love and laughs shared with my family and friends in Malta, the UK and the US. I write this book for them, even if this comes across to them only as a strange, undecipherable and quite unasked-for gift. And that includes Fílos, the 'dog', who has patiently watched me work on this book this past year. To my mother and my aunt, who make their lives harder so that mine may be easier: thank you.

Last but not least, I am grateful for my partner AJHM, whose endless love, encouragement and belief in my capacities hold me steady.

Abbreviations

The following works are cited with these abbreviations in text and endnotes.

A	'Antigone', Sophocles	
AP	*Aporias*, Jacques Derrida	
BSI	*The Beast and the Sovereign, Volume 1*, Jacques Derrida	
BSII	*The Beast and the Sovereign, Volume 2*, Jacques Derrida	
BT	*Being and Time*, Martin Heidegger	
D	*Demeure: Fiction and Testimony*, Jacques Derrida	
DPI	*The Death Penalty, Volume 1*, Jacques Derrida	
DPII	*The Death Penalty, Volume 2*, Jacques Derrida	
EE	*Existence and Existents*, Emmanuel Levinas	
GD	*The Gift of Death*, Jacques Derrida	
HS	*Homo Sacer: Sovereign Power and Bare Life*, Giorgio Agamben	
IB	*Invitation to a Beheading*, Vladimir Nabokov	
ID	*The Instant of My Death*, Maurice Blanchot	
LD	*The Last Day of a Condemned Man*, Victor Hugo	
LPS	*Introduction to the Reading of Hegel: Lectures on the Phenomenology of Spirit*, Alexandre Kojève	
LRD	'Literature and the Right to Death', Maurice Blanchot	
PS	*Phenomenology of Spirit*, Georg Wilhelm Friedrich Hegel	
TC	*A Tale of Two Cities*, Charles Dickens	
TI	*The Idiot*, Fyodor Dostoevsky	
TM	*The Tenth Man*, Graham Greene	
TW	'The Wall', Jean-Paul Sartre	

Introduction
Literature, questions, death

In the history of the ancient Near East, from as early as the Isin-Larsa period up until around the time of Alexander the Great, its influential cultures manifested an odd practice that has since come to be called the ritual of the substitute king.[1]

An eclipse, likely in conjunction with other omens, heralds calamities that only the death of the king will appease. At this point, fearing for his life, the king and his counsellors call for the enthronement of an appointed substitute (*šar pūḫi*) who is to die in his stead. The surrogate, often a commoner (*saklu*) or even a prisoner or criminal (*dābibu*), is now clad in robes and diadem, and, subsequently, there are enacted specific traditions in front of the god Šamaš – including recitations, sign-making, ceremonial eating, burnt offerings, libations and ablutions – which prepare this substitute king for his fated death (referred to as *ana šimtīšu*). Once killed, the surrogate's corpse is washed with litanies, psalms and wailing, and, after his honoured burial, there are performed exorcistic rites and the consequent burning of the original king's regalia, insignias, furniture and other possessions.

Throughout the reign of this substitute, whose duration as monarch differed depending on the circumstances but never lasted more than a hundred days, the man who used to be king completely withdraws from all royal engagements and hides in the palace. His abstention is, however, only public; the original king retains the power of governance, and, after the substitute king's death, he is quickly reinstated. Šamaš is appeased – a king has died, after all – and, as always, life will go on after death.

Through this opening example of the substitute king, this book acknowledges a complex and long-standing interrelation of death and politics, one which finds itself reconfigured across times and cultures in a myriad of forms. Here, even religious beliefs, at least in their social performance, are subsumed under the exhaustive dynamics of power, for while the ritual is indeed indebted to religious reasons for its (surprisingly not so rare) enactment, it nonetheless remains undeniably political at core. As Jean Bottéro sees it, the substitute's office was to 'serve as a lightning rod [. . .] in order *to take upon himself* [. . .] the evil fate that threatened his master', and what emerges as being of utmost importance is not the appeasement of the gods but rather the facilitation of the sovereign's survival.[2] The ritual's spiritual aspects, therefore, find their mediation through the political control and regulation of death – one that extends, even, to its *exchange*. As a whole, in fact, what this project aims to consider are the dynamics of this latter problematic: that is, of how and why one may exchange one's death with an Other's, what this reveals of the borders of life and how this reconfigures what one may understand by that perennially ambiguous syntagm, the 'human being'.

Such a discussion implicates vast questions and territories that are perhaps unexplorable, seeing as how death is often considered as what lies strictly at or beyond the limits of our knowledge. More so than cultural, historical or even religious concerns, this idea of dying 'in-stead' (instead of, in someone's stead) also raises wide and disconcerting philosophical questions. What is our *relation* to death – our own or someone else's – assuming there can be such a thing? How does politics, or more specifically sovereignty, affect this relation? What are the significations of the death sentence, when one is *made to die* just like the substitute? Can death be given and thus taken, and what might that possibility even signify? Ultimately, could death be thus understood as a potential horizon that undoes not only the subject but perhaps the category of subjectivity itself? After all, philosophical accounts of the mortal subject often serve only to fortify or concretize the subject rather than disperse it.[3]

There are still more questions since, in the possibilities of death's exchange, one inversely finds also the counter-intuitive complexities of the continuation of life when death is no longer in the future: that is, when death is somehow in the now or even in one's past. What happens – on phenomenological, existential and ontological grounds – when one, like the king, survives 'their own death'?

As such, in the first section of this introduction, what shall be addressed in the manner of scene-setting are some aspects of this relation between death and sovereign politics, and the positioning of death within, or without, the political sphere. It will be noted how death can be utilized in the grips of politics to control life, but also always elsewhere, beyond our grasp. From this, the second section of this introduction shall turn to these dynamics as they might appear in literature, where, it shall be intimated, literary works both mirror and challenge the multifarious implications of this politically anomalous death.

Yet how does literature represent this dangerous game of finalities? And why even turn to literature at all? It would be unwise to state that literature and the politics of death have some unique and unshakeable communion, but it might not be too grandiloquent to claim that death may place the very idea of literature into question, or, vice versa, that literature questions death. One might, in good humour, point out that it is after all these same Sumerians of lower Mesopotamia, the practitioners of mortality's exchange, who also invented writing.[4]

Dead politics

In an act of complete power, the late-Assyrian king appoints a substitute to die in his place. Let us, for a moment, take a step back and try and ascertain what the role of sovereignty signifies in this context.

As made clear in Achille Mbembe's influential essay 'Necropolitics' – which builds upon the seminal thoughts of Frantz Fanon, Carl Schmitt, Michel Foucault and Giorgio Agamben – this kingly act of choosing who is to live or die, 'who is *disposable* and who is not', translates to 'the ultimate expression of sovereignty'.[5] While sovereignty as 'absolute kingship' might at first seem to us an anachronistic concept, Mbembe turns to the present manifestations of power in (post-)colonial occupations and beyond to challenge the late-modern 'normative reading of the politics of sovereignty': that is, how diverse institutions paradoxically posit the subject as a fully autonomous agent while at the same time demanding collective agreement throughout society.[6] Effectively, what Mbembe underscores is the continuous reassertion of sovereign power, throughout history as well as in our own time, through the constant transgression of its own prohibition against killing.

Through this point, we are able to draw the first few lines between the ancient Near Eastern context and that of contemporary occupations and warfare – such as the insidious domination of Palestine, the assaults on Ukraine, the militarization of borders, or the 'war on terror' – in recognizing how sovereignty can to a great degree be trans-temporally and trans-culturally defined as that which decides the state of exception.[7] Wherever there is the choice of who lives or dies, wherever there lingers the spectre of punishment or retribution, there is also the figure of the sovereign – and this choice, this spectre, is alive and well. Perhaps Bottéro's opinion that 'the procedure of substitution [. . .] betrays [. . .] a sensibility that [is] diametrically opposed to ours' is not entirely accurate, and one can begin to understand that the absolute political power of the sovereign is not simply a thing of the past.[8] As Mbembe makes clear, the intertwining history of death and politics recalls not only medieval heads on spikes or the French Revolution but also gas chambers, slave plantations and contemporary terrorism. The state of exception, therefore, wherein life finds itself subjugated to death, still finds effect globally and contemporarily. This is why it is with Mbembe's argument, here, that we begin to traverse our initial questions, still in the process of being formed; his thought threads the past with our present through the constant kernel of violence and suffering (the manifestations of sovereign tyranny) and shall continue to influence this study more generally, if only at times implicitly, by leading us to the thought of Heidegger and Hegel, to an understanding of the living dead, of how 'human' may become 'thing', and, ultimately, towards a means of reading death and politics otherwise. From a more specific angle, Mbembe's essay is written in response to Foucault's idea that biopolitics – which can summarily be defined as the 'numerous and diverse techniques for achieving the subjugations of bodies and the control of population' – has long since emerged from and transformed the dynamics of sovereignty.[9] On the nature of said sovereignty, at least, Mbembe and Foucault seem to be in accordance. In his 1976 lectures, 'Society Must Be Defended', Foucault describes how '[s]overeign power's effect on life is exercised only when the sovereign can kill',[10] which he locates (in 'Right of Death and Power over Life', published that same year) as originating from the ancient Roman *patria potestas* – and, as we have already seen, this particular form of power can be traced much further back, too.[11] Consequently, the 'very essence of the right of life and death is actually the right to kill: it is at the moment when the sovereign can kill that he exercises his right over life', and in the political sphere, then, 'there is no real symmetry in the right over life and death'.[12] In effect, Foucault ponders the troublesome idea that, while there is a death penalty, there can be no such thing as a life penalty. Death is the power of the sovereign, and it is in this way that Mbembe describes necropolitics to be the 'subjugation of life to the power of death'.[13] Dead politics, as the above subheading suggests, is not where politics is dead, but rather where politics lives on and works through death and the dead.

On the other hand, it might well be a distortion of emphasis to talk of the politics of death as if it overshadows the politics of life. After all, Foucault would suggest that death is what is negated through biopolitics, which rests not on classical sovereignty but biopower, a life-power and power-over-life which he somewhat ambiguously demarcates as emerging around the time of the French Revolution and more overtly through the agricultural revolution. If the symbol of sovereignty's power 'was the sword', as Foucault asserts, it has contemporarily been transformed into the needle or vaccine: 'a power that exerts a positive influence on life, that endeavors to administer, optimize, and multiply it, subjecting it to precise controls and comprehensive regulations'.[14] From the advent of biohistory, the *droit de glaive* is blunted; or, rather, the sword is no longer wielded as a threat but exhibited as an implement of defence. Life is its own ultimate value, life above all, even above death; the sovereign's right to 'take life or let live' is not exactly undone, writes Foucault, but rather supplemented by the biopolitical right to 'make live and to let die'.[15] Biopolitics, then, takes over from sovereignty and treats subjects not as individuals that may be killed but as a population to be managed, regulated and normalized ('a sort of homeostasis', Foucault explains), where death – that which should be avoided at all cost – recedes either into taboo or simply into what the enemy must face if the state is to survive.[16] The sword no longer calls for the blood of its subjects but for that of the other.

We emerged into biohistory, Foucault contends, to escape the tyranny of death manifested as wars or epidemics – and already, in the irony of this, we can see why Mbembe re-politicizes Foucault's views.[17] We desired the management of our lives for the sake of our protection and at the cost of the enemy's lives; ultimately, '[i]t is in order to live that [we subjects] constitute a sovereign'.[18] As we have seen, however, Mbembe questions whether the notion of biopower is 'sufficient to account for the contemporary [sovereign] ways in which the political, under the guise of war, of resistance, or of the fight against terror, makes the murder of the enemy its primary and absolute objective'.[19] Here is a clear and more practical echo of Agamben's thoughts on the persistence of sovereignty, who underscores how '*the production of a biopolitical body is the original activity of sovereign power*', and thus biopolitics marks neither the disappearance nor transformative nullification of sovereignty (*HS*, 6).

Mbembe's point on the construction of alterity as enmity consciously recalls, too, Schmitt's understanding of sovereignty. According to Schmitt, classical sovereignty has, in modern times, receded into secularized institutionalization and a liberal pluralism apparently devoid of the figure of the sovereign, where its 'technological progress has no need for individual persons'.[20] However, even this neutral and technological ground of liberal democracy, Schmitt admits, quickly and continually re-becomes 'an arena of struggle', one where 'friend-enemy groupings' are decided through the power of the political;[21] as such, if the sovereign can be summed up as 'the action of "us" against "them" – friends versus enemies', as Tracy B. Strong writes, then we have not changed as much as we would like to think we have.[22] This Hobbesian (and to a degree Hegelian) characterization of the contemporary milieu is what, for Schmitt, defines politics (as opposed, for instance, to economics, where one does not have enemies but only competitors), which is always, in the words of George Schwab, 'governed by the ever-present possibility of conflict' – and thus the haunting figure of the sovereign, never dead.[23]

Monarchical rule has indeed been dissipated in the modern age by 'the [democratic] division of power' – that is, 'the notion that power must be checked by power', an idea quite at home in Foucault's sketch of the biopolitical episteme; however, and through Schmitt, one can nonetheless read the 'indivisible' power of the sword that persists through the historical development of the political, for the exception never ceases to come.[24] If 'the state's *raison d'être* [is] to maintain its integrity in order to ensure order and stability' (the homeostasis of biopower), there remains today the constant creation and deployment of dichotomies (us/them, friend/enemy), breaking through liberalist procedures and calling for the 'resolute action [. . .] necessary to combat threats'.[25]

This decisive action – deciding, in times of crisis or siege, what the exception is and what to do about it – is constituted by (and in turn constitutes) the aspect of sovereignty still present in the contemporary 'life-affirming' political state. Quite simply, then, sovereignty emerges as the exercise of 'the monopoly to decide'[26], and its violence amounts to an 'arbitrariness that accomplishes its own work and validates itself through its own sovereignty, and thereby permits power to be exercised as a right to kill'.[27] The biopolitical 'legal order', as the writings of Schmitt, Agamben and Mbembe evidence, can only be defined against the ever-present anarchical or chaotic threat of enmity and emergency, and death is thus the irreplaceable currency that allows the state to afford life.

As Mbembe goes on to argue, when sovereignty is read as '*the generalized instrumentalization of human existence and the material destruction of human bodies and populations*', then '[s]uch figures of sovereignty [. . .] are what constitute the *nomos* of the political space in which we still live'.[28] In short, while Foucault observes the gradual appearance of life displacing death in the political, Mbembe reveals the latter still at the centre.

For Foucault, death 'is outside the power relationship' and the contemporary state 'has no control over death, [even if] it can control mortality'; biopolitics, therefore, 'literally ignores' and 'no longer recognizes death'.[29] For Mbembe, on the other hand, '[p]olitics is death that lives a human life', where death does not recede into the background but, rather, is that through which 'power [. . .] continually refers and appeals to exception, emergency, and a fictionalized notion of the enemy' in order to function; this function is 'the work of death'.[30] As he states, this is perhaps most evident in war, as understood on the basis of Schmitt's state of siege. Indeed, war is not where the state's biopower is exercised in order to prolong the life of its citizens but is 'as much a means of achieving sovereignty as a way of exercising the right to kill', a clear echo and reversal of Carl von Clausewitz's famous aphorism.³¹ We now have, then, the formulation that politics is the continuation of war, where political order can exist only through sovereignty's power to decide the state of exception, where 'the entirety of one's life' is always at risk. Thus, rather than subjects being controlled, regulated and managed by life (biopolitics), they are controlled by death (necropolitics), which Mbembe claims comes to mean, ultimately, 'conferring upon them the status of the *living dead*' – a particular and difficult turn of phrase which this book shall examine in considerable detail.³² Already, however, when coming to terms with a political order that rests solely on the power of deciding the exception, of who is living and who is living dead, the fact that the death penalty is foundational for human society begins to emerge.

The sword of sovereignty, then, is never simply defensively pointed at the enemy. For Mbembe, to be a political subject means that one's very life is already punctured by the sword, where existence is not shielded by the blade but rather always already pierced by it through and through. As Agamben explains, 'human life is included in the political order in being exposed to an unconditional capacity to be killed', and 'the absolute capacity of the subjects' bodies to be killed forms the new political body of the West' (*HS*, 85, 125).

However, the wielder of the sword, the sovereign, seems immune to its point. Georges Bataille expands on this idea:

> The sovereign is he who is, as if death were not. [. . .]. He has no more regard for the limits of identity than he does for limits of death, or rather these limits are the same; he is the transgression of all such limits.³³

And is this not exactly the decisive action of the ancient king, who plainly and easily transgresses even the limits of identity so that his fated death would, for him, simply not be? And, because of this, is not the poor substitute one of the *living dead*, living only so that he may die in-stead?

In this vein, it is also true that the sovereign joins the living dead in the continuation of his life after his own supposed death. However, surely the ancient Near Eastern king does, eventually, die his own bodily and *proper* death (in the sense of the 'correct' subject this time around, as well as in the sense of death's property and/or the property of death).³⁴ Death not only is the power of sovereignty but also takes place as its inevitable end – 'death becomes, insofar as it is the end of life, the term, the limit, or the end of power too' (much the point of Shelley's 'Ozymandias').³⁵ As such, this book also acknowledges, as does Stuart

J. Murray, the diverse possibilities in which 'death exceeds [...] the juridical logic of the exception' and how it may be 'a way to interrupt, to momentarily suspend, or to meaningfully subvert biopolitical logic through thanatopolitics'.[36]

Of biopolitics and the appearance of death, Murray writes:

> I believe we are invited to read 'biopolitics' not in Agamben's usual sense of the term but as Foucault understands it. Agamben's conception of biopolitical power draws on Schmitt, and is understood as negative: namely, the decisive power of the sovereign ban that he sees as continuous from antiquity to the present. Foucault, on the other hand, sees a shift occurring in modernity, when modern biopolitics becomes productive or enabling.[37]

Therefore, Murray's thanatopolitics – closer to Foucault's biopolitics than to Mbembe's necropolitics – retains within its field a certain productivity or enabling of the political subject (to wallow in Foucauldian language, this might be termed 'reverse productivity') to *resist*, even if through the complete unproductivity and negativity of death. This manner of resistance, interruption and suspension is crucial, and shall be returned to. Indeed, if such (reverse) discourse is even possible, exploring the thanatopolitical would enable one 'to speak in the name of death'[38] and 'to discuss the status of *death-as-such* or, more precisely, of death's life or *the life of death*'.[39] Death thus 'proliferates and remains', and, closer than we presume it to be, it 'punctuates the language of everyday life'.[40]

In the shared realm of death and politics, of the living dead and the life of death, there is a distinction to be made between 'necropolitics' and 'thanatopolitics'.[41] In most critical studies, the use of 'necropolitics' is used to open up a space of discussion where the political working of death is scrutinized on the basis of the oppression of minorities (whether economic, racial, gendered and so on), essentially following Mbembe's transposition of Foucault's work into colonized and postcolonial spaces. On the other hand, this study aims to look at the mutual interpolations of death and politics as they emerge in literature, where, as shall be seen, these are often deeply troubling of a one-sided domination of politics over death. Literature, which speaks before it is spoken to, speaks also with the voice of the dead, the very ones who should be voiceless. As Murray notes, '[t]here is, then, an ambivalent specter of death that remains inassimilable and incomprehensible within sovereignty's hermetically self-referential discourse'.[42] It is this spectre that shall be unearthed here.

Therefore, while retaining the understanding of sovereign power as that which decides the state of exception, 'thanatopolitics' shall hereon be used to signify the additional possibility of death as a response to politics outside the sovereign's absolute power, which it breaks and interrupts. It was earlier stated that dead politics is not where politics is dead but where politics *works* death, as if completely believing that 'life and death are not natural or immediate phenomena which are primal or radical, and which fall outside the field of power', but rather solely elements that can be manipulated through the political.⁴³ It would not necessarily be counter-intuitive or contradictory, then, to add that dead(-)politics – thanatopolitics – thus also signifies the ways in which death kills, or *unworks*, politics itself. Is this where there emerges, as Murray tentatively suggests, 'maybe [. . .] a postsovereign subject?'⁴⁴

The compelling idea of postsovereignty (where death has put an end to that which has always defined the political and ontological order) shall be returned to in the last chapter, necessarily hand in hand with the idea of postsubjectivity. However, given the inescapability of sovereignty, a fact compellingly underscored by Mbembe, Agamben and others, can such a concept as 'postsovereignty' be anything but an empty vision? One tentative answer to this question lies, rather unsurprisingly, back within Foucault. If the sketch of postsovereignty begins to emerge through these different politicizations of power over/from life and death, one begins to think of other, similar spaces that fall outside the onto-political order, and this is exactly what one finds already intimated by Foucault.

Indeed, Arthur Bradley, likewise reading Foucault's 'Society Must Be Defended' in *Unbearable Life*, highlights Foucault's awareness of a particular aporia: that 'sovereignty over life and death logically requires that the sovereign place the political subject in a position outside the order of the living: the subject is paradoxically neither dead nor alive until the sovereign takes the decision one way or another'.⁴⁵ Through this, Bradley identifies sovereignty's 'more originary and fundamental power to decide upon the living and the non-living, upon what *counts* as being alive and what does not', and how 'what is socially, politically, or philosophically intolerable in the eyes of the state, for whatever reason, is simply deemed to be ontologically or politically nonexistent in the first place'.⁴⁶ Such power, which Bradley terms nihilopolitical, assures the (philosophical, political and social) subject its place under the thumb of sovereignty as much as it simultaneously offers an outside of the order of sovereignty and subjecthood: the subject may exist beyond the reach of the sovereign power to kill only insofar as it is *pre*-subject, or *non*-subject, and we are returned to the life that should not exist, the paradoxical 'life of death', the dead man walking and the living dead. Sovereignty's 'dramatic and somber absolute power', Foucault writes, is one that can be exercised 'over men insofar as they are living beings'.⁴⁷ The question we are left with, then, is of who rules the living dead, and whether the condition of living death is *the* space of resistance against this rulership – a resistance characterized not by vigour or passion but rather by neutral indifference, and which has been inaccurately yet 'consistently named "life"'.[48]

In briefly comparing bio-, necro- and thanatopolitics, death's troublesome position in relation to politics becomes only more worrying. Death is, respectively, that which is ignored, that which is utilized and that which escapes and ends all power that seeks to either ignore or utilize it. These simultaneous flourishes of the sword reveal that a closer look at death's invisible and minute dynamics needs to be undertaken – one not far removed from the thinkers already discussed here or indeed from Maurice Blanchot, Jacques Derrida, Martin Heidegger, G. W. F. Hegel and Emmanuel Levinas, among others. This point of examination, however, would retain as its principal concern the potential political, existential and ontological implications of the possibilities of death's exchange, where death is no longer solely mine: what this study tentatively calls a *relational death*, a death paradoxically lived on by the living dead, *in relation*.

Literature's sword

To examine this principal concern – the exchange of death and its ramifications – this book turns to fictional literature of the death penalty in order to bring forward figures who resist the political kernel of sovereignty and, in so doing, trouble a long-standing ontological understanding of the place of death as that outside or beyond the human experience.

One may begin with the understanding that, like death, literature too 'punctuates the language of the everyday life'. While this destructive understanding of language shall be discussed further on, it is well beyond the scope of this introduction to examine the multitudinous definitions of the literary, or how and why this punctuation even occurs. An explanation is required, however, as to why the questions previously raised – mainly philosophical and political in nature – are here to be refracted through the lens of literature. After all, Plato's infamous exile of the injurious poets from the ideal, sovereign Republic still finds its resonances today.[49]

It would perhaps be wisest to steer clear of a circular debate around real or constructed dichotomies between literature and philosophy and, seeing as how we have already invoked Plato, instead extrapolate his idea of the *meletē thanatou*: that is, the manner of 'a true disciple of philosophy [. . .] always practicing how to die without complaint', one who leads a 'life [that is] the practice of death'.[50]

In other words, a preparing for death through a living of death. This Platonic 'concern for dying as a relation to self and *an assembling of self*, as Derrida describes it, reveals how '[p]hilosophy isn't something that comes to the soul by accident, for it is nothing other than this vigil over death that watches out for death and watches over death, as if over the very life of the soul' (GD, 14–15).[51] Leaving to one side, for now, this powerful idea of self-assemblage within the realm of death, we witness the ancient understanding that philosophy can only begin from the end. On this, one may recall Cicero, who similarly believes that 'to philosophize is to learn how to die'.[52]

Philosophy thus starts from the end, from death. The thanatopolitical sovereign, through the *droit de glaive*, likewise founds, and is founded by, death. And so what of literature? Does it too watch over death, and is its sword protectively and biopolitically pointed outwards, or thanatopolitically inwards?

It is easy enough to make the case for death's seminal role in the literature of the death penalty henceforth examined, and of us being urged to think of – or even practice – death through these particular works. As poet and dramatist Joanna Baillie puts it:

> If man is an object of so much attention to man, engaged in the ordinary occurrences of life, how much more does he excite his curiosity and interest when placed in extraordinary situations of difficulty and distress? It cannot be any pleasure we receive from the sufferings of a fellow creature which attracts such multitudes of people to a publick execution, though it is the horrour we conceive. To see a human being bearing himself up under such circumstances [. . .] must be the powerful incentive, which makes us press forward to behold what we shrink from, and wait with trembling expectation for what we dread.[53]

Baillie here presses the idea of one of literature's roles, that of preparing for death, in much the same way that Plato positions philosophy. If literature can be described, now in Blanchot's words, as 'the highest form of work' – and this, counter-intuitively, because it '*ruins action*' in its refusal of concrete work/activity in favour of literary imagining and the fantastical freedom to say everything and be nothing – then the idea of a *work* of literature quickly erodes beneath our feet, and one is left with a literature that begins only 'at the moment when literature becomes a question' (LRD, 313, 316, 300).[54] Literature, Blanchot writes, is not so much a productive work or working of something as it is 'the element of emptiness present in all', being both before and beyond the particularities of its authors and perennially open to and transformed by the universal and the futural, continually 'made and unmade' and thus always unworking, emptied and disappearing (*LRD*, 302, 306). That is, as per Blanchot's implication: literature is the art of living death.

Thus, we already begin to glimpse here literature's inextricable ties to death and dying – two terms that must be differentiated later on – through its innate hollowness. As such, this book does not here turn to literature to provide answers but, rather, to help shape the questions.

Blanchot goes on to write how literature's constitutive emptiness is made unmistakably clear through its inevitable grounding in language. 'Literature is bound to language', and language is, in itself, a death sentence: to name something is to murder it (*LRD*, 322). Blanchot explains this thus:

> For me to be able to say 'This woman', I must take her flesh-and-blood reality away from her, cause her to be absent, annihilate her. The word gives me the being, but it gives it to me deprived of being. The word is the absence of that being, its nothingness, what is left of it when it has lost being – the very fact that it does not exist. (*LRD*, 322)

In Adam's naming of the animals of Eden, therefore, there is at 'work' not only the dynamics of hierarchical and political (and masculine) power but also the unworking dynamics of death, that is, losing being. Language's universalization, then, condemns to death the particular, where the woman – the 'she' – becomes merely an 'it', the universal and empty 'it' of a neutral statement like 'it is raining'.[55] In so long as it remains bound to language, then, literature, much like philosophy, cannot but begin from the end. In seeing death at the origin of each point in the present triangulation of politics, philosophy and literature, the idea that the politics and philosophy of the death penalty can be accurately and insightfully interrogated through literature holds firm.

Crucial here is the following from Derrida:

> This is why all the things we're dealing with here, sovereignty, [. . .] the living dead, the buried alive, etc., the spectral and the posthumous – well, the dream, the oneiric, fiction, so-called literary fiction, so-called fantastic literature will always be less inappropriate, more relevant, if you prefer, than the authority of wakefulness, and the vigilance of the ego, and the consciousness of so-called philosophical discourse. (*BSII*, 185)

This powerful pro-literature sentiment, which might recall Levinas's claim that 'the whole of philosophy is but a meditation of Shakespeare', seems to place literature as prior to philosophy and thus enforce the notion of a dichotomy between the two.[56] However, the present Blanchovian definition of literature – as that which constantly makes and unmakes, invents and destroys, meditates and erases the very meaning of 'human' through its emphasis on the absence (death) within presence (life) – troubles any such distinctions that might be drawn as lines in the sand. It is with this mindset that, in attempting to understand the human condition in relation to death, we here turn to the fictional literature of the death penalty.

This is not to say that reading non-fictional literature of the penalty would garner no relevant insights to the present discussion. One might include journalistic and biographical accounts of condemned inmates (such as Sister Helen Prejean's *Dead Man Walking*) as well as non-fictional memoirs from death-row prisoners themselves (such as Mumia Abu-Jamal's *Live from Death Row*, Richard M. Rossi's *Waiting to Die* or Billy Neal Moore's *I Shall Not Die*). Norman Mailer's *The Executioner's Song*, representing the case of Gary Gilmore, would be of particular interest in terms of the momentous reinstatement of the death penalty in the United States in 1976. The list of potential texts can go on indefinitely, and indeed the reader might already have in mind a cluster of works that would be pertinently placed in this reading, and which they are encouraged to keep in mind as this book progresses.

There are two notable disadvantages in choosing not to read non-fictional texts as well as one advantage that outweighs both. Let us start with the drawbacks. First, non-fictional texts afford us great perspective on the global-historical development of the death penalty and its matrix of interconnected problems: its strained relationships with local and international law as well as with the concepts of justice and cruelty; its mutability in social opinion and party politics alongside struggles for either abolition or retention; its relation to developments in popular psychoanalysis in terms of criminal profiles and definitions of insanity; its biased deployment when it comes to race, gender or social class; its technological developments, 'progress' in techniques of execution and evolving medical determinations of pain and death; its place in religious, ethical and humanistic debates, and ones on punishment and mass incarceration more generally; its relation to theatricality and visibility and so on.[57] Not including the multiple literary forms that can reflect these issues – such as court transcripts, periodicals, speeches, propagandist material, newspapers, articles, essays, eyewitness accounts, medical studies, biographies and autobiographies from death row – means that such topics shall only remain a background to our current discussion.

The second disadvantage in leaving non-fictional texts to one side is the risk of forgetting, or worse ignoring, how the death penalty contemporarily targets equal subjects unequally – specifically, and especially in the United States, immigrants, Black people and ethnic minorities. As Geoffrey Adelsberg writes, the death penalty as institutionalized in the West 'reveals a continuing differential exposure of Black and Brown people to sovereign decision', whereby 'the sovereign repurposes the white imaginary of Black and Brown criminality to frame certain people as always already a threat and thus deserving of sacrifice for the sake of protecting the polity'.[58] On this matter, a significant amount has been written – including by Foucault and Mbembe themselves[59] – and the fact that 'racism is [. . .] inseparable from the logic of the death penalty' should not be minimized.[60]

Rather than justify the exclusion of non-fictional writing, one may instead understand the advantage in prioritizing fictional literature: in sum, fictional works allow us to go beyond individual cases of condemnation and begin to understand how the death penalty operates on a universal rather than particular (personal, historical) level. Death row, as shall be seen, is not reserved for those condemned to death.

On this, one may begin with the point that several fictional narratives of the death penalty present us with an unnamed protagonist. This nameless everyman – as presented in Blanchot's *The Instant of My Death*, Victor Hugo's *The Last Day of a Condemned Man* or Franz Kafka's 'In the Penal Colony' (all discussed later on), as well as in other works such as George Orwell's 'A Hanging' – allows us to glimpse not a condemned individual paraded as someone entirely removed from our own situation, at whom one can gawk and tremble in expectation, but rather an image of ourselves. The 'nameless' shall gain additional signification as this study progresses, its nuances developing in terms of not only universality but also anonymity. For now, it is sufficient to state that the fiction of the death penalty – because it is fiction – is here read, in Hugo's words, as 'eliminat[ing] the contingent, the accidental, the particular, the special, the relative, the modifiable, the episodic, the anecdotal, the event, [and most importantly] the proper name'.[61] Transposing what Ève Morisi writes when discussing Hugo's *Last Day*, fiction 'destabilizes spatiotemporal coordinates, [. . .] empties out character, represents an unexpected subject';[62] indeed, it empties out the singular subject itself, and one can see how, in the words of Peggy Kamuf, 'literature is the other name of singular universality/ universal singularity'.[63] This universalization – that is, the universalization of the literary that Blanchot speaks of, empty of all particulars – puts us on death row ourselves, and we find ourselves always already slain through a literature which provides us only with the example and never with the exemplary.

The sovereign's decision to kill – an act that can hardly escape the resonance of 'making an example' out of someone – in this way begins to falter in its significations and power, as literature dilutes the decision of eliminating the exceptional subject into the generalized experience of those already hollowed or emptied, neutrally living a death sentence that names no one in particular. Kamuf's *Literature and the Remains of the Death Penalty*, following Derrida, makes the case for literature's unique position in interrogating these glimpsed limits of sovereignty: 'It is in fact literature's fundamental ambiguity', she suggests, 'that allows for the creation of a space outside of sovereign power', and '[l]iterature can thus speak back to sovereign power'.[64] Writing of Albert Camus's *The Stranger*, Kamuf sees this 'fundamental ambiguity' as literature's embrace of 'the incommensurability between an experience of events and their narration'; rather than attempt some (impossible) totalitarian account or analysis of living death, the literary narratives of those condemned to death allow for the paradox, the aporia, the present absence to remain unresolved.[65] As she writes:

> Literature, then, would come to be lodged in this 'time of the bandages' between death and resurrection, beyond life and yet still there, still appearing as Jesus appears to Mary Magdalene when she turns away from the mouth of the empty tomb and sees a man whom she at first mistakes for a gardener (John 20:14-15). Like the bandages, then, literature signals as trace of an absence and in a time suspended between all the modes of presence.[66]

In line with Morisi, too, one can see within the death penalty – that supposed ultimate assertion of sovereignty – the paradoxical undoing of this same sovereignty. Morisi, also reading Hugo's *LD* (now in conjunction with Agamben's *Homo Sacer*), notes how many instances within the novella 'indicate that the death-bound prisoner loses his sociopolitical existence'.[67] Leaving to one side the debatable accuracy of the term 'death-bound', one may forward the difficult paradox implicit in Morisi's point that she leaves undeveloped: if 'sociopolitical existence' is not only upheld but generated through sovereign power, why is it that, in the death penalty, in the apex manifestation of sovereign power, it is markedly absent? We are back within the realm of the non-subject, stripped of all ontological and political signification, which can only inhabit a space which is non-sovereign: death row.

This book, then, is not concerned with 'the use of fiction for activism',[68] or with how 'Western literature has infiltrated both the abolitionist and retentionist arguments', or how literary fictions both reflect and shape cultural politics, law, philosophy and societies in terms of the multiple background elements listed earlier, from policies to psychoanalysis to medicine.[69] Instead, literature is here the catalyst due to its capacity to not only question but also empty the subject, and, in so doing, embody the potential nullification of the sovereign that condemns it.

All in all, then, it seems, that we find ourselves in a rather bleak situation, apparently already dead and perennially threatened – and thus (un)defined – by a death penalty that is here understood as boundless, spilling over the confines of both prison cells and fiction. And yet there is the possibility of speaking back to the sovereign, of annulling the sovereign from the place of death itself. This book contemplates, understands and expands this dual, ambiguous position of the human experience.

In just the five years prior to the publication of this book, there emerged multiple important publications on the death penalty. These include, among others: Kelly Oliver and Stephanie M. Straub's collection, *Deconstructing the Death Penalty* (2018); Birte Christ and Ève Morisi's collection, *Death Sentences: Literature and State Killing* (2019); Peggy Kamuf's *Literature and the Remains of the Death Penalty* (2019); David Wills's *Killing Times* (2019); Ève Morisi's *Capital Letters* (2020); and Katherine Ebury's *Modern Literature and the Death Penalty* (2021), each to some extent already incorporated earlier. One could here include, too, Arthur Bradley's *Unbearable Life* (2019), also grappled with the notion of the living dead. Such interventions cannot be said to owe their impetus solely to the recent translations of Derrida's *Death Penalty* seminars (2014 and 2017), and this developing constellation of works successfully attests to the persistent contemporaneousness of the issue of the death penalty, even if one is tempted to think of it as merely an archaic practice, maybe even irrelevant to our quotidian lives.

It shall be left to the reader to discover the many different strengths of the works named above. What this book offers that is yet unexplored is not only an analysis of several fictions previously under-considered within the context of the death penalty (such as Sophocles's, Greene's, Sartre's and Nabokov's), or novel readings of seminal ones (such as Blanchot's, Hugo's and Dickens's). Rather, in putting to one side all the commonly discussed aspects of the death penalty as listed above, as well as not participating in the recurring yet warping focus on the contemporary situation in the United States, or the historical backdrop of France, or the role of the realist novel, for instance, this book finds the space to ask the wider question of how we are to understand ourselves – politically and ontologically, as humans – if death is not something entirely removed from our lives but rather held constantly *in relation*, if death is always already here as we live and breathe as made evident by the temporal and spatial recurrence of the death penalty. It is in light of this principal question that the complex conceptual matrices of the penalty are foregrounded and developed towards a notion of postsovereignty, a concept not usually considered in the context of the penalty as the assumed epitome of sovereign power. If all this recent research only partially touches (psychologically, legally and sociologically) on the death penalty's serious challenge to any sense of self or identity, then this book makes its political and ontological destabilization the central focus.

The death penalty, traditionally discussed as only an aspect of society rather than its foundation, or as only something that society enacts rather than that which allows society to act in the first place, is here scrutinized in a way that philosophy has neglected: that is, as a way of thinking otherwise the human relation to death and, subsequently, the ontology of the human itself. It is for this reason that this book turns not to the socio-politico-historical context of fictional works, but rather to the destabilizing power of literature itself.

To this end, the second chapter begins by asking what, first of all, is to be understood by the term 'death penalty'. Here, definitions are proffered through Immanuel Kant and Derrida, circling questions of sovereignty, law and the certainty of the time of death, which the penalty seemingly affords the condemned. This supposed certainty is, ironically, the first step in our questioning of whether we are, as Heidegger defines us, beings-towards-death, since, at least for those condemned, it seems death is here already. Led by the literary works at hand, therefore, this project undertakes a lengthy examination of Heidegger's concept of 'my death' and explores an alternative conception of death – a relational death – which necessitates a re-evaluation of Heideggerian ontology.

The third chapter then defines both the idea and context of the 'relational death' through a discussion of the problematic temporality of the death penalty which, like the French Revolution that popularized its terror, seems to turn in on itself to the point of paradox. Through a reading of *Antigone* and Hegel's Lord and Bondsman dialectic, the relationship between sovereignty and its condemned subjects is explored, allowing us to begin to understand the matrices of relations simultaneously and paradoxically withheld and erased, rather than simply severed, in death. These relations – with the figure of the sovereign, with that of the commoner-substitute who dies in-stead, and with death itself – are further illuminated through three literary texts, namely Graham Greene's *The Tenth Man*, Charles Dickens's *A Tale of Two Cities* and Victor Hugo's *The Last Day of a Condemned Man*. It begins to emerge that we are all living corpses, condemned to death – and yet what is one to make of these relations in death, or of their political nature? Ultimately, what is 'me' and 'my death' now?

With these questions at the forefront, the fourth chapter seeks to understand the consequence of the collapse of distinction between Self and Other following the elimination of the living dead subject. Through the thought of

Levinas, and beyond it, a reading of Jean-Paul Sartre's 'The Wall' and Vladimir Nabokov's *Invitation to a Beheading* illuminates what it would mean were we to understand the subject as one already deceased, decomposing and shedding off the Heideggerian world and our thrownness into mortality. The Levinasian command 'thou shalt not kill' is in this context transformed into 'thou shalt not die', and human sociality is thus further revealed as being founded not on ethics but through sovereignty's ultimate decree. Here, we are met with not the impossibility of death, but the impossibility of life. In being beyond Heideggerian structures of Being, then, one must further question *how* we are (for the ontological question is not a deliberation of whether we *are* or *are not*), and Levinas's idea of the *il y a*, along with Derrida's notion of *chora*, here allows us to conceptualize the human beyond Heideggerian Being: not, then, the human *being* but rather the human *thing*, manifesting some sort of 'assembling of self', as Derrida puts it, possible only in death.

At this point, there remains the irresolvable tension between the dead human and the voice that nonetheless speaks on: for to survive, as the idiom goes, means also that one must tell the tale. This paradoxical literary voice, speaking from beyond the tomb to utter the impossible phrase 'I am dead', is what is explored in the fifth chapter, both through the genre of autothanatography and the Blanchovian concept of the Neuter. This 'I' that belongs not to a productive narrative but rather, as it were, to the epilogue or even epitaph might be a way of thinking beyond, as well as resisting, the sovereignty that condemned it, towards a postsovereign subject that several thinkers – including Agamben, who is at length conversed with in this final chapter – have tried and failed to sketch.

Prior to these four chapters, the upcoming first chapter shall take on the questions that have been raised in this introduction and add some more through a close reading of Blanchot's short literary work *The Instant of My Death*. His narrative is here read as manifesting and in several ways deepening the manifold philosophical, political and literary questions around death that were all too briefly addressed in this introduction, and an analysis of the text's main conceptual gestures, therefore, shall help this study extend outward and more broadly, expounding these questions in the four chapters that follow.

Without being forgotten, the ritual of the substitute king shall intermittently, and almost uncannily, be brought to bear on this work at perhaps unexpected points, as if it were a haunting, like that of the other dead king who returns from the grave and belies 'the most famous fiction of sovereign power from the Christian Middle Ages: "the king never dies" (*le Roi ne meurt jamais*)'.[70]

'Long live the king!' Barnardo enigmatically yells at Elsinore.[71] Yes, long live the dead king!

1

The Instant of My Death

In 1944, a young man sits within an estate of evident wealth, contemplating a manuscript. He is interrupted by a soft knock at the door. He answers it and finds in front of him a Nazi lieutenant whose formidable stature had been masked by the tenderness of his knocking. The lieutenant yells. He wants everyone inside the house to go outside. The young man stands demurely aside as his elderly relatives cross the mansion's ornate doorway first, followed by two young women. He too then follows them, calmly, onto well-maintained lawns that have now become a killing field. The lieutenant bares his teeth, his weapons and his soldiers, and the young man knows that he is going to die. His one last request is to ask that his family be allowed to go back inside. The soldiers assent, and the young man ignores the hushed shuffling of the women's clothes, perhaps thinking instead of the mistake he has made in having assumed these soldiers to be German – they are, in fact, members of the Russian Liberation Army. Or maybe he thinks of his manuscript. Or of God, or of nothing at all, because as the soldiers take aim he feels only peace. He is not happy, and maybe he is not even a little surprised that he is not distressed. Peace might not be the right word for what he is feeling – he is already dead. He does not know how long he has been a corpse, there with his eyes closed, but an explosion in the distance resurrects him. He is dismissed by the lieutenant. There are more urgent matters than that of his execution; other things are happening, clamouring, banging for immediate address. The young man walks away. Without knowing how, he ends up in the shadows of a forested heath. Sometime later, he learns of how the soldiers had burned everything, except his house, but three young sons of famers and some horses have been killed. He leaves for Paris, still unsure of whether he is even alive.

This is, of course, the story recounted in Blanchot's *The Instant of My Death*.[1] As made obvious through its title, what concerns this narrative is the seemingly impossible phrase 'my death' and its realization in what Blanchot insinuates was his own actual experience during the war. It is a narrative that explores what is here considered to be a very significant transposition: when death, which we so often associate with what is to come and which lies in wait for us in the future, is made to be present, brought into the right now or even the past. Alternatively, we think of death as that which happens to other people; surely, death might well be happening *right now*, but it is not happening *to me*. One recalls Epicurus's famous 'Letter to Menoceus', where he writes of how death, 'the most awful of evils, is nothing to us, seeing that, when we are, death is not come, and, when death is come, we are not'.[2] The instant of my death, then, somehow never seems to coincide with my life, and it is this disassociation of death and self that Blanchot's narrative successfully manages to displace in the short space of five pages.

What, then, does *The Instant of My Death* reveal of the present moment of my death?

Perhaps, due to the very nature of what is being explored, not very much at all. As Michael Dillon and Paul Fletcher contend: 'The present moment; the moment of death: both are always "in-between" conditions, and therefore intractable to definition or appropriation.'[3] It seems, then, one cannot define this immediate instant of death, and yet such radical ambiguity is very often fecund. This lapsed time of death-made-present is what Dillon and Fletcher interrogate in their essay. Looking at Blanchot's short narrative, they see in the account an impossible representation of the ahistorical and exceptional instant, where our experience of the present – that which always escapes determination – may amount to 'not the death of time [. . .] but the time of death'.[4]

This book recognizes in *The Instant of My Death* a radical rethinking of writing and fiction, life and politics, time and death. It can be confidently asserted that this narrative tightly encapsulates all the questions put forward in the introductory chapter, and more, and thus its analysis could easily take up the entirety of this study. But a problem is immediately manifest, for how does one even begin to address the in(de)terminable – that is, the interminable and indeterminable – alterity of death, that which is, by definition, beyond definition? And can one reasonably expect every desired answer from *The Instant of My Death*? While the question of one's own death might not be the most appropriate place to start, is not literature only literature, as Blanchot writes in 'Literature and the Right to Death', when it 'becomes a question'? Let us, then, begin with Blanchot's own questions.

It is difficult to read Blanchot's narrative without there also being – if only at the back of one's mind – Derrida's *Demeure*, a critical work which proffers an analysis of the concepts of fiction and death through a particularly close reading of this austere narrative, first published in 1994.[5] Pairing these texts – as publishers have since done – is not necessarily or solely restrictive and may even be more than apt, considering the close dialogue, one revolving especially around the space of literariness, which irreversibly binds the two thinkers.

Indeed, in an article that looks at *Demeure*'s problematization of 'the borders that pass between fiction and testimony', Ginette Michaud rightly notes that Derrida is perhaps the philosopher who 'has lent the most attentive ear to Blanchot's thought, following closely its narrative and theoretical dimensions'.[6] Meeting for the first time due to an unhappy incident involving Jean Beaufret, Derrida and Blanchot were to become and remain friends,[7] to the point, even, of *Demeure* itself being 'a gesture of friendship' due to *The Instant of My Death*'s troubled publication process.[8] Thus, according to Michaud, 'Derrida's text can also be read as a *response*', where 'such restitution of Blanchot's literary (and perhaps political) testimony makes Derrida not only the host, but also the heir'.[9] Reading Blanchot through *Demeure*, then, seems not only a preliminary step towards the narrative but a supplementary one.[10]

Of *Demeure*, Derrida writes: 'Literature and death, truth and death: this is the subject' (*D*, 22). His commentary takes upon itself the ideas evoked in Blanchot's (questionably) autobiographical narrative, traversing from the position of the witness being-before-the-law and the implications of testimony and passion to the more presently seminal notions of irreplaceability, justice and the problematization of death. And yet, despite Derrida's symbolic and exhaustive reception of *The Instant of My Death*, there is a particular detail from the narrative to which no attention is paid, and it is from this oversight that the following discussion recognizes a possible other reading which seems inherent to Blanchot's text itself. Therefore, it is through Derrida – unavoidably – that the present argument is led towards an analysis of what are here taken to be the two most important phrases: 'the instant' and 'my death'.

The five-page narrative is much more complex than it appears. Although marked by its brevity, it is nonetheless 'an enormous text' (*D*, 43). The reader is immediately presented with formal complexities, such as the framing device which nests the rest of the narrative: 'I remember a young man', it starts in the manner of a recounting (*ID*, 3). After this, however, the narrative problematically continues with the third person singular 'he' while retaining certain interjections by this unnamed first narrator ('In his place, I will not try to analyze', for instance) (*ID*, 5). The last sentence of the narrative (before a paragraph that may be termed an epilogue, situated an indeterminate time later) loosely but somewhat unsuccessfully conjoins this 'I' with the 'he', as when the narrator thinks: '"I am alive. No, you are dead'" (*ID*, 11). Already, therefore, one can acknowledge the intricacy of Blanchot's text despite its 'parsimony [*principe d'epargne*]' (*D*, 56). It is a narrative saturated with the Blanchovian ideas of writing, time, death and the Neuter; it echoes Fyodor Dostoevsky's experience, whose writings Blanchot often critically addresses; it marks overt ties to Hegel, André Malraux and Jean Paulhan; and its language is deceptively terse.[11] These are aspects that shall be returned to in due course. Let us start, however, with the aforementioned absence in Derrida's analysis.

The complexity of the opening sentence is noteworthy: 'I remember a young man – a man still young – prevented from dying by death itself – and perhaps the error of injustice' (*ID*, 3). Although the exact nature of this injustice will be discussed slightly further on, this first line nonetheless forcibly halts the reader. 'One could spend years on this sentence', Derrida admits (*D*, 54). *Demeure*, in fact, can be said to revolve in its entirety around this pivotal and counter-intuitive sentence, with Derrida's reading of it situating the condemnation to death – wherein the commanding officer 'placed his men in a row in order to hit [. . .] the human target', at whom the soldiers 'were already aiming' – as a manifestation of the impossible experience of dying (*ID*, 5).

> By this [first sentence] we understand that what happens to him is not the dying, it is not dying. It is not dying but following a verdict that is an order to die: die, you are dead, you are going to die. The order to die comes to prevent him from dying ('prevented from dying by death itself'), and the testimony will in some sense recount this division, in its dividend and its divisor. From dying, he is prevented by death itself. This singular division is the true theme of a testimony that will testify, in sum, to an 'unexperienced experience'. (*D*, 54)[12]

What is this experience that cannot be experienced? Here, Derrida sees the officer's condemnation of the protagonist as just that: although the man is not physically killed, there is nonetheless the feeling that he has died through an unspoken (death) sentence. 'Death has already taken place, however unexperienced its experience may remain in the absolute acceleration of time infinitely contracted into the point of an instant'; in other words, '[t]here has already been an instant in which death happened to him. Everything was preprogramed; it was inevitable and fatal, it has thus already arrived – death' (*D*, 62, 70). As Derrida states years later: 'To die, basically, [. . .] is to be exposed to death' (*BSI*, 137). As a result, the young man 'lives, but he is no longer living. Because he is already dead, it is a life without life' (*D*, 88). Blanchot's work, therefore, allows us to begin questioning commonplace assumptions about death – that it is, supposedly, always the cessation of metabolism, that it is only biological and that there is only one way to die.

One can thus understand why *The Instant of My Death* is often referred to as an autothanatography: as opposed to autobiography, this is a writing of one's death rather than one's life. In her introduction to a special issue on the autothanatographical, Susan Bainbrigge is quick to note that '[t]he term [. . .] might appear to be a contradictory one, since death cannot be known to the self, much less written about', but concludes that 'when *thanatos* replaces the *bios* in autobiography', the focus is 'on dying, rather than living, [which] makes plain the reality of the mortal self. Death itself, though "unknowable", still prompts attempts to grasp – through writing – its nature and meaning'.[13] It is a term Derrida uses only once in *Demeure*, although somewhat hesitantly, parenthetically: according to him, Blanchot's fiction is 'testimonial and autobiographical in appearance (autothanatographical in truth)' (*D*, 55). Although the accuracy of such a term (along with these precursory definitions) remains to be ascertained, Derrida's description seems to hold so far: the account indeed seems to be written '*from* my death, *from* the place and *from* the taking-place, better yet, from the *having-taken-place*, already, of my death' (*D*, 45).

As suggested earlier, what makes such claims especially opaque is 'the viewpoint of common sense', according to which – understandably, one might add – 'I should not be able to say: I died or I am dead'. One can supposedly only 'testify to the imminence of [. . .] death', and, therefore, '[n]othing seems more absurd to common sense, in effect, than an unexperienced experience' and its (auto)thanatographical and thanatopolitical consequences. Derrida, however, underscores the importance of thinking through this paradox in order to properly 'read or hear Blanchot' (*D*, 46–7).

From the outset, one recognizes that 'death' and the 'instant', however problematic these terms quickly become, are clearly and inextricably knotted together in this particular (non-)experience. The moment the decision is made to shoot the man is the instant that the man dies, the instant when he feels 'extraordinary lightness, a sort of beatitude (nothing happy, however). [. . .] The encounter of death with death' (*ID*, 5). This last phrase, writes Derrida, reveals 'death itself [. . .] at the tip of the instant of imminence, at gun point, *at the moment when* and *from the moment that* death was going to arrive'. It is an encounter which is 'only ever [. . .] an anticipation, the encounter of death as anticipation with death itself, with a death that has already arrived according to the inescapable: an encounter between what is going to arrive and what has already arrived', and death, therefore, 'has just come from the instant it is going to come. [...] *It has just finished coming.* Death encounters itself' (*D*, 64–5).

As Derrida acknowledges, perhaps the clearest exemplification of this is the protagonist's 'last' wish that his family go inside so that they might not witness his execution. This being granted – and the fulfilment of one's last wish signifies an end that is already here – his family assents in 'a long, slow procession, silent, *as if everything had already been done*' (*ID*, 5).[14] Although death has not come, the experience of certain death has: this is the unexperienced experience, which lies not only on phenomenological lines but also on ontological ones. Additionally, '[o]ne is not resuscitated from this experience of inescapable death, even if one survives it. One can only survive it without surviving it' (*D*, 62–3). Ebury acknowledges how several fictional works, in fact, acknowledge this impossibility of survival and the sense of posthumousness that cannot be exorcized: 'in these narratives, even if the person was imprisoned or exonerated, their sense of self and their bodily integrity appears to be reduced by the threat of the death penalty. These plots represent an anxiety that the person threatened with the death penalty is no longer a subject or citizen', and this point shall be here developed throughout.[15] Summarily, then, despite the risk of being overly reductive when taking such terms at face value, the moment that death is made inevitable, the instant when one is condemned to death, is the moment that one dies.[16] Hence, one can begin to grasp the words spoken between the indeterminate and almost-converging 'I' and 'he' along with the last line of the epilogue: '[a]ll that remains is the feeling of lightness that is death itself or, to put it more precisely, the instant of my death henceforth always in abeyance' (*ID*, 11).

However, the meaning of these two phrases that we have here been discussing – 'prevented from dying by death itself' and 'the encounter of death with death' – are in Derrida's reading extensively conflated. As already discussed, both the former and the latter phrases are read by Derrida as referring to the 'interruption of the death sentence' through the very instant of 'what will already have taken place', and this is correct (*D*, 49). Both, after all, concern death meeting death, a thanatopolitical interruption of sovereignty's sword. On the other hand, and now is the time to bring in what Derrida does not, one is led to wonder whether such conflation misses out on other nuances in Blanchot's narrative: that is, the vital significance of the death of 'three young men, sons of farmers – truly strangers to all combat, whose only fault was their youth – [and who] had been slaughtered' (*ID*, 5, 7).[17]

Derrida says very little of these three, almost nothing. In an extensive commentary on a five-page narrative about death, the neglect of these deaths is strange. In *Demeure*, only one sentence addresses them directly and summarily: 'The farms are burned; the young farmers, who had nothing to do with the whole thing, have been executed', and one other reference mentions them indirectly in terms of the trauma of war (*D*, 86; see also *D*, 80). Evidently, Derrida does not acknowledge their place in Blanchot's text as a seminal one, equating their narrative positioning to that of 'the bloated horses, on the road, in the fields' as an attestation to the event of violence (*ID*, 7). This is despite the fact that the three sons can be said to have been in the exact same position as that of the narrator – who similarly had nothing to do with anything, a stranger 'to all combat', who was also a young man like them, and who *has also died* – with the sole difference being that the Château to which the protagonist is linked, and what it represents in terms of social standing and history, commands 'a respect or consideration that the farms did not arouse' (*ID*, 7).

It is odd that Derrida mirrors the soldiers' violence in his lack of consideration of the three sons. In this he is not alone. Very often *The Instant of My Death* is read in such a way that the sons' deaths are understood as being chronologically anterior to the young man's trial. They are the already dead. For instance, in a review article of *The Instant of My Death/Demeure*, Rei Terada writes: 'A roving band of soldiers pillages [the protagonist's] region of the French countryside, burning farms and killing the farmers' sons. The Lieutenant orders his men to execute the young man, then moves away, distracted by the noise of an explosion'.[18] Even Dillon and Fletcher, in whose article death is so closely related to the instant, forget about these other deaths. The explosion of the 'nearby battle' and the three deaths are, therefore, separated by these readers not only spatially but also chronologically, or even pictured as entirely disparate. And thus the latter are seen – when they are even seen at all – simply as either an allusion to class difference or a testament to the horror of war, or else their mere mention is read as the literal incarnation of survivor's guilt on the part of the protagonist, 'the feeling that he was only living because, in the eyes of the Russians, he belonged to a noble class' (*ID*, 5, 7).

However, and this is the crux of the present argument, the reading here proposed is that, chronologically, those three sons died in that same explosive battle which led to the dismissal of the protagonist. In a text which foregrounds the instant to such an extent, and which disturbs the very idea of 'chronology' in significant ways, the deaths of the three other young men can reasonably be read as having happened *instant*aneously to the protagonist's execution, and, consequently, the implication is that it was their death which deferred his own. Thus, that first paradoxical aphorism – 'prevented from dying by death itself' – here gains further meaning in it being the death of the three sons which prevented the protagonist from dying, who dies nonetheless. As such, what Derrida writes of Blanchot's first line remains exceedingly insightful: one can indeed spend years in its contemplation.

This is not saying that no other reader has acknowledged this simultaneous death. 'Blanchot's life is indebted to the death of innocent farmers, whose failure to belong to a certain class costs them their life', writes Jungah Kim, although once more – despite even the title of her essay – the sons of farmers are left to the side (one is tempted to add: of the road, with the horses) in the survivor's favour.[19] Even *Demeure* itself can be read as gesturing at this possibility left unread, where, as quoted previously, Derrida tellingly refers to the three men as having been 'executed'. Nothing more about them, however, is said, and, in a last twist of the knife, the title of Blanchot's narrative itself ('*my* death') hides away these other deaths as if they were something secret. It is here deemed important that, just like the protagonist, one not ignore the 'feeling of compassion for suffering humanity' (*ID*, 5).

Christopher Fynsk, too, acknowledges the vital significance of this feeling. In his book *Last Steps*, Fynsk sees in *The Instant of My Death* 'an affective knowledge of being-with [and "dying-with"] that will be coupled with an enigmatic relation to death'.[20] Despite aiming to understand how the protagonist's realization of mortality is tied to this 'feeling of compassion', Fynsk's 'humanity' effectively remains a disembodied and human-less one. He writes how, for the young man, '[s]uffering [. . .] has become a passion of the Outside: this is what the young man knows with those caught in the affliction of the ongoing struggle, which in the neighbourhood is general [. . .] and measureless'.[21] As we have seen, however, it is difficult to maintain that suffering in *The Instant of My Death* is 'general' or 'measureless'. There is, indeed, a certain universality to the dead body's symbolic gestures, but Blanchot by no means ignores the particular to focus only on the general. The three dead sons are foregrounded, clearly given a marked place as who they are – or were. Fynsk, unfortunately, only sees 'the young peasants from his neighbourhood' as ones that suffered from a lack of social advantage, and as such the protagonist is narrowly read by Fynsk as sharing his suffering with everyone at once, and thus with no one in particular at all.[22]

At this point, one must stop and query the manifold implications of these simultaneous deaths in the narrative. What kinds of different death sentences are at play here, and have the farmers been slaughtered, assassinated or executed? Is there any difference? What of innocence – after all, their 'only fault was their youth' – and the 'error of injustice'? In what other ways does the 'instant' make 'my death' problematic, or even impossible? How are death and dying to be understood on this basis of time, especially when the intended survives and someone else, someone other or a third party, dies? And, ultimately, how justified is Derrida in calling *The Instant of My Death* an autothanatography ('in truth', he adds), when the term's prefix denotes some kind of unbreakable solitude in, and possession of, death?[23]

Before progressing, it is worth noting that such a series of questions essentially sums up the main concerns of this book, as has been intimated in the introduction. But let us start, at least, with the first of these questions, and contemplate with Derrida for a while longer.

On the one hand, Blanchot refers to the three young men as having been 'slaughtered' (*abattus*), and then later as having been assassinated (*assassinat, assasiné*): 'This was war: life for some, for others, the cruelty of assassination' (*ID*, 6, 7). On the other hand, however, Derrida refers to them as having 'been executed' (*exécuté*) – a word never used in the narrative – and such different nuances open up an ambiguity which calls for some form of address. Blanchot's first term stems from *abattre*, that is, to beat down (hence the other meanings of *abattus* and *abattu*: despondent, dejected, depressed), and reminds the reader of the abattoir, a slaughterhouse for animals; seemingly, then, the sons are no different from 'the bloated horses', having been fatally flogged and beaten (in its dual meanings of 'defeat' and 'corporal violence'). The second word, however, makes us pause in implying a certain purpose to – or more precisely put, a certain purposiveness in – their death, since one does not assassinate the arbitrary animal but rather an identified 'human target'. These two words as used by Blanchot thus immediately seem at great odds: the first demotes, literally depresses, the victims by highlighting their animality – animals being traditionally scaled on some lower Aristotelian tier than human beings – whereas 'assassination' brings to the fore an affirmative estimation of their prominence, seemingly and contradictorily suggesting that they too somehow belonged to 'the noble class'.

In fact, to return once more to Shakespeare and dead kings, the first recorded literary use of 'assassination' stems from *Macbeth*, where the target is none other than King Duncan.[24] He seemingly sits on the opposite end of the social spectrum from those simple sons of farmers, and thus the word 'assassination' in the context of Blanchot's narrative serves to point us towards reassessing these social polarities in relation to manners of death. Similarities can already be drawn in the representation of King Duncan as Macbeth's first *innocent* victim. One could also tease out the parallels between the regicide and the killing of the three young men – for is (the literary version of) King Duncan not also, to a certain extent, a stranger to all combat as he awaits his soldiers to inform him of the events of the battle, or in the naïve, unbounded trust he puts in his hosts?[25] – and it would not be a fruitless endeavour to further examine the shared ground between the concepts found in both *The Instant of My Death* and *Macbeth*.[26] Why would such purpose be ascribed to the death of the three farmers if not to suggest, in some manner, that their deaths were not merely the unimportant or accidental by-products of war? There is, then, a certain suitability that presents itself in the concept of the assassinated commoner against the backdrop of innocence, although this does not disaffirm the protagonist's class guilt in the face of the soldiers' slaughter. In the appositeness of seeing both slaughter and assassination in the killing of the young men, there perseveres the apparent self-contradiction of the protagonist's view of their death.

The matter is further confounded in Derrida's referring to the three sons as *exécuté*; he writes that '[e]xecution here is a matter of assassination', questioning the possibility that the narrative distinguishes between 'the rules of war, war crime, and then murder pure and simple' (*D*, 87–8). But one must stop and ask whether 'execution' and 'assassination' are interchangeable terms; Kamuf, too, remarks on their difference: a person may be assassinated, yet '[i]t is not a person but a *sentence*, the sentence of death, that is executed, in other words, carried or followed out to the end'.[27] Moreover, while assassination is almost exclusively restricted to the eminent, execution seems to be the great equalizer, historically bringing an end to the lives of commoners and kings alike; it was not only those such as Maximilien Robespierre or Marie Antoinette who were executed but also countless common citizens killed under the most uncertain accusations.[28] Therefore – to play with what Derrida meant by '*principe d'épargne*' – execution and assassination cannot be balanced without dividend.

There is still, however, a certain depth to Derrida's choice of *exécuté*. Despite not acknowledging the simultaneity of these deaths, his reference to 'execution' seems extremely pertinent in that, as the great equalizer, it not only contains within it the idea of assassination but also that of slaughter, and so captures and maintains the ambiguity that arises from this juxtaposition of terms diametrically opposed. The idea of social classes, ones differentiated even by the manner of their killing, thus collapses under 'execution'. While the first step towards this is Blanchot's use of 'assassination', where the young men are placed alongside the protagonist in social standing, the concept of execution also turns the other way round in allowing the reader to see that the soldiers' act of violence towards the protagonist can also appropriately be considered slaughter. The consequences of 'social class', then – as that which takes some form of strict stratification – are here not the most pressing issue.[29]

Indeed, the soldiers' actions relegate the protagonist's association with the Château to the life before his death, and after the slaughter of his former life he has merely the Bois des bruyères, as if he were the son of a farmer – or an animal – inheriting the land and nothing else.[30] Simultaneously, the sons of farmers are elevated and it is now they who are nobility, through their 'assassination' commanding the protagonist's respect, who now looks at the sons as they might have looked at him. This is not simply a reversal of roles. Crucially, what the text reveals is *a simultaneous experience of the same death by both parties* – both nobility and commoners, both assassinated and slaughtered – and hence the execution of one necessarily always implicates the other. And yet one ends up 'living on'.

In this way, the shared death and dying-with that this current discussion speaks for is doubly underscored. First, this death is still 'in abeyance' ('*toujours en instance*') while at the same time being-present – the execution has and has not taken place. This is where a particular nuance of 'abeyance' emerges most clearly: as the OED has it, 'abeyance' (originally 'to gape' or 'open wide') is not only a 'state of suspension, *temporary non-existence* or inactivity' but also 'the position of waiting for or temporarily *being* without a claimant or owner'.[31] The protagonist can thus never claim his death – '*désormais toujours en instance*' – nor his being-after-death, as death is now paradoxically both *past* and *pending*, and which has instead been suffered by the three sons (*ID*, 10). After his execution, the protagonist is non-existent, emptied of being – and this, Blanchot suggests, is not only temporary.

Second, in this execution, the prior (social) difference between the victims is annulled through the shared unexperienced experience of death. It is almost as if alterity itself were under erasure – although, it is vital to add, only or perhaps necessarily through the decisive *a priori* presence of alterity itself. Therefore, while the fact remains that the young man was not killed, but survives, identifying what happens in the narrative as an act of 'execution' does bring to the forefront this sense of a conjoint experience of death, a death in common.

It might not be too glib to comment on the appropriateness of how the young man is, in this common death, bound to *common*ers. After all, as Queen Gertrude, the wife of a dead king, remarks, death is ultimately 'common'.[32] Once more speaking of dead kings, one could also mention, if only in the mood of the purely coincidental, how the ancient Near Eastern king, while substituted, both called himself and was referred to as 'farmer' (*ikkāru*), keeping that title (or lack thereof) until his reinstatement.[33] Indeed, the substitute chosen to take on the king's death was almost always the common man; as Walton notes, '[i]n the earliest extant text referring to the substitute king, a common gardener was chosen as the substitute'.[34] The one who took the king's death had to be someone who, in Bottéro's words, 'was simple, naïve' or *innocent*, and 'who was without importance on the social level and whose fate really could not be of interest to anyone'.[35] Thus, once more highlighting the dynamics of dying in-stead as going beyond class- or role-reversal, the ritual is not simply the manifestation of how a king becomes both commoner and 'subject' to the commoner, while this same commoner is removed from his position of subject in order to be subjected to death through execution. It is not social prestige that is at stake but (im)mortality as stemming from social role *and indeed surpassing it* into a continuation of life after death, the nullification of the borders of death and identity. What separates the protagonist from the sons of farmers, then, is alterity, of which social class is only a superficial aspect, and what conjoins them is death.

It must be noted that the substitute king ritual is not to be perfectly equated with Blanchot's narrative, despite there also being parallels to the ancient Near Eastern master–slave relationship that will be explored in the third chapter. The difference here, of course, is that the death of the three young men was in no way an appointed or idealized sacrifice; indeed, there is something explicitly anti-sacrificial in the sons' corpses (and the horses' bloated ones). If the three sons were indeed 'lightning rods' for death, no one placed them there. Ultimately, from this non-social but nonetheless communal death, there emerges the irreducible difference of the protagonist's survival. One is thus led to ask whether this is the reason why there persists the notion of 'the error of injustice', and why, after execution, 'what then began for the young man was the torment of injustice' (*ID*, 7).

What becomes apparent is that the protagonist does not, in fact, survive, since what is implied by that word, 'survive', is a complete foregoing of the experience of death. A more appropriate turn of phrase, therefore, might be to say that the protagonist 'lives on', which denotes having gone through the unexperienced experience of death. To quote Derrida again, 'one can only survive [an execution] without surviving it'. The protagonist is no longer alive, he has gone through death: the 'life for some' that he speaks of in contrast with execution is not the continuation of one's life before death but rather the start of one's life after it, or its return. Disconcertingly, after-life and after-death are perfect synonyms.

Survival is thus best understood as 'living on', *sur-vivre*, and here we turn to Derrida's essay of that same name to illuminate the problem of how the living on of one and the non-living of the Other – in a manner that is erroneous and/ or unjust – troubles the idea of 'my death'.[36] After all, as Derrida suggests in *Demeure* but leaves unaddressed, Blanchot often appears 'troublesome even to the *Jemeinigkeit*, the "mine every time", which according to Heidegger characterizes [. . .] being-for-death' (*D*, 51). This is crucial, and this ontological troubling will be returned to.

In 'Living On' – where Derrida (primarily) reads Blanchot's earlier works *The Madness of the Day* and *Death Sentence* along with Percy Bysshe Shelley's 'The Triumph of Life' – he writes: 'Survival and *revenance*, living on and returning from the dead: living on goes beyond both living and dying.'[37] Derrida expounds that living on is 'the very progression that belongs, without belonging, to the progression of life and death. Living on is not the opposite of living, just as it is not identical with living'. This relation, he adds, is 'undecided, or, in a very rigorous sense, "vague".'[38] Although Derrida is here commenting on *Death Sentence*, written well over four decades before *The Instant of My Death*, one can see the continued relevance of his idea of 'living on' from the former to the latter, outlining one of the many possible readings of that particularly problematic line from Blanchot: 'Dead – immortal' (*ID*, 5). The young protagonist dies and lives on. He is the *revenant*, living on beyond the sovereignty that decreed his death.[39]

The distinction between living and living on must remain vague if it is not to reinforce some indivisible border between life and death, for that would not be hearing Blanchot. However, if what creates this ambiguous state of living on is 'the error of injustice' – hence Derrida's assertion that '*The Instant of My Death* is also a meditation on justice' – then necessarily one must define the parameters of this justice (*D*, 86).

Notably, in effect here is not civil law but military law, *jus in bello*, where justice bears a unique relation to the politics of death, a thanatopolitics (or even Bradley's nihilopolitics), which may be located at the core of Blanchot's narrative. However, trying to decide whether the killings can be classified as 'war crime[s]' or 'murder pure and simple' through an analysis of military justice would be to launch a tangential (moral) discussion centred on the soldiers' actions: whether they were wrong to kill anyone even during war time, or (as Derrida hints) wrong in not killing the young man as well – one might even be returned to the discussion of the justice or injustice of the killing act in both historic and contemporary culture. What is being foregrounded in the narrative itself, however, is the very mechanisms of the death sentence – that is, the prior certainty of one's coming time of death, with the added complication of how, in certain cases, one survives one's own sentencing and thus lives on through one's own political fate and exceptionalism. The focus is thus not only on the soldiers' impromptu condemnation of the protagonist but also, and even more prominently, on those condemned and their knowledge of a certain time of death. One of the fundamental problems thus becomes the question of the appropriation and abeyance of death: to whom does death belong when one has already been condemned to death, and what are the ramifications of a third party claiming it instead? Indeed, can one even speak of death as belonging to anyone at all?

Does death belong to the young protagonist and the three sons, or does it instead belong to the sovereign power that decides life and death through execution, which in this case takes the form of the Russian soldiers who have declared him enemy? Although, of course, the farmers' sons do not suffer the protagonist's unexperienced experience (at least from what we are shown), the question remains of how one can say 'my death' when it is the judge or executioner – in this time of war, the soldiers act as both – who speaks the sentence as well as engraves death's time and place. Initially, this might lead us back to the idea of injustice, which, as demonstrated, is in some respects wider than how Derrida reads it; he writes of *The Instant* that, '[t]hrough his own personal salvation, the saving of his life, [. . .] a young man experiences political and social injustice. [. . .] He has benefitted from an injustice, and he will not cease to suffer from this privilege' (*D*, 86–7). However, especially because both mentions of 'injustice' in the narrative are in actuality related directly to the unseen farmers' sons, the erroneously unjust is also the question of death's possession, the wavering between *l'instant/instance* of '*my* death' and the interruption or irruption of the political sovereign by what shall be addressed as the Third (the third party here is, aptly, *three* sons). This does not mean that death is an error (or not), or something of an injustice (or not), but what is indeed 'the error of injustice' that the protagonist speaks of is the fact that the farmers die in the young man's stead; the confusion that the 'nearby battle' creates leads to the fatal error where others are killed in-stead. This may be what allows Derrida to enigmatically write that, in *The Instant*, 'injustice would have been a mistake, would have been done by mistake; in other words, it would have been just for [the young man] to die – perhaps' (*D*, 54).

The young men are not, though, killed *instead*; there was no ultimatum of 'your life or theirs'. Had not the protagonist been at that instantaneous time both about to die and dead, their killing would not pose such a problem to the reader; one would not be able to say that they were killed 'instead', but simply that they were 'killed' or 'killed also'. However, in having, through their deaths, created a revenant – and, to reiterate, this happens without any intention of self-sacrifice or martyrdom – the reader is presented not only with the superficial problem of who has or has not died, and whether this was right or wrong, but rather more worryingly with how dying-in-stead puts into question the sovereign's power to determine the where and when of the death of those condemned: in other words, to determine the exception and subsume it into the political order. To Derrida's previous remark, in fact, one can respond: why, then, did this perhaps-justice not take place? What kind of interrupting revolution or resistance has overthrown this justice? And if it is commoners who can interrupt the (in)justice of the death sentence of the sovereign, what does this say of the limits of sovereignty? After all, the protagonist's survival was not the result of a sovereign decision or 'pardon'. His living on maintains itself in a space utterly devoid of decision and of the political; it is the consequence of what Dillon and Fletcher call a '[r]evolution [but one with neither action nor agency] [which] is fundamentally threatening because it lies before or beyond the limits of politics'.[40] Of note here is an obsolete connotation of 'interrupt', specifically meaning to infringe or suspend a law.[41] It might be, then, that in *The Instant* we see an interruption (of death) that allows for the possibility of the non-political space of postsovereignty, where there stands, as Murray alludes, the 'postsovereign subject' beyond the reach of the sovereign's sword.

Important in this connection is Dillon and Fletcher's claim that

> 'the instant of my death' engenders a being who is subject to the movement of a departure (for which she is already behind schedule), rather than one whose being is intimately tied to the self-securing of time [. . .]. The political subject of living beyond life [. . .] is not the transcendental ego of self-consciousness in life but an interruption of death.[42]

What is almost overwhelmingly disturbing about *The Instant of My Death* is that, while the protagonist is indeed this subject who lives beyond his life(-)time, the event of the 'interruption of death' is another death, at one and the same time a death which is *one and the same* and that happens *at the same time*; it is the death of the three sons of farmers which is the 'interruption of death' and of the sovereign's decision. To echo one of Dillon and Fletcher's more trenchant points, this 'lapse of time, time's remainder' – or, in other words, death in abeyance – really is 'the time of the possibility of politics in the making'.[43] This potentiality, perhaps, can be found in the postsovereign subject who is nonetheless not post-political.

By way of closing off this initial discussion in order to examine all the questions raised thus far, this study shall very briefly put forward an outline of a further few possible problems that arise from the other dying in-stead and which thus call for thorough exploration in the following chapters.

With the *revenant*, is there not also the possibility of the *arrivant*? In *Aporias*, Derrida is struck by the weight of this term, writing that it denotes 'he or she who comes, coming to be where s/he was not expected, where one was awaiting him or her without waiting for him or her, without expecting it [*s'y attendre*]' (*AP*, 33).⁴⁴ This guest, stranger or Other 'does not simply cross a given threshold' but 'affects the very experience of the threshold', and one can already see how the three sons are indeed new arrivals, as the following extract makes especially clear (*AP*, 33–4).

> [T]he absolute *arrivant* [. . .] surprises the host – who is not yet a host or an inviting power – enough to call into question, to the point of annihilating or rendering indeterminate, *all the distinctive signs of a prior identity, beginning with the very border that delineated a legitimate home and assured lineage* [. . .]. The absolute *arrivant* does not yet have a *name* or *identity*. [. . .]. This is why I call it simply the *arrivant*, and not someone or something that arrives, a subject, a person, an individual, *or a living thing* (*AP*, 34).⁴⁵

The threshold which the three men affect (who are dead, *no longer even living things*) is that of death, what Derrida calls the '*final* extremity, with the finality par excellence of the *telos* or of the *eskhaton*'. Ultimately, together, they are the *arrivant* who (or which) 'makes the event arrive', the event that is the transgression of the border of my death. And, as Derrida's remarks of *The Instant*, 'this border will always keep one from discriminating among the figures of the *arrivant*, the dead, and the *revenant*' (*AP*, 34–5).

There is in *The Instant*, therefore, an intriguing relation between arriving and returning. But how is *l'arrivant* to be distinguished from the Third, which is so tightly bound to the concept of justice? After all, '[j]ustice is this very presence of the third party', as Levinas notes.⁴⁶ According to Derrida, '[t]he third arrives without waiting. Without waiting, the third comes to affect the experience of the face in the face to face. [. . .]. For the third does not wait'.⁴⁷ Perhaps, then, it is no accident that there were *three* sons of farmers, especially given Blanchot's close and formative friendship with Levinas.⁴⁸ Notably, though, Derrida does discriminate between the *arrivant* and the *revenant* in his sole preoccupation with the protagonist, and thus, for him, the third *does* wait.

We should here note that, for Derrida, the *arrivant* is also 'the neutrality of *that which* arrives' (*AP*, 33), a claim which recalls Blanchot's formulation of the anonymous and radical passivity of the Neuter, and thus also the passivity of both the young men – again stressing their non-identities (the plural here indicating a community or assembly of the Neuter, perhaps) – and the protagonist, who 'did not try to flee but advanced slowly, in an almost priestly manner' (*ID*, 3).⁴⁹ This archi-passivity is perhaps one of the most seminal bridges between the thought of Blanchot and Derrida (as well as Levinas and Agamben, whose ideas shall be discussed more centrally in the fourth and fifth chapter, respectively). It is here, at this crossroads of thought, that this introduction concludes its analysis of *The Instant of My Death*.

This book has begun to explore such broad questions as the dynamics of the death sentence and its interruption, the potentialities of thanatopolitics and the postsovereign subject, the *arrivant* and the *revenant*, the Third and the Neuter, identity and passivity. What has been evidenced so far should not be taken for more than it is: *one* literary work has provided the reader with *one* example of a thinking through death, albeit on several levels. And yet, one can already hear in this discussion the echoes of a vast range of literary works, all in their own way thinking through the human and our relation to death. Furthermore, if all this is '[thanato]politics in the making', what form of politics does this literature suggest? Is it that which is postsovereign? Ultimately, this literary thinking-through of death and its politics is what must be discussed, and these interrelated issues trouble even the concept of autothanatography, which must be rethought on its own literary and philosophical terms rather than from the common-sense view of its apparent contradictions. To get to this, one must first begin with the self-contradictions of the death penalty.

2

Death penalties

Horses

The previous chapter has expounded several preliminary ideas on the possibilities and implications of a death shared with that of the excluded Other. However, it might be said that it did so while itself excluding that Other all too often forgotten: the animal. Indeed, another instance of death in Blanchot's narrative – this time absolutely ignored by its critics – is that of the 'bloated horses'.

It would be the purpose of a different book to delve into the age-old association of death and the equine. Here it might be sufficient to point out how easily we may forget, in light of contemporary tensions, that the majority of violent death throughout history has been wrought not with buttons and machines but on horseback, or even from the insides of a wooden horse.[1] Among other art forms, several works of literature underscore this relation; one recalls, for instance, how it is a horse that King Richard III famously pleads for, hastening towards his prophesized death, and it is the horses that 'eat each other' upon the death of King Duncan.[2] In philosophy, one happens upon Silenus in the forested heath, the half-man, half-horse god whose words Friedrich Nietzsche contemplates, and who advises us that, if we are to insist on *being*, then it would be best for us 'to die soon'.[3] We are reminded that, while we may try and hold rein of horses, it is death that reigns over us. All we can do, perhaps, is prepare ourselves for death and assume the tender features of the 'Hippocratic face', a medical term (still in usage) that denotes the facial expression often taken on just before death.[4] Inevitably, 'Hippocratic' literally translates to 'one superior in horses'.[5]

Humanity and the nonhuman animal have been cleaved time and again. The exclusion of the horse in the first chapter inadvertently mirrors how we are traditionally distinguished from animals by way of rationality, consciousness, logos, politics, 'language, tool use, the inheritance of cultural behaviors, and so on' – what Cary Wolfe describes as 'the old saws of anthropocentrism'.[6] While holding to the porousness of this dichotomy, what is of primary concern here is the death of the *human*, as bare, unbearable or animalistic as it may be, and this as a death which happens in a political context.[7] It was previously stated that death reigns over us, and it is indeed the problematic connotation of royalty and sovereign power that this chapter foregrounds: to whom does death belong under the sovereign sentence of the death penalty, and is death truly one's own when the sovereign decrees it and the Third interrupts it? How does this problematization pave the way towards conceptualizing the relational death that *The Instant* foregrounds? And while the horse must, once more, be left to one side in order to pursue these questions – however much the gibbet resembles the abattoir, and even if animal deaths were also often substituted for human ones in the ancient Near East[8] – it might be worth keeping in mind a particularly revealing English idiom which winks, playfully, with the knowledge that horses will never be too far removed from this exploration of relational death: namely, to 'ride a horse that was foaled of an acorn' meant that one is executed on the gallows.[9]

For whom the bell tolls

At the intersections of the animal and the death penalty is Kant. In the first two sentences of his foundational *Anthropology*, he writes: 'The fact that the human being can have the "I" in his representations raises him infinitely above all other living beings on Earth. Because of this he is a person [. . .] an entirely different being from *things*, such as irrational animals, with which one can do as one likes.'[10]

Animals, or *things* as Kant's technical terminology requires him to call them, are thus principally set apart from man on the basis of (their lack of) autonomy and rational will.[11] Human beings, therefore, are not only embodied life living in the world of sense, acting under empirical Euclidian and Newtonian laws (the zoological aspect of man which Kant terms *homo phaenomenon*), but also living a life extended into the realm of Right, that is, rational and moral law (this being the *homo noumenon*).[12] For Kant, however, there are two ways (arguably, these are the *same* way) in which man may revert back to animal, and this can be seen as actually quite revolutionary thinking considering Kant's time: first, through the enactment of suicide, and, second, through the enactment of a crime which merits capital punishment, generally being – though not without exception – homicide. In these cases, according to Kant, man becomes some*thing* less than man. Of suicide, applicable also to the criminal who kills, he writes that while 'man is no thing', he 'who fails to respect humanity [. . .] turns himself into a thing, becomes an object of free choice for everyone', and thus 'can be treated by others as an animal or a thing; he can be dealt with like a *horse* or a dog, for he is no longer a man'.[13]

Kant's fervent advocacy of the death penalty – based also on the premises of the concept of Right, coercion, and the idea that punishment and crime must be equivalent (*jus talionis*) – hinges, indeed, on the idea that man can become some 'thing' perhaps even 'below the beasts', and that which is killed is no longer the Aristotelian political animal.[14] Capital punishment is thus justified in the Kantian framework; it is not, according to Kant, the *homo noumenon* who is the subject of the condemnation to death. Indeed, this rational aspect of man actually collaborates with the sovereignty that sentences him, and this in the capacity of a 'colegislator' endowed with 'pure reason'.[15] The subject of the sentence, rather, is the *homo phaenomenon*: that thing that receives punishment, which cannot be one and the same with the law due to the impossibility of *willing* punishment (for that would not be punishment at all) and which has been expunged of its innate and civic humanity. This is why Kant accuses Cesare Beccaria of both sophistry and of 'overly compassionate feelings of an affected humanity': Kant upholds that 'man can have no duties to beings other than man'.[16]

This particular defence of capital punishment has proven to be a divisive one. For instance, for all his criticisms of Kantian philosophy and his deep-seated dislike of the brand of Neo-Kantianism popularized by J. G. Fichte, Arthur Schopenhauer here falls in line with this reasoning, even explicitly criticizing Beccaria. He states, very clearly, that 'everyone is justified in demanding the pledge of the life of another as a guarantee for the security of his own life'. Although not exactly seeing eye to eye with Kant on the idea of *jus talionis* or even on the *phaenomenon/noumenon* distinction, Schopenhauer, thinking more on the lines of this binding guarantee, concludes that '[f]or the security of the life of the citizens capital punishment is therefore absolutely necessary'.[17]

This is not to say that Kant remains without powerful criticisms.[18] Attila Ataner, for one, probes insightfully and lengthily into Kant's contradictory stance – the simultaneous approval of the (thanato)politics of capital punishment and the ethical disavowal of suicide – writing that not only is there 'very little in Kant's writing that explains how this [reversal to thing-ness] could possibly transpire', but also that Kant 'simply cannot escape the fact that execution extinguishes an autonomous will'.[19] In effect, as Ataner argues, the death penalty kills not only the *phaenomenon* but also the *noumenon*, an act incongruous with the

Universal Principle of Right (hence Kant's condemnation of suicide as self-killing *noumenon*). Derrida, too, proclaims 'the extraordinary rationality but also the stupid uselessness of this Kantian logic', a logic 'as rigorous as it is absurd' (*DPI*, 127).[20] In the first volume of his seminars on the death penalty, in fact, Derrida strongly criticizes Kant's prioritization of 'hypothetical imperatives' over the survival of the *homo phaenomenon*, who 'clings to life and to the motives of vital interest', who is a thing and yet 'nothing and nobody, in a certain way' – which, in sum, places the Categorical Imperative above any 'attachment to phenomenal life' or 'value of life' (*DPI*, 124–5, 127–8).

Despite its deep fallibilities, the Kantian distinction and the emphasis on thingness shall need revisiting. However, before that, it is worthwhile to further examine Derrida's seminars as a way of returning to the main question of this chapter, and it is now necessary to make clear, through these same seminars, just what this book understands by 'death penalty'.

First, 'death penalty' (or 'death sentence' or 'condemnation') will here and throughout be used in preference to 'capital punishment' for two reasons. This is not only because of the latter term's ties with the 'head'[21] – and it is worth keeping in mind, as Derrida remarks, that '[w]ithin the legal procedure of execution, putting to death has not always involved attacking the head, decapitating, practicing decollation, hanging or strangulation of the condemned one, or again by a firing squad aiming at the condemned one's face' (*DPI*, 41) – but also because 'capital punishment' brings to the very forefront the idea of *method*, which of course connotes also histories of execution, cultures, religions, theatricalities, technologies, arguments for abolition or retention, legal frameworks, medical realities and consequences such as burial rites, mourning and so on.[22]

The second important clarification is that here, with Derrida, this investigation holds a distinction between being 'condemned to die' and 'condemned to death', although these may at first seem indistinguishable. Indeed, in his second book of *The Discourses*, Epictetus asks us to imagine ourselves in prison, sentenced to die, when another prisoner offers to read us poetry. We reply: '"You think I can listen to poetry in my position?"'. We are in turn asked: '"Why, what is it?"', to which we once again reply: '"I'm sentenced to death!"'. We are then dealt the cutting, and seemingly irrefutable, response: '"And the rest of us aren't?"'.[23] However, while we are all condemned to *die* someday, only the ones condemned to *death* know 'in all certitude [. . .] that the hour of [their] death is fixed, by *others*, by *a third party*, at a certain day, a certain hour, a certain second' (*DPI*, 218; see also *DPII*, 68).[24] Moreover, 'to be "condemned to death" implies a calculating decision as decision of the other' – that is, the sovereign (*DPII*, 137). This is the uniqueness

Derrida attributes to the death sentence, and the decisions and certainty that define it cannot be transposed to similar situations, such as the cases of the battlefield or terminal illness. In the latter situation, prognosis offers no more certitude of one's time of death than that possessed by the (relatively) healthy. Although of course the condition of terminality is itself unique, and questions the human relation to death in a powerful and sometimes even similar manner (as Dostoevsky shows us),[25] it is a state that 'may, in fact, go on for a number of years. Terminal does not mean immediate', and nor does it signify death at a fixed point in time.[26] We can thus respectfully disagree with our fellow inmate, no matter how impressively erudite he is.

A question thus presents itself: Why should this chapter be titled 'death penalties'? – in the plural, if not in reference to execution's multifarious methods or to a broadening out of the term so as to include, for instance, the terminally ill? To put it simply, this is because there is never only one death in the death penalty. Here the emphasis this book places on Derrida's insistence – that, under the death penalty, death is the 'decision of the other' – begins to make some degree of sense. As it shall be argued, there is always necessarily implicated someone else: *the other*, and/or *the third party*. In the case of the death penalty, death can never be singular.

The idea of law in relation to the death penalty is key here, and this is a relation that has already been foregrounded in the previous chapter. Derrida's seminars very much deal with the historical and contemporary situations of the death sentence, especially in terms of legislation (such as the case of Buffet and Bontems, the rather strange situation of the United States and the figure of the president, and the 1948 Declaration of Human Rights), and hence recognizes in the death penalty (as Agamben does a few years earlier, both to a great extent following Walter Benjamin) a uniqueness apart from the element of certitude: that is, its ability to be simultaneously inscribed in law while being also on its outside.[27] This latter aspect manifests, after Schmitt, through 'sovereignty [. . .] marked by the right of life and death over the citizen [turned *enemy* of the state], by the power of deciding, laying down the law, judging, and *executing* the order' (*DPI*, 5, 4). The death penalty, therefore, has always been marked by the political, ever since Plato's time – the supreme council who oversaw Socrates' death makes the 'theologico-political' underpinning of the sentence more than lucid – or even as far back as the time of the ancient Near Eastern king. In fact, according to Harrold Tarrant, Plato strives to 'establish that Socrates would have been unjust in escaping [his punishment], not because he owed it to his accusers and jurymen to stay, but because he owed it to the city and its legal system considered in the abstract'.[28] Sovereignty, then, is at the very heart of the death penalty, and its justice pursues us to the death. As Derrida clarifies: 'If one wants to ask oneself "What is the death penalty?" or "What is the essence and meaning of the death penalty?" it will indeed be necessary to reconstitute this history of sovereignty as the hyphen in the theologico-political' (*DPI*, 22–3). In sum, as Derrida writes, if '[t]here is always the theologico-political wherever there is the death penalty', there is also always its hyphen, the sovereign (*DPI*, 23). Without the law, there can be no death penalty.

On the other hand, Derrida sees the inverse to be simultaneously true. He ponders the thought of 'the birth of law as birth of the death penalty', where one finds 'the very structure of absolute law as founded on the death penalty' which is 'at the origin of the social contract or the contract of the nation-state, *at the origin of any sovereignty, any community, or any genealogy, any people*' (*DPI*, 20–1).[29] Later on, crucially – but added only as an afterthought during the oral presentation of the fifth seminar itself – Derrida says of Blanchot:

> This is a logic that we saw in Blanchot as well. There is no law without death penalty. That's it! The concept of law in itself would not be coherent without a death penalty. One cannot think a code of law without death penalty. This is the logic that runs from Kant to Blanchot in a certain way. (*DPI*, 124, footnote 3)

It is thus also true to say that, without the death penalty, there can be no law. As Benjamin writes in his seminal 'Critique of Violence', those who argued against the death penalty's abolition 'felt, perhaps without knowing why and probably involuntarily, that an attack on capital punishment assails, not legal measures, not laws, but law itself in its origin'.[30] To hear Kant once more: '[t]he mere Idea of a civil constitution among *men* carries with it the concept of punitive justice belonging to the supreme authority', and so what we call society, in its diverse permutations, cannot be distinguished from the penalty.[31] The death of the condemned, then, has us always already implicated within in. This logic, 'which is that of absolute sovereignty and the self-preservation of the political body, [authorizes] the absolute maintenance, *even though or because it is exceptional*, of the death penalty, in the name of the self-preservation of [this same] sociopolitical body' (*DPI*, 86).

The death sentence is thus what founds the very structure of law; hence Derrida's claim that 'it will always be vain to conclude that the universal abolition of the death penalty, if it comes about one day, means the effective end of any death penalty'; for 'even when the death penalty [. . .] will have been purely and simply, absolutely and unconditionally, abolished on earth [*sic*], it will survive:

there will still be some death penalty', and 'it will have other lives [. . .] to sink its teeth into' (*DPI*, 282–3).³² Condemnation to death, as the foundation of human society, always denotes and necessitates a social and 'collective experience of putting to death'. This is why the focus of this book, alongside other contemporary works that concentrate on the death penalty, cannot ever be anachronistic – the death penalty is what founds the very idea of lawful society.

This needs some further unpacking. Adelsberg describes this foundation clearly: 'No matter how many international organizations a nation joins, no matter how much one sovereign state submits to the strictures of the laws of these institutions, the sovereign only retains her/his sovereignty if she/he holds the right of exception, the right to put these laws aside and decide over life and death'.³³ In order for a state to remain a state, therefore, it must be haunted by the spectre of the death penalty. As such, while the sovereign 'may lose her/his capacity to decide on the life and death of citizens in the realm of criminal law', it will retain the penalty 'as recourse when the stability of society and law itself is supposedly at stake. This leads to a partial, merely conditional abolition that leaves the sovereign power of decision over life and death violently intact'.³⁴

One is thus never fortunate enough to live in a nation where the penalty has been abolished; so long as there exist the intertwined concepts of law, punishment and society, the ultimate punishment remains alive, the spine of the body of law that oversees all our lives – and deaths. It is from the death penalty that all punishment derives; incarceration for life, the policeman's baton, censorship, a parking fine: punishment gains its degrees only in light of its capital form and borrows its reality only because the death penalty created the lawful society in which these punishments can be enacted in the first place. The death penalty, then, is not *a* punishment, but rather *the* 'paradigm of punishment' itself, the true abolition of which would 'remove the very foundation of law'; as Christina Howells writes, the penalty 'is not one punishment among others. It is exceptional'.³⁵

We must now return to the certitude of the time of death in the death penalty: this may at first seem in many ways more fundamental than its complex relation with law (and with*out*), seeing as how the death penalty persists regardless, whether in common civil law (*jus commune* and *jus civile*), *The Instant*'s wartime law (*jus in bello*), the law of the eye for an eye (*jus talionis*) or even in what can be termed '*jus in absentia*' and being outlawed.³⁶ The certainty of death in the death penalty, then, seemingly runs even deeper than its entrenchment in law and lawlessness, where even lawful abolition fails to kill the killing sentence; that is to say, while the death penalty can survive without the codifications of law, it cannot survive without death. As John Cyril Barton notes, this is the 'arresting peculiarity of capital punishment: that the death penalty is virtually the only means of death (the one universal human experience) in which the subject knows beforehand exactly how, by what means, and precisely when his or her life will end'.[37]

However, it is this certitude – that the condemned one knows, fully and absolutely, the time of their death – that this book nonetheless reads as uncertain. How am *I* to know of *my* death, when the death penalty involves always more than the (ontological) one? If the penalty has incorporated within it society in general – as discussed above, it is omnipresent and omnisocial – then there always remains an openness in death row, through which the other, the third, the *arrivant*, may infiltrate and interrupt the sovereign's 'mastery over the time of life and death' (*DPI*, 220). Indeed, Derrida acknowledges the phantasmagoric nature of this certitude, making the point that this 'calculating decision [. . .] seems, paradoxically, to put an end to finitude; it affirms its power over time; it masters the future; it protects against the irruption of the other' (*DPI*, 258). This is, however, mere illusion, fiction, as *The Instant* has demonstrated; the Other irrupts without being expected. Kamuf, too, puts her finger on this. Building on Derrida's above points and discussing the intended uncertainties within Robert Coover's *The Public Burning*, she writes of how such interruptions of the sovereign sentence reveal its permanent openness, even one for the future: 'Finitude, which means above all that I can never "know what to expect", is canceled, suspended, ended – *finie la finitude* – in-finitized, *as it were*. This "as it were" is the remains and trace of the phantasm, which [. . .] fiction retrieves and registers for us to read'.[38] The condemned are thus rescued from this fiction of certainty peddled by sovereignty and in this manner maintained in that paradoxical state: 'Dead – immortal'.

If, then, the death penalty and its literature so trouble the idea of the singular, self-enclosed death, instead sketching the idea of a relational one – where an other may step in at any point, not ever protected against – it is thus best to thoroughly examine the thoughts of an immediate antagonist to this sketched 'relational death'.

The first chapter presented this notion of relationality in light of death's frequent and perhaps entirely misconstrued disassociation from that which is called 'myself'. For Heidegger, this is anything but the case. For him, death is always one's own, and 'therefore never send to know for whom the bell tolls; It tolls for thee' and for thee only.[39] This Heidegger presents most clearly in *Being and Time*, where there is undertaken 'a thinking of the finitude of human life' and the always 'implicit but fundamental [. . .] possibility of death'.[40]

For Heidegger, we die because we live – or, rather, because we *are*. Silenus's words become a tautology. '"As soon as man comes to life, he is at once old enough to die"', writes Heidegger, quoting the German medieval poetry of Johannes von Tepl (*BT*, 289).⁴¹ But what does it mean *to be*, and how *are* we? These are, of course, Heidegger's questions in *Being and Time*, where he argues that there are two 'different ways of maintaining oneself in this Being [*Dasein*]': either authentically, with the courageous '"knowledge"' that we ourselves are condemned to die, or inauthentically, in '"ignorance"', where one flees '*in the face* of [death]' and only acknowledges death with the idle chatter [*das Gerede*] of the public – whom Heidegger terms the 'they' [*Das Man*] – which understands death as 'a mishap which is constantly occurring'; in other words, as an inconspicuous, indefinite and 'well-known event occurring within-the-world' and which 'belongs to nobody in particular' (*BT*, 295–7). However, as Heidegger advocates, one may gain the authentic knowledge of one's own death through anxiety [*Angst*]. 'Anxiety brings Dasein face to face with [. . .] the authenticity of its Being', he writes, and this is an idea he repeats even in his 1960 public lectures in Meßkirch, more than thirty years later, when he suggests that we make a habit of visiting graveyards in order for us to master 'the art of dying daily', here echoing the Platonic *meletē thanatou* (*BT*, 232).⁴² If we are born to life, and all life dies, then our existence – our *Being-in-the-world* – is also necessarily one that is *Being-towards-death* [*Sein-zum-Tode*]. This is why we should think about death: because of its equivalence to thinking the very structures of life itself (*BT*, 276). In short: 'Being-towards-death is essentially anxiety', and death is thus revealed not as a certain event that happens to other people and which we can experience in our lifetime, as the 'they' would have it with their alienating talk, but as a possibility that constitutes my very Being and which remains wholly outside of my experience (*BT*, 310–11).

Heidegger goes on to characterize this death that is a necessary and constitutive foundation of our being. Unlike animals, we do not simply 'perish' [*Verenden*]. Instead, our death is more of a 'demise' [*Ableben*], which is the way Dasein 'can end without authentically dying', since existence can never no-longer-be [*Nicht-mehr-da-sein*] or be 'annihilated'; it would then no longer be existence (*BT*, 280). We thus die *properly* [*Sterben*]. This is not to say that, for Heidegger, differentiating between human and nonhuman death relies on a belief in some sort of afterlife. *Being and Time* can in fact accurately be described as where 'God has been methodologically ruled out' or as an 'anti-theological' work where there is the wilful exclusion of all such problems.⁴³

Our death encompasses the physiological or 'biological signification' of death (the existentiell-ontic level) as well as the existential-ontological, and it is what is 'not-yet' (we are still alive, not dead yet) (*BT*, 292, 280). However, while it will never be made present(-at-hand) – because death cannot be made present, because non-Being cannot *be* – it is nonetheless an always present 'possibility of no-longer-being-able-to-be-there', when 'all [Dasein's] relations have been undone'. Furthermore, '[t]his ownmost *non-relational* [*unbezügliche*] possibility is at the same time the uttermost one'.[44] And so, famously, Heidegger states: 'Death is the possibility of the absolute impossibility of Dasein', a *'possibility which is one's ownmost, which is non-relational, and which is not to be outstripped'* (*BT*, 294–5). It is this contradictorily individualizing definition of death that this book questions.

Heidegger's authentic anxiety reveals that I am a singular individual only because I die.[45] Aphoristically pronounced, *I am* because *I die*.[46] Consequently, only I can die this ownmost death-of-mine; according to Heidegger, 'death *lays claim* to [. . .] an *individual* Dasein', and death is what is mine every time [the *Jemeinigkeit*] (*BT*, 308). He states this vehemently and very clearly:

> *No one can take the Other's dying away from him*. Of course someone can 'go to his death for another'. But that always means to sacrifice oneself for the Other *'in some definite affair'*. Such 'dying for' can never signify that the Other has thus had his death taken away in even the slightest degree. Dying is something that every Dasein itself must take upon itself at the time. By its very essence, death is in every case mine, in so far as it 'is' at all. (*BT*, 284)

Thus, if '[t]he Being of any such entity is *in each case mine*', 'mineness and existence are ontologically constitutive for death' (*BT*, 67, 284). The same, of course, goes for me: no one can take my death. The Other, then, not only cannot substitute my existence for my death but also cannot help me come to an authentic grasp of my Being-towards-death. Although 'Dasein is essentially Being-with [*Mitsein*] others', witnessing 'a termination [*Deendigung*] of Dasein' when the Other dies in front of me is still not equivalent to me authentically taking up my death (*BT*, 281). In the death of the Other, we still do not encounter the nothing of *Nicht-mehr-da-sein*: we only encounter 'a mere corporeal Thing' (the corpse, on which Kant and Heidegger will later convene) (*BT*, 282).

Already there are here echoes of dispute from the first chapter, namely: the 'not-yet' individuation of death as opposed to Blanchot's common, de-individuating death 'in abeyance'; the unexperienced experience; and survival as a paradoxical manifestation of how Dasein 'lives on' or even 'outlasts' itself. Derrida is correct to observe in Blanchot a troubling of the *Jemeinigkeit* (see *D*, 51).

Aside from these prior problematizations, there are two further points of contention that this study shall expound in the next section: Heidegger's disconnect of the other's death from my own, and his reluctance to think of a period after death. Both these points can be understood from a Greek point of view, to which Heidegger repeatedly returns in his undoing of Western metaphysics. Here we shall return to the myth of Narcissus.

We are all familiar with Ovid's telling of it in the third book of the *Metamorphoses*: after spurning yet another lover, Narcissus is cursed by Nemesis into falling in love with his own reflection in a still pool. In anguish over his inability to reach his lover, and then realizing that he has pitifully fallen in love only with himself, he 'melts [. . .] and languishes away': his body goes to the underworld, and in our world there remains only a flower.[47]

Narcissus falls 'in love with [his own] fantastick shade'.[48] Inauthentically, he takes his reflection – which can be read as an indefinite and never-present possibility – as substantive, material certainty. As Ovid's narrator reminds him, however, it is only '[t]hy own warm blush [which] within the water glows', and only '[w]ith thee the colour'd shadow comes and goes'.[49] Narcissus, with the illusion that what belongs to him (his reflection) is removed from him (another being), is in Heideggerian terms trapped in the talk of the 'they' which distances death from our own being. However, the youth does subsequently take the leap from inauthenticity to authenticity: he realizes that, in truth, it is only his shadow, and that, moreover, it is *his* shadow. Belonging to him, like death, his reflection makes him himself, coming and leaving with him. It is wholly his ownmost, non-relational possession; it cannot be stripped from himself. However, the fact remains that the reflection does not belong to him, no matter how constitutive it is – for he can neither caress it nor possess it – and Narcissus is thus here revealed as authentic.

What is contrapuntal in this myth is that authenticity does not strike the reader as any better. Narcissus persists in his love for himself: 'Let me still feed the flame by which I die; | Let me still see, tho' I'm no further blest', he adamantly proclaims.[50] Just as Heidegger argues one should, he continues to view his reflection, his shadow, as both his own (possibility) and not his own (impossibility) – and remains plagued by the fever of self-love. No matter how relational his realization seems to be, with an object and subject – 'It is my self I love, my self I see' – he is tied only to himself, not to any other.[51] Narcissus is chained to non-relationality. From this arises his poignant and particular wish to both depart from and multiply himself: 'How gladly would I from my self remove! | And at a distance set the thing I love'.[52] Charles Martin's translation, which is at times less faithful to the original but also less moralistic than the Joseph Addison version cited above, renders this wish as follows: 'Oh, would that I were able to secede', and thus 'from my own body, depart from what I love!'[53]

The spatial gap between 'my' and 'self' retained in Addison's former translation uncovers a Narcissus who wants to be not just without body but also without self; he seeks a departure not at the existentiell-ontic level but at the existential-ontological: it is not just in life that he seeks the distance of the *Mitsein*. Moreover, he is seeking not death but a cessation of Being-towards-death – and, with this cessation, Being-towards-death's solitary non-relationality. He cries: 'I see his fate involv'd in mine.'[54]

Even in the after death, that realm Heidegger prohibits us from thinking lest we end up in theology, Narcissus gazes at the water: his 'flitting ghost retires, | And in the Stygian waves itself admires'.[55] Martin's version, however, preserves an ambiguity: 'On the ferry ride across the Styx', Narcissus's 'gaze into its current did not waver'.[56] The first translation leads us to affirm Heidegger's view of death; in the persevering reflection in the waters of the Styx, death remains non-relational: it is that which makes us *be* as well as *not-be*. In death, we authentically see non-relationality as the everlasting (or, sacrilegiously for Heidegger, 'immortal') reflection of ourselves. Yet there nonetheless remains an ambiguity through another meaning of 'stygian': that is, the 'very dark' and thus unreflective.[57] As the Martin translation suggests, though Narcissus gazes, he may no longer, in death, see himself. While Heidegger asserts that 'mineness and existence are ontologically constitutive for death', Narcissus now exists – in the after(-)life, after(-)death – without solitary mineness, no longer non-relational. His is being-in-abeyance. Heidegger's death, in negating the 'I', at the same time constitutes it – and, to quote Ovid, 'its empty being on thy self relies'.[58] Heidegger's death, like his 'self', is ultimately 'hermetically self-referential', Narcissistic.[59]

The impossibility of my death

'[M]ust one start out from the question of the death penalty [. . .] in order to pose the question of death in general?', Derrida asks (*DPI*, 238). The penalty is a question, he states, of which the 'great thinkers of death never seriously spoke and which they no doubt held to be a circumscribable and relatively dependant, secondary question' (*DPI*, 237).[60] Of Heidegger, Derrida in fact somewhat cuttingly remarks that 'this great thinker of being-toward-death never shows any interest in the death penalty' (*DPII*, 148).

Any answer to the question of why the death penalty is not merely 'secondary' needs to go via literature. Aside from the links drawn in the introduction to this study, one may also turn to Derrida's remarks on how the 'modern history of the institution named literature in Europe over the last three or four centuries is contemporary with and indissociable from a contestation of the death penalty', as well as tied to 'an abolitionist struggle that, to be sure, is uneven, heterogeneous, discontinuous, but irreversible' (*DPI*, 30). This movement towards abolition is more relevant to his seminars than revisiting 'those large veins that are "literature and death", "literature and the right to death", or the trail of countless literary or poetic works that put crime and punishment, and that punishment called the death penalty, to work or onstage' – which are, indeed, precisely at stake in this present book (*DPI*, 29–30). Derrida explores the political nuances, manifestations and struggles of the lives and works of not only Jean Genet and Hugo but also writers like Shelley and Camus. This study, however, will focus not on the socio-historical, autobiographical and legislative but rather the existential-ontological-(thanato)political – and this through the literary which Derrida, despite acknowledging its crucial position, chooses to leave largely unaddressed in his seminars. As such, as this book progresses, literature shall come to bear more and more, necessarily not limited to one particular author or era in light of the very timelessness and universality of death and condemnation. It would be straightforward enough to remain with Blanchot's *The Instant of My Death*; or even, perhaps, to limit oneself to other works of his, such as *The Madness of the Day*, where a man is living death, or *Death Sentence*, where the revenant emerges once more.[61] But one must remember that Blanchot (or his protagonists, at least) has not been the only one condemned to death.

And so we shall turn to literature in general to examine 'death in general' and this notion of the relational death. But surely Heidegger has already stopped us in our tracks, has been convincing enough to dissuade any such endeavour despite the opening but hounding questions of the first chapter? It is incoherent to insist on any sort of relational death, Heidegger tells us, because if I do not die then I am not I.

But perhaps this insistence is not so outrageous. In the death penalty seminars, for instance, Derrida not only sees the question of 'what is death?' as 'perhaps not preliminary to the question of death given or life taken', placing the mechanisms of the death penalty before Heidegger's ontological death, but also questions the very logic of the structure with which Heidegger endows the concept of death. This Derrida does by pointing out how 'every calculation of this type supposes the possibility of calculating and mastering the instant of death'

– and, from the previous chapter, we can already see the folly in this (*DPI*, 237, 239). '[N]ever more so than today', Derrida continues in light of this presumed mastery, 'has objective knowledge as to the delimitation of death [. . .] been as problematic, debatable, fragile, and deconstructible down to the minimal semantic kernel of the word death' (*DPI*, 239). Derrida, to some extent, carries out this deconstruction earlier on in *Aporias* (and in this work we are reminded that the 'semantic kernel of the word death' is also the 'one word that remains absolutely unassignable'), where he takes issue with Heidegger's 'ontological delimitation among the fields of inquiry concerning death', questioning 'how much one can trust the powerful apparatus of conceptual distinctions put forth by Heidegger' (*AP*, 22, 30, 39).

This present argument unambiguously holds with Derrida's critiques of Heidegger on these counts. It perhaps follows the suggestion of Derrida's angel: not the angel of death but an angel who whispers that, 'at bottom[,] that's the dream of deconstruction, a convulsive movement to have done with death, to deconstruct death itself', 'to come to blows with death [. . .]. Death to death' (*DPI*, 240–1). It is almost a dream of immortality, even if Derrida states, in the seminars, that he is not interested in the question of '[w]hat comes afterward', and (rightly) acknowledges that 'neither does life come out unscathed by this deconstruction' (*DPI*, 241). As he states in *Aporias*, in direct contradiction to these later sentiments of his, one cannot 'think being-to-death without starting from immortality' (*AP*, 55). Possibly, then, if Heidegger can be called 'antitheological', then always at the heart of the act of deconstruction rests the theological as the radical unsaid.[62]

However, alongside the fact of *Demeure*'s misreading of *The Instant of My Death*, Derrida cannot truly be said to think relational death as is configured here. He is never as far from Heidegger as he is often assumed to be. On the other hand, the point must be made that, although he does not think of death as relational, he nevertheless concedes the possibility of thinking it (as primarily evidenced by his angel of deconstruction). This is especially true of two of his works.

The first is the aforementioned *Aporias*. Here, despite the problems he identifies with the Heideggerian structure of death, Derrida fully endorses its non-relationality: 'If death [. . .] names the very irreplaceability of absolute singularity (no one can die in my place or in the place of the other), then all the *examples* in the world can precisely illustrate this singularity. Everyone's death [. . .] is irreplaceable. So is "my life." Every other is completely other [*Tout autre est tout autre*]' (*AP*, 22).

This is why Derrida terms death a 'secret, since it signs the irreplaceable singularity' on the basis of the now-famous dictum '*tout autre est tout autre*', a paradoxical statement of relation or symmetry that is nonetheless radically asymmetrical (*AP*, 74). And so, in light of Heideggerian inauthenticity, he states that 'nothing is more substitutable and yet nothing is less so than the syntagm "my death"' (*AP*, 22). Nothing is less so than any kind of substitution or dying in-stead; nothing more so than Heideggerian non-relational death.[63]

Derrida adds that 'any form of survival or return [*revenance*] [. . .] is not opposed to being-toward-death, it does not contradict it [. . .] because it is conditioned by being-toward-death and confirms it at every moment' – meaning that, essentially, only mortals both think of, and 'achieve', immortality. Thus, '[t]he incontestability of being-toward-death, the non-derivation of certainty concerning being-toward-death [. . .] would not leave any other methodologically rigorous choice than that of starting from "this side" [that is, this life]' (*AP*, 55–6). Indeed, reinforcing what we have already seen:

> In *Being and Time*, the existential analysis does not want to know anything about the ghost [*revenant*] [. . .]. Everything that can be said about them, as interesting as it may sometimes sound, would certainly stem, in Heidegger's view, from derivative disciplines [such as theology]. It would concern the figures or the experiences of demise [*Ableben*] rather than death properly speaking. Such would be his fast answer (too fast for me) to whoever would be tempted to consider [. . .] spectrality or living-on, surviving. (*AP*, 60–1)

With that parenthetical interjection – '(too fast for me)' – Derrida signals that he does not firmly hold that any thinking of survival, *revenance*, or of that which lives on, on the other side, is fundamentally flawed, and thus the matter of non-relationality might not be as incontestable as it seems. Despite being rather unrelenting on the possibility or even thought of 'dying in-stead', one of the central thoughts explored here, such an investigation is, then, possible within the ethos of a deconstruction that comes to blows with death. Derrida, in fact, leaves 'suspended' the possibility of 'draw[ing] the necessary consequences' when talking of how, '[i]f *Jemeinigkeit*, that of *Dasein* or that of the ego [. . .], is constituted in its ipseity [. . .], then this self-relation welcomes or supposes the other within its being-itself as different from itself', and, inversely, 'the relation to the other (in itself outside myself, outside myself in myself)' (*AP*, 61). It is also an examination, Derrida points out, that 'may even engage the political' – here read as sovereignty, the exception and the death penalty, where one is condemned to death and expects nothing more ('*du s'attendre à la mort*'): that is, a political which is from its inception thanatopolitical (*AP*, 72).

Thus, if 'dying would be the aporia' – that is 'the impossibility of being dead, the impossibility of living or rather "existing" one's death, as well as the impossibility of existing once one is dead, or, in Heidegger's terms, the impossibility for *Dasein* to be what it is' – then the aporetic itself, by its very porousness, includes within it not just the end of 'dying-properly but, and it is quite different, the end of the properly-dying' (*AP*, 73–4). This second end opens up the insight with which Derrida approaches the conclusion of *Aporias*: that 'man, or man as *Dasein*, never has a relation to death as such, but only to perishing [the animal], to demising [*Ableben*], and to the death of the other, who is not the other' [*Sterben*] – and so '[t]he death of the other thus becomes again "first", always first'. Therefore, '[t]he death of the other, this death of the other in "me", is fundamentally the only death that is named in the syntagm "my death", with all the consequences that one can draw from this' (*AP*, 76). The non-relationality of Heidegger's death is pushed to the impossibility of a relation with one's ownmost and not-to-be-outstripped death, and in this way a certain shade of relationality can begin to come to light.

The Gift of Death, published one year after *Aporias*, can almost be read as a sequel which (mainly through an engagement with Czech philosopher Jan Patočka) makes more overt the secret that is theology, faith and religion. Derrida here sees death as '*the gift that is not present*', and this idea of the gift, which one awaits with the 'attentive anticipation of death', offers 'a new significance for death, a new apprehension of death' (*GD*, 29, 12, 31). Is this, Derrida asks, what amounts to *dying for the other*?

This is the notion of sacrifice that Derrida explores, a dying for the other which is (definitively) not a dying instead of the other: '*for* is not *pro* in the sense of "in place of the other"' (*GD*, 43). The notions of responsibility and religion, at the heart of sacrifice, can only come 'from the site of death as the place of my irreplaceability, that is, of my singularity', and so 'existence excludes every possible substitution' (*GD*, 41). Responsibility, for Derrida, amounts to the self 'who looks without the subject-who-says-I being able to reach that other': in short, responsibility is existence and to exist is to be responsible (*GD*, 25). Being always existentially different from the other, one always dies one's own death. On this he is stubborn: 'I can give my whole life for another, I can *offer* my death to the other, but in doing this I will only be replacing or saving something partial in a particular situation (there will be a nonexhaustive exchange or sacrifice [. . .])' (*GD*, 43). This repeats what Heidegger says of sacrifice, and further reiterations of one's irreplaceable mortality abound.[64] Death, therefore, is here configured as a gift that one can only give oneself, 'for it can only be mine alone, irreplaceably':

'to give oneself death or to put oneself to death [*se donner la mort*]' is to give oneself singularity or individuality, wherein we are 'ready to receive death', and it is a gift, a secret, because the 'I myself' cannot come to ever truly know or possess death (*GD*, 45, 31, 40).

In *The Gift of Death*, Derrida once more (and this time more pronouncedly) critiques Levinas. Levinas's idea of responsibility as being first and foremost entwined with the other's mortality, 'to the extent of including myself in that death', prompts some questions for Derrida: 'How can one not *be*?', and 'how can we think of death starting from *adieu* rather than the inverse' (*GD*, 46–7)?[65] Derrida dismisses Levinas's proposition – that death is not what constitutes us but rather that the Other does – and postpones thinking from death-to-life as opposed to life-to-death (or Being-toward-death) by stating that he 'cannot effect such a displacement here [in *The Gift of Death*]' (*GD*, 47). It is Derrida's dismissal of Levinas that now appears 'too fast'.

This not *being*, this thinking from death, and the implicit Levinasian possibility of dying *with* the other – or even *in-stead* – is broadly categorized by Derrida as being 'in the ethical dimension of sacrifice' (*GD*, 48). If existence is responsibility (because death constitutes me as individual, and thus I am able to be responsible *as* such an individual), then this other side is irresponsibility (which Derrida troublingly associates with temptation and the 'demonic'). One is justified in wondering whether irresponsibility finds its place in ethical sacrifice. 'The ethical', Derrida writes, 'involves me in a substitution, as does speaking', and this is because, 'in speaking [or in language more generally], I renounce at the same time my liberty and my responsibility. Once I speak I am never and no longer myself, alone and unique'. And thus, '[t]he ethical can therefore end up making us irresponsible', and the elision of the other with the 'subject-who-says-I' is 'a lack of responsibility' (*GD*, 60–1, 25). And so the absolute alterity of the other – *tout autre est tout autre* – which 'signifies that every other is singular' and thus irreplaceable in death, also 'seems to contain the very possibility of a secret that hides and reveals itself at the same time', thus being a 'secret [which] doesn't belong, [which] can never be said to be at home or in its place' in the singular, non-relational mortality of the irreplaceable individual (*GD*, 87, 92).

To conclude with regard to Derrida's (quasi-)thinking of relational death: this present work takes up what Derrida hopes someone would, or what he never seemed to be able to find time for in *The Death Penalty* seminars, *Aporias*, and (to a much lesser extent) *The Gift of Death*: that is, an examination of the figure or revenant who is replaceable and non-singular, who comes to blows with death and survives, who starts not from this side of life but from that other side of death, whose death is not his ownmost, who starts from a dying *with* (and its epitome, dying *in-stead*), opening the gift of death and annulling its secrecy, who not only lives on but *speaks* on as well, who is irresponsible, more demonic and less secretly theological. In sum, this book shall sketch the figure which brings to light the impossibility of 'my death', a figure at the limit of deconstruction (and ontological structures) that seems already present in the literary works examined here. This figure – bearing considerable similarities to the *homo sacer* – has already, and inevitably, to some extent been always already conceived of (even if often postponed) in Derrida's writings. All this is something which consistently troubled him at least throughout the 1990s, especially if 'to deconstruct' is, ultimately, 'to deconstruct death'. This is not to say that what is intended here is a comprehensive deconstruction of death – unless, that is, one takes breaking off the handle of a vase as equivalent to breaking the whole vase itself.

Relational death, then, is only ever intimated in Derrida's work, and never thought out to its consequences. In this light, one must converse with other arguments that more directly attempt to collapse the harshly defined boundaries of the non-relational death. Stefano Cochetti, for instance, similarly picks up on the Narcissism implicit in Heidegger's view of death, if only superficially so and in a rather misconstrued manner, and sees a potential break from this 'self-referential mechanism' of death. He writes that while, '[s]trictly speaking, there is no togetherness or social being in death', there may 'in broad terms' be 'something analogous to that in the form of ritual blood sacrifice and of dying in war'.[66] Although he identifies these two modes of dying as attempting 'to conjure away, or at least alleviate, the social gaps of death, striving to realize the paradox of a social death' and granting one 'the ability to stand in for another in death', he makes the wrong assumption that death can be crystallized into a communicable event (and, in the case of ritual sacrifice, a sacrificial one at that), rather than as something that must be kept as possibility. In 'striving to release both death from its exile in the isolation of *Dasein*, and *Dasein* itself from its oppressive vacillation between meaninglessness and incommunicability in the face of death', Cochetti forgets that, for Heidegger, authentic death is not at all meaningless, and indeed *Being and Time* was itself in part written as a counterargument to the nihilism Cochetti seems to identify within it.[67] Ultimately, it is not enough to say that 'in war, one often dies replacing the death of others' (presumably those still at home) – since this in no way allows these others to survive their own deaths, but merely postpone them; moreover, to uphold ritual blood sacrifice as 'orientated towards conferring a meaning on the communication of death, thereby contributing to the socialization of death itself', is to be trapped in the idle chatter of the 'they'.[68]

Among others, significantly more nuanced arguments for a relational death are propounded by Alison Stone and George Pattison. Stone forwards her thoughts on this, initially, by thinking with Adriana Cavarero (and Hannah Arendt) in terms of natality, that 'peculiar' gift of birth, where 'feminist ideas about birth may instead be taken as opening up possibilities for rethinking death and mortality'.[69] Seeing that Cavarero's impersonally materialist 'views of birth and death actually conflict', Stone reads into this conflict a relationality *within* the singular that works on the Derridean lines of the Other, that is, that which is 'in itself outside myself [and] outside myself in myself'; indeed, she writes that 'each singular being, within itself, is the holding together, the concrescence, of a determinate and in each case unique set of relations', which constitute the self. Thus we find here a repetition of Heidegger's statement that 'Dasein is essentially Being-with [*Mitsein*] others', a repetition that reaffirms Heideggerian uniqueness while simultaneously relocating it to an outside of the self (though Heidegger himself does not do this, but keeps it within, Narcissistically). Stone writes: 'If someone's birth is their entrance into a shared world with others, then their death must equally be their irreversible departure from this *shared* world', where one 'will cease to be there *with these others*' and thus, '[i]n this sense, one's death [. . .] is constitutively social'.[70] And so, through Cavarero, Stone challenges Heidegger in lucid terms:

> If I am constituted of a web of relations with others, then when I die, these relations end, relations that were equally parts of the webs of relations that constituted each of those other people. So something of each of those people does die at the same time. Conversely, when others die part of me dies; our deaths are not separate from one another.[71]

Thus, Stone continues, if 'my death is the end of my existence *as* the unique concrescence of relations that I am, then for one of those relations to end is for me to undergo, already in life, a part of my death'; therefore, 'our deaths are not separate [. . .], it is a *we* who die: a death shared'.[72] Later, in her 2016 essay "The Relationality of Death", Stone reiterates this view of death as one which is 'shared' (and not only one's ownmost possibility) 'insofar as each person is constituted of a web of relationships unfolding over time' – for this reason, when a person dies, a part of us literally dies with them; death 'will be *ours* – shared'.[73] If the Other constitutes the World in which I am being, then the loss of the Other changes my very Being-in-the-world. Stone thus departs from Heidegger's impersonal gaze at the corpse of the Other.

But, even if this argument holds water, does this necessarily entail a change in my Being-towards-death? One suspects that Heidegger's rebuttal to Stone's conception of death would be to accuse her of prioritizing the existentiell-ontic level of death, and not its existential-ontological terms, especially in relation to her figuring of death as corporeal mortality (mainly through a reading of Simone de Beauvoir's *A Very Easy Death*). According to Stone, we relate to others that are embodied – 'we are [. . .] relational beings *qua* living bodies' – and so 'our deaths are continuous with one another as physical occurrences', where 'death is relational *as* a corporeal phenomenon that befalls human beings as bodies entwined organically'.[74] For Heidegger, though, ontology takes precedence over biology; thinking otherwise would be a mistake (even if for some, like Kevin A. Aho and presumably Stone herself, the mistake is in *not* thinking about the body).[75] Yes, death cannot happen without biological destruction – '[t]o die [. . .] is to undergo a biological process' – and so let us not commit a transposition of Kant's belief that the *noumenon* can somehow be disassociated from the *phaenomenon*.[76] Crucially, however, death does not happen *only* in biological cessation of function (the existentiell-ontic face of death) but happens throughout one's life (existentially, ontologically), from the beginning of the self and as long as the self *is* the self. One dies even in the prime of one's biology, which Stone seems to skim over in her focus on a relational death that emerges in biological death.[77] Furthermore, even if one delineates the problems of the body, *one dies precisely as one forms these relations with the other*, because it is 'I', as constituted by my death, that makes such relations. In a part of me dying *with* the other who becomes a corpse or a thing, it is only a quality of the self that dies, and not the self as a whole self; only a part of one's psychological, social and ethical self – in Stone's words, a 'dimension', 'strand' or 'part of this person', a part of one's narrative or 'story' – comes to an end.[78] While her idea of death does challenge Heidegger's sharp delineation between my death and the other's, especially in seeing the perseverance of *Mitsein* in death (and even going so far as to ponder the 'possibility of post-mortem survival' through mourning), Stone thinks of a death that concludes a chapter of one's life, not its book.[79]

Pattison takes a similar position, as evidenced by a reference he makes to Donne's Meditation which reveals it to be a poem that paradoxically posits both a non-relational and a relational death: 'No man is an island, entire of itself; [. . .] any man's death diminishes me, because I am involved in mankind.'[80] The bell may toll for thee, but the rest of us can hear it anyway.

Pattison writes of the possible 'reasons for thinking that the distinction Heidegger draws between my "experience" of the deaths of others and the prospect of my own death is not as sharp as he claims'. In noting, as Stone does, that the death of the other confronts me with a change to my very Being(-in-the-world), and thus one is not just '"there alongside"' the other's death, as Heidegger contends, Pattison concludes that the 'cocoon of I-ness is irrevocably broken open'.[81] Thus, he writes: 'Life will never be the same. I will never be the same. The deaths of others and my consciousness of their having died effects a diremption at the heart of Dasein'. In this elevation of the other's death, Pattison holds that 'our own death is something we discover only in relation to the deaths of others', or, 'perhaps even more correctly, bestowed by others'.[82] He elaborates:

> That is, it is bestowed in the language that I am given to speak [. . .] whatever thoughts I have about death. Of course, the mediation of our relation to death through language makes us prone to the idle [chatter of the 'they'] – but does it not at the same time give us the [. . .] more authentic possibility of talking about our own death and about the deaths of others? And [. . .] does it not also disclose the commonness of our mortality? [. . .] If Heidegger's fundamental contention is that each of us must die alone, is it not equally credible to consider that, especially with regard to death, 'we're all in it together'?[83]

This does not only recall the bestowal of the gift of death (this time not a self-gifting but rather a gift to/from the other), but also Derrida's claim that '[o]nce I speak I am never and no longer myself, alone and unique'. Thus, with Sartre's counterarguments to Heidegger in *Being and Nothingness* in mind, Pattison writes:

> I will always fail in my attempt to authentically ground my own existence by grasping and owning my responsibility for being the thrown nullity that I am [i.e. an authentic Being-towards-death], since in every case I will end up being handed over to others and being irredeemably reified in how they remember me. [. . .] Where Heidegger insists on the 'always my own'; quality of an authentic comportment towards death, Sartre sees such 'mineness' as always being wrested away from me and my death – and my life with it – being reduced to just one more event in the world.[84]

For Pattison, then, death is relational insofar as it does not close off, as Heidegger believes, the 'I' that it constitutes; rather, he argues, the self is, in death, 'handed over to a contingent and indeterminate future' in the hands of the other, where the 'I' 'could become just about anyone', and thus 'society [. . .] reaches out to include the dead as well as the living'.[85] While Pattison raises very interesting claims, especially on the lines of subjectivity, he remains subject to the same counterarguments made to Stone above. Furthermore, his discussion is shrouded in ideas of remembrance and love: the ethical demand of the other for love is 'perhaps stronger' than death, he believes.[86] Apart from the fact that his discussion of Heidegger comes from a Christian perspective, where the ethical relation to the other is first and foremost a relation to God as love, it is not clear why this is so. In terms of the loss of the other as amounting to the loss of what I love, the loss of what I hate or despise (a Nemesis), for instance, can be equally powerful.

Apart from Heidegger (and the case of Narcissus's own love), Derrida too can be read as forwarding a refutation of Patterson's position, here formulated rather pithily: love and remembrance work psychologically, not existentially or ontologically.[87] As he writes in his 'Foreword' to Nicolas Abraham and Maria Torok's psychological analysis of Sergei Pankejeff (more famously known by the pseudonym endowed him by Sigmund Freud, 'Wolf Man'), ideas like those expressed by Pattison amount to the psychological processes of incorporation and introjection, where the self tries to identify with the lost other, where one 'pretend[s] to keep the dead alive, intact, *safe* [. . .] *inside me*, [. . .] to love the dead as a living part of me' as if in a crypt.[88] This, Derrida writes, is the question of 'whether or not [. . .] mourning preserves the object *as other* (a living person dead) inside me'; he concludes that this ultimately 'leads to the paradox of a foreign body preserved as foreign but by the same token excluded from a self that thenceforth deals not with the other, but only with itself'; as such, '[t]he more the self keeps the foreign element as a foreigner inside itself, the more it excludes it'.[89] As he writes elsewhere, mourning 'makes the other a *part* of us [. . .] and then the other no longer quite seems to be other'.[90] Pattison's idea of love trumping death ignores the fact that, at the heart of the crypt, is 'a deathly silence, a blackout' – the crypt, one can say, is not reflective but stygian. Pattison's incorporated and introjected love for the other in death does not love the other, but the self.

As has been argued, Derrida does not, however, think relational death: indeed, in this same 'Foreword', he locates once more 'an undecidable irresolution that forever prevents the two [the self and the other] from closing over their *rightful, ideal, proper* coherence [. . .] over *their* death ("their" corpse)', and this undecidability can be located in the many paradigms of the crypt.[91] In contrast, what is attempted in this book is what Derrida briefly alludes to only in his notes to the 'Foreword', when he writes that 'heterocryptography calls for a completely different way of listening from that appropriate to the cryptic incorporation of the self'.[92] Here is, therefore, highlighted a cryptography that listens differently to difference.

Nonetheless, both Stone and Pattison provide us with plenty to consider beyond Heidegger himself. Through Stone's departure from natality, for instance, the already outlandish proposition of the possibility of dying in-stead is made even more so in reversing the question: can someone be born instead of someone else? To this question, this study's previous answers can perhaps be similarly deployed: is birth really our own, given that this supposedly singular 'I' is re(-)produced from two individuals, the *two* who give birth to another, the Other or the *third* party? Is birth (or even, more problematically, conception) not, then, also relational, in that it is, as Stone remarks, 'the conclusion of the process by which a unique set of relations has cohered into, and as, the gestating fetus'?[93] This project holds that death and birth are not simply or diametrically antithetical, but nor do they amount to the same thing: it is a different set of questions to think about whether sexual reproduction condemns one to life.[94] Besides, the idea of life penalties perhaps becomes secondary to the present one of death penalties if one holds that those who are born are *beings* at all only because of the possibility of them *not-being*.

Therefore, while Derrida, Stone and Pattison certainly pave the way for an idea of the relational death, this idea is here posed more radically: that is, that someone else can die in-stead. Both Stone and Pattison indeed trouble Heidegger's 'ownmost' death, and ask questions that follow in the wake of poststructuralist contentions that the subject is not a closed off unity but rather relationally constituted: then is not the subject's death, they ask, also relational? This thinking can be linked not only to Derrida, as above, but also to thinkers like Judith Butler, who writes:

> It is not as if an 'I' exists independently over here and then simply loses a 'you' over there, especially if the attachment to 'you' is part of what composes who 'I' am. If I lose you [. . .] then I not only mourn the loss, but I become inscrutable to myself. Who 'am' I, without you?[95]

Butler even addresses the familiar problems of the idea of (self-)narration; as she states, 'I am gripped and undone by these very relations. My narrative falters, as it must' – and here looms on the horizon, once more, the question of autothanatography as the beyond of narrative, the writing that is simultaneously the end of writing, the epilogue.[96] However, both Stone and Pattison are here read as retaining a Heideggerian degree of self-possession, where, no matter how relational death can be configured, it remains, indelibly, my own. Both see the death of the other as reducing (Stone) or deeply and irrevocably changing (Pattison) my world – but not *my* death. Even if it is relational, my ownmost death is still my own 'not-yet', and, crucially in this discussion, it is only in the wake of dying one's own death – *and not in the instant* – that relationality is exposed; in other words, it is death's consequences that are re-evaluated in terms of Being as *Mitsein*, and not death in and of itself. In short, Stone and Pattison speak of a self-defeating *Mitsein* that it is contained only within one(-)self since the Other is now already dead. If there is to be conceived a truly relational death, therefore, both parties must be dead; and we recall that even if one survives death, it is solely on the basis of not surviving the unexperienced experience. Thus, although to a considerably lesser degree than Heidegger, Stone's and Pattison's views of death both deal 'not with the other, but only with [the Self] itself', and 'obey a conservative, "Narcissistic" finality'.[97]

To conclude this chapter: in the absence of a proper examination of relational death, one has to turn to the literature that 'birthed' such death, the relational death that may also be here glimpsed through *Mitsterben* (dying-with, following *Mitsein*), a term which, as of yet, remains revealingly unthought of in philosophy.[98]

One literary figure that Heidegger consistently avoids, Pattison reminds us, is Dostoevsky. Dealing instead with Leo Tolstoy's *The Death of Ivan Ilyich* – where the protagonist is 'in continual despair' as he struggles to come to an authentic understanding of his Being-towards-death – Heidegger refrains from engaging Dostoevsky despite the literary, cultural and political influence the Russian author held in Germany in the interim between the World Wars.[99] With Pattison, this study asks: 'Does Dostoevsky have a question for Heidegger that Heidegger would not like to have had asked?'[100]

This question, perhaps, is that of the death penalty. Prince Myshkin asks whether the death penalty undoes human nature itself: 'Who can tell whether human nature is able to bear this without madness?' (*TI*, 20). His reflections in *The Idiot* are congruent with what this chapter has foregrounded. Execution, he states, is 'done in an *instant*', although even then death will have already happened. This is because 'the chief and worst pain may not be in the bodily suffering' but rather 'in one's knowing *for certain* that in an hour, and then in ten minutes, and then in half a minute, and then *now, at the very moment*, the soul will leave the body'. At this instant, 'one will *cease to be a man* and [. . .] that's bound to happen; the worst part of it is that it's *certain*' (*TI*, 18–19).[101] In the unexperienced experience, this Kantian idea of man ceasing to be man must for now remain postponed – of course, Dostoevsky only had in mind the straightforward idea that man ceases to be man once dead, and bluntly states *contra* Kant that '[t]o kill for murder is punishment incomparably worse than the crime itself' – although his questioning of human nature under the pressure of the death penalty does make us pause, along with further reflections by

Myshkin, and shall be re-examined in the final two chapters. The Prince explains how one 'may lead a soldier out and set him facing the cannon in battle [. . .] and he'll still hope; but read a sentence of certain death over that same soldier, and he will go out of his mind' (*TI*, 20). Being *condemned to death* is here re-verified as a unique and troubling state, far different from the hope still entrenched in being *condemned to die*, that is, in Being-towards-death. Perhaps, in refusing to allow death its Heideggerian manifestation as possibility, by turning it into certitude, the penalty transmutes death into a term Heidegger does not consider: the impossible impossibility.[102] The death penalty makes death no longer both perennially possible (always *à-venir* in the *avenir*) and simultaneously impossible (because it can never happen, as an event, to you), but rather impossible to be impossible; death cannot *not* happen since, indeed, it has just happened through the foundation of the lawful society in which we live.

It is true that there is no obviously relational death in *The Idiot*, but the novel might manifest Stone's (and Butler's) idea of the faltering narrative. Pattison reminds us of Mikhail Bakhtin's analysis of Dostoevsky's style as one which is understood best in its heteroglossia and polyphony, whereby each narrative voice is 'very disconnected' from the other (an accusation made against the Prince himself during the telling of a story about the death sentence) (*TI*, 54).[103] Thinking of other voices, Myshkin hypothesizes a scenario: 'Perhaps there is some man who has been sentenced to death, been exposed to this torture and has then been told "you can go, you are pardoned." Perhaps such a man could tell us [what it was like]' (*TI*, 20). In alluding to himself, Dostoevsky recalls not only his own unexperienced experience but also Blanchot's (or his protagonist's), along with the myriad other literary voices who 'could tell us' of surviving – but first *waiting under* – the death penalty, a loud and vast polyphony of difference as shall be heard, or overheard, in the following chapters. 'Death', Pattison writes, 'comprising dying, the moment of death, and whatever may be "beyond" death', is thus 'as subject to the polyphonic, variform indeterminacy of the novelistic world as any of this world's other great themes'.[104] The pluralized heteroglossia of death *penalties* indeed asks many questions – in that other voice of the Other – that Heidegger might not, or cannot, answer, demonstrating a subject who is not unified with its ownmost reflection in the pool but rather one already in Hades, looking for a reflection and finding none. And so let us hear the questions.

If, in the first chapter, we have seen how literature opens up a space for a different, radical (relational) conception of death, and if, in this second chapter, rejections of Heideggerian existential-ontological Narcissism have been read as not adequately recognizing this space, then the next chapter must return to a literary questioning that is nonetheless deeply informed by such rejections of the idea of one's ownmost, non-relational death. These are the questions: before surviving the death penalty, what does it mean to await a death that is certain because it has already happened as the unexperienced experience? When death is no longer able to be the anticipated Heideggerian possibility, but is instead the impossible impossibility – what does *waiting* mean, then, under the death penalty? Does the duration of *waiting* rebuff the *instant*? What does this waiting reveal of death, its possession, and of the sovereign and *other* parties involved in the condemnation? Does waiting – or abeyance – stretch on to immortality? Ultimately, accusingly, is this present concern with surviving death just more chatter, an inauthentic way of escaping one's fear of it?

Or is it, perhaps, another, no less authentic, understanding of death? St Paul exultantly states that, in Christ, the 'mortal shall have put on immortality' and '[d]eath is swallowed up in victory'; indeed, he cries: 'O death, where is thy sting? O grave, where is thy victory?'[105] But perhaps immortality, or having death in abeyance – where the 'I' is suspended on the stratum of the impossible impossibility – is not the triumphant inauthenticity it may seem to be. In the sovereign condemning the subject to death, what is also condemned, in the same sense that a building or structure is condemned, may be the very category of subjectivity itself, the 'cocoon of I-ness', ipseity, the self-enclosed finitude, the Narcissistic and authoritarian totalization of the 'one'. The sting of death, then, more overwhelming than Heidegger thinks it to be, stings not 'you' or 'me' but the 'I' itself.

3

Missing death

Station: Limbo

What is 'relational death'? It is 'living the death one has already died', where the subject persists in a manner that is not towards-death and which so has its being in question.

Relational death is, then, perhaps most evident during the period of *waiting* under the death penalty, when living on without surviving. It is this period of waiting that shall now be explored, with particular attention to how this 'time' of abeyance relates to the previous discussions on the relationship between sovereignty and the death penalty, the idea of 'life without life', the interruption of the Third and dying in-stead, the possibility of starting from *adieu* and, ultimately, the seemingly impossible thought of conceiving the human otherwise than being-towards-death.

Let us return, for a moment, to Heidegger, as he checks his watch and waits for the train. In *The Fundamental Concepts of Metaphysics*, a lecture course presented not long after the publication of *Being and Time*, he speaks of a waiting at a desolate train station that is oppressed by boredom (*Langweile*), whereby one finds oneself 'wanting to kill time'.[1] He asks: 'What do we really want in constantly looking at the clock? We merely want to see time passed'.[2] It is immediately quite apparent that this impatience is not the case for the condemned subject. Prince Myshkin, for instance, tells his captive audience of a friend who, condemned to death and out on the scaffold, 'had only five minutes more to live', and although those 'five minutes seemed to him an infinite time', it was not a time for boredom; rather, 'he divided his time up', planning how best to devote his last thoughts and trying to make every moment count as 'eternity' (*TI*, 53–4). Living life without life (the relational death) is not a matter of killing time, but living under a time that kills with every second. As Blanchot writes:

Through waiting, he who waits dies waiting. He maintains waiting in death and seems to make of death the waiting for that which is still awaited when one dies. Death, considered as an event that one awaits, is incapable of putting an end to waiting. [...]. Waiting is what allows us to know that death cannot be awaited.³

Under the death penalty, one does not die of boredom.

Heidegger's 'various forms of boredom', as the translators of the lectures remark, can all be characterized as '"being held in limbo" [*Hingehaltenheit*]'; indeed, they note that 'boredom' is only the best English approximation of *Langweile* – which literally translates to 'long while', and which inherently carries 'the temporal sense which Heidegger makes central to his phenomenological analyses'.⁴ Heidegger does acknowledge that 'waiting can be full of suspense', and indeed the state of limbo seems to map well onto the state of being condemned to death, where time seems to stretch on eternally, between proper life and proper death; however, the key difference remains the issue of relationality.⁵ His limbo is an empty one, self-enclosed; it is the 'long while' which '*holds us in limbo and yet leaves us empty*'.⁶ This time of bored waiting, of non-relationality or Narcissism, is empty because there is only the waiting of something to come (the train), and one is meanwhile faced only with oneself (as if in a mirror or reflective pool). As with anxiety – and Heidegger places *Langweile* alongside *Angst* as fundamental attunement (that mood or voice which 'gives us the possibility of grasping the Da-sein of man as such') – waiting leans *towards*, future-oriented, secure of an end point and concerned solely with the emptiness of the mean*while*.⁷ Heidegger elaborates: 'Being held in limbo does not happen over any course of time whatsoever, but over this particular interval of time that drags between our arrival and the departure of the train.'⁸ In boredom, 'the while [*Weile*] becomes long [*lang*]. Which while? Any short while? No, but rather *that while whilst Dasein is as such*, the while that measures out that tarrying awhile [*Verweilen*] which is allotted to Dasein as such'.⁹ Heideggerian boredom is not something one can go in and out of, and the time in question, then, is the finite time of Dasein: not finitude, but mortality. It is important to point out that the state of being condemned does not belong to the everydayness that Heidegger speaks of here – indeed, condemnation is generally regarded as the opposite, as event, whereas boredom is 'uneventfulness' – and so to claim that the mood of boredom does not adequately describe that of living on seems of limited value. However, the intrinsic attunement of boredom in Dasein, discussed earlier, reveals that to talk of boredom is also to talk of Being-towards-death; a 'breaking out' of the latter must, therefore, also entail a breaking with the former (while also problematizing the dichotomy between the event and the mundane).¹⁰ Both boredom and Being-towards-death deal with the temporality of Dasein as finitude and the individuation (or 'solitude') that Heidegger contends comes with it.

The next step is to ask how the time of the condemned man differs from this empty limbo of boredom. An answer, perhaps, lies in Heidegger's meditation on the train station itself – and here one recalls, incidentally, the shared etymological roots of 'station' and 'stasis':¹¹ 'What do we expect of the station? That it be a station in general? No – but rather that we can use it as a station, i.e., that at this station we can immediately enter the train and depart as quickly as possible.'¹²

As such, what bores us is not only the fact that the station is 'not yet offering anything'. As he clarifies, 'the station in itself does not bore us [. . .] but does so only insofar as the train is not yet there'.¹³ In this context, the station – where one waits for a promised, scheduled departure, one's own 'not-yet' – works along the same lines as the death penalty. The difference, here, is that the time of the relational death is not only a waiting for what is to come but also for what has already passed; it is to wait for a train that has already departed, and which might never come again. If the death penalty, like the train station, promises us the 'calculable knowledge' of our time of death and makes us expect a death that will arrive, the time of waiting under the death penalty is simultaneously pregnant with this death, which has already come to pass as the unexperienced experience at the instant of condemnation. It is not empty time because it is full of what has already arrived. If, then, for Foucault, the train is relational, it is apparently not so for Heidegger.¹⁴

While David Wills's reading of Heidegger's temporality somewhat differs from the one forwarded here, his understanding of this time of death, this dead time as one awaits proper death, finds itself perfectly at home in, and very pertinent to, this discussion:

> [S]entencing to death and thereby determining the precise 'now' of the end of life means that the lived nows of the condemned person's everyday existence no longer function as moments in which death is possible, and which *potentialize* being. Instead, those lived nows come to constitute 'dead' instants, instants of nonbeing that restrict or imprison a condemned person in a time devoid of, vacated by life. [. . .] [T]he present now comes to be staged as instant of death.¹⁵

Relational death starts, then, to emerge as not only a death that withholds relations (to sovereignty, to the other and/or to the third party) as opposed to annulling them – hence threatening the category of the contained, purely individual self – but also that which rethinks the problems of our *'relation to time'*, and to our death, on temporal (train-)lines.[16] As Kelly Oliver writes, 'the death sentence brings with it a life defined by waiting for death. But this waiting is not like the "natural" waiting for death that accompanies human life. Indeed, the law requires that it be unnatural'.[17] Time becomes unnatural in this manner: the past becomes where one has died already, the future when one may not die and when finitude is infinitized – that is, the possibility of living on in abeyance, a prolonged interruption of sovereignty in which '[t]he death sentence is deferred but never rescinded in a moment that changes temporality itself'.[18] The question changes from 'when will death come?' to 'will death ever come?' (because the sovereign's condemnation has already answered the first question, and very precisely at that); moreover, the tension between the 'instant' and the 'while' is reversed: within the mechanisms of the death penalty, it is not the case that there is a long while until the instant of one's death, but that there is the instant of death followed by the long while itself. Moreover, this is not the persistence of limbo in Heidegger's sense: time here does not leave us empty or hollow, but rather full of relations and full of its own individual fragments. If, through Heideggerian boredom, the 'self is recognized in and through its inability to see past itself', and so can fully be-in-the-world, then through the waiting of the death penalty subjectivity can look past itself and at its past self, recognizing itself as having already exited its being-in-the-world.[19]

We now turn to see how certain other literary works come to manifest this temporality of the relational death, which is intrinsically bound to the idea of 'missing': (i) as absent, not found, no longer possessed, in abeyance; (ii) as desiring something that should be there but is not, in the sense of wistfulness and yearning (for proper death); and (iii) as missing the train, where one does not go onto death's promised and scheduled departure, where one fails to die, where one waits for the death one has already died.

Living corpses

Unlike these fundamental moods of Heideggerian solitude (boredom and anxiety), the death penalty does not 'abandon us to ourselves'.[20] What follows is a reading of condemnation as staged in Sophocles' *Antigone*, which stands slightly apart from its more traditional interpretations, ones carried out in terms of law and ethics (and which surprisingly discuss the death penalty only very scarcely, taking it as given ground). This reading, then, will reveal how *Antigone* may allow us to discern just how the condemned figure is indeed not 'abandoned' to the non-relationality of Heideggerian singular death.

Antigone is a radical figure who 'dare[s] to transgress [Creon's] laws' and buries 'the unhappy corpse' of her brother Polynices not once but twice, first by covering him 'with a light dust' and later with 'a threefold libation' (*A*, 7, 43, 27). Ismene, worried, thus proclaims her sister 'in love with the impossible'; indeed, while the Chorus assumes that '[t]here is no one foolish enough to desire death', Antigone is revealed, in part through this instance of dramatic irony, as already residing within the impossible impossibility of the death sentence (*A*, 13, 23).

When caught, Antigone is told by Creon that there is 'no hope that the sentence will not be accomplished'; however, the sovereign heeds – to an extent – his son Haemon's news of the people's support of Antigone's cause and decides instead to 'hide her, still living, in a rocky cavern', where she might die (*A*, 89, 77).[21] This merits some rumination: the sentence of stoning is transmuted into one of being buried alive; in short, the stones are not to be taken to her but, rather, she is to be taken to the stones. This is a move that in many ways pre-empts (and undermines) the Foucauldian account of the supposed transformation of sovereignty, where 'taking life' is transformed into 'letting die', for Creon is very much sovereign.[22] This demonstrates once more, therefore, Mbembe's reasoning in departing from this particular biopolitical understanding (vis-à-vis sovereign power) of how the drama of 'letting die' only disguises what continues to take place: that is, an unmitigated condemnation to death whenever the sovereign declares it. Creon remains the paramount thanatopolitical sovereign, he who has power over not only the living but the dead. As the Chorus affirms, the sovereign has the 'power to observe every rule with regard to the dead and to us who are alive'; he consistently considers (the Schmittian) 'enemy [as] never a friend, even when he is dead' (*A*, 23, 51).

Because of the instantly effectual sentence of 'stoning', even though she is not caught immediately, Antigone is condemned from the moment of transgression.[23] In consciously handing herself over to the death sentence she knows lies in wait for those who defy the sovereign, she becomes the already dead. In fact, this first instant of death is perhaps even more important than her later, proper death, which is quite literally in the dark: in the cavern, Creon finds her 'hanging by the neck, caught in the woven noose of a piece of linen', and it is unclear whether she has hanged herself or had Haemon hang her (*A*, 115). As Jacques Lacan rightly notes in his discussion of the play in *The Ethics of Psychoanalysis*, 'we don't know what happened in Antigone's tomb', and our focus is, therefore, turned to the prior and eminently more visible death/s which Sophocles foregrounds.[24]

Lacan, as noted by Paul Allen Miller, understands 'that Antigone, in her decision to defy Creon, consciously seeks death'. It might not, however, be that simple, as this would seem to suggest some indivisible dichotomy between life and death, and, as Miller himself goes on, Antigone 'transcends the comfortable binary oppositions that structure our daily ethical and social lives' and can even be situated as 'already belonging to the realm of the dead'.[25] Indeed, from the broader context of his articulations on desire, ethics, the sublime and the Kantian *Begriff*, Lacan writes that Antigone's death is one 'lived by anticipation, a death that crosses over into the sphere of life, a life that moves into the realm of death', and this in itself is an apt description of living (the relational) death, living on death's abeyance.[26] On the other hand, however, he identifies Antigone as a 'self-willed victim', seeing in her a 'martyrdom'.[27] Following his discussion of Aristotle's tripartite account of tragedy – that of fear, pity and catharsis – Lacan claims that Antigone, 'right through to the end[,] feels neither fear nor pity', and it is 'only the martyrs [who] know neither pity nor fear'.[28]

Implicit in this concept of martyrdom, however, is the idea that one gives one's life to the point of death, when one knows that performing an action – a 'holy' crime in this case – will with certainty result in one's death (and this works similarly to Levinasian sacrifice, especially in its moral resonances). While agreeing that Antigone does trouble the borders of life and death, Lacan's reading of the play is contestable on this point of martyrdom: while, for Lacan, Antigone's martyrdom ends in the tomb where she is buried alive, one can argue that her martyrdom ends (and not begins) with the first handful of dust on Polynices' corpse. If martyrdom is bearing witness, generally through the sacrifice of one's own life, this life was instantaneously sacrificed when Antigone first attempted to pay tribute to Polynices, when death became a certainty and her transgression put her under the tyranny of the death sentence.

In his last lecture on the play, Lacan does see Antigone as being 'between two deaths' – hence him calling her beautiful – and this recalls the lived relational death 'between what is to going to arrive and what has already arrived'. Lacan, however, once more argues that the idea of Antigone having already been dead 'is consecrated' only when her punishment is effected.[29] It is only at that point of being buried alive, Lacan asserts, that Antigone is 'shut up or suspended in the zone between life and death. Although she is not yet dead, she is eliminated from the world of the living. And it is from that moment on [the burial and her knowledge of it] that her complaint begins, her lamentation on life'.[30]

What is being presently argued is that Antigone, along with all the other polyphonic voices of those condemned, has in fact been living under the death sentence since her first act of transgression, and she thus 'lives on' not when she is buried alive or when Creon refuses to grant pardon, but from that instant when she defies the sovereign. In defying Creon, she is not, as Miller writes, seeking or desiring death, but rather becoming already dead, already 'shut up or suspended in the zone between life and death'. This is what in part leads Butler to describe Antigone as 'half-dead' and 'bound not to survive', seeing her fate in this death-in-life as being destined 'not to have a life to live, [but rather] to be condemned to death prior to any possibility of life'.[31]

In line with the foregoing, while Antigone does assert that she 'come[s] living, poor creature, to the caverns of the dead', it does not seem that she thinks herself alive *properly* (A, 89). It seems as if she misses her death, in all senses previously outlined. Earlier on, in fact, Antigone states how 'it is no way painful for [her] to meet this death' because she is already a corpse; she 'has long been dead, so as to help the dead' (A, 45, 55). She continues, crucially: 'I knew that I would die, of course I knew, even if you had made no proclamation' (A, 45). Here, then, is the death sentence that comes even before sovereignty and which constitutes it, a sentence which does not await Creon's pardon or affirmation. Antigone already knows she is dead at the instant of transgression and does not need to await Creon's final say: it is under the lawlessness of the death penalty, the punitive power that makes human society possible in the first place and not those of the lawful system of sovereignty, that she departs 'to the heaped-up mound of [her] strange tomb', 'living neither among mortals nor as a shade among the shades, neither with the living nor with the dead' (A, 83).

With this understanding, there is now both an added dimension to Lacan's categorization of Antigone as one who goes 'beyond the limits of the human' (and who is thus 'inhuman') as well as the added question of how there can be a death-drive from one already dead.[32] More immediately relevant, however, might be the possibility of re-reading *Antigone* through Hegel. Often criticized for its emphasis on the dialectical collision and reconciliation of one-sidedness, the Hegelian understanding of time and the relation between self and other nonetheless allow us to develop the present concerns. The question is of how, in this reading of Antigone as the living dead, the famous (and 'tragic') Lord–Bondsman opposition – which is the historical and political equivalent of the Hellenic *polis* serving as the bedrock of this tragic drama – enables us better to understand the intricate and ancient machinery of the death penalty (*LPS*, 19).

As a tragic work, *Antigone* drew Hegel's attention when formulating his theory of tragedy, as made manifest through works like the *Lectures on the History of Philosophy*, *Lectures on the Philosophy of Religion* and, most prominently, the *Aesthetics*. The drama, which he deems one of the 'most excellent works of all time', receives central consideration in his *Philosophy of*

Right and the *Phenomenology*.[33] For Hegel, *Antigone* is the paramount enactment of ethical progress, and the protagonist 'is revealed as the paradigmatic figure of womanhood and family life in both the ancient and modern worlds' – an incarnation of Woman pure, divine and simultaneously subversive, dialectically opposed to man and human law.[34] This is a conflict that, for Hegel, must result in the death of the individual (hence Antigone being a tragic figure) in order for history to progress dialectically towards its rational goal.[35]

A crucial step in this progression is Hegel's account of 'Lordship and Bondage', which depicts a struggle between two self-conscious-to-be entities.[36] Because both self and other inevitably mirror each other's desire (to be recognized as self-conscious), 'each seeks the death of the other', and this 'involves the staking of its own life' in order to 'rid itself of its own self-externality'. At the end of this trial or struggle to the death (*Kampf auf Leben und Tod*), the victorious self-consciousness emerges as Lord, independent and *for itself*, while the loser becomes the Bondsman, the dependent consciousness living for its Master. However, the lord is nonetheless still mediated and recognized through the bondsman, 'for which thinghood is an essential characteristic', and thus, because the bondsman is a slave who has been beaten to the brink of death, his affirmation counts for nothing (*PS*, 113–15; cf. 116–17). There is, therefore, still a dependency at work: the Master is only a master because there is a slave; Creon is only sovereign because Antigone is held in his subjection. As Derrida states, albeit while talking of more concretized forms of sovereignty, 'unconditional sovereignty is conditional' (*DPII*, 57).

The dialectical struggle can be further exhumed through Alexandre Kojève, one of the foremost 'commentators' on Hegel.[37] In his *Introduction to the Reading of Hegel*, he repeats Hegel by writing that, to become human (i.e. self-conscious), '[t]he "first" anthropogenic action necessarily takes the form of a fight', one which both parties must survive since the Lord 'is unable to be "recognized" by the dead adversary' and 'can no longer expect anything from it for himself' (*LPS*, 11, 8, 14). He agrees that the 'warlike and idle' state of Mastery is an 'existential impasse', showing how it is the slave, through (forced) labour and time spent working for the master (after losing the fight), that finally leads himself out to freedom and true self-consciousness (*LPS*, 58, 46).

Why must it, however, 'necessarily' be a fight, and one to the death, but which both must survive? In the fight unto the death, writes Kojève, each entity is 'ready to risk its life' and 'to put the life of the other in danger'; both 'must introduce death into [their] existence, by consciously and voluntarily risking [their] life, while knowing that [they are] mortal' (*LPS*, 7). However, the two entities must also behave differently if they are not to end up both dead: 'one must fear the other, must give in to the other, must refuse to risk his life for the satisfaction of his desire for "recognition"' (*LPS*, 69). This defeat, as Kojève (with Hegel) concludes, births human society: 'society is human – at least in its origin – only on the basis of its implying an element of Mastery and an element of Slavery' (*LPS*, 8).

And thus, in line with Kant's, Benjamin's and Derrida's understanding of the death penalty as undeniably foundational of sociopolitical existence, we see this struggle to the death at the origin of human society. For this to happen, the slave must survive without surviving; or, rather, he must live on but not survive. The lord 'must leave him life and consciousness, and destroy only his autonomy', which means, effectively, that the slave 'who has been defeated and spared' remains '*a living corpse*' – and here we are returned to Mbembe's living dead (*LPS*, 15–16).[38] It is easy to see the condemned Antigone in the figure of the Slave, defeated, lamenting the loss of her autonomy, a living corpse – and yet ultimately undoing the Master, the sovereign. She even admits as much herself. Antigone is a living corpse because she is the condemned subject of the thanatopolitical sovereign, and the slave is a living corpse because, while he has not died *properly* (or, more precisely, has retreated from dying *properly*), he has gone through the unexperienced experience of death.

To equate Antigone and the Bondsman, however, overlooks rather more problematic nuances that the tragedy puts forward – not least in the fact that Antigone, condemned, can no longer retreat from properly dying. The gate of life has been shut behind her, entombing her. Moreover, although Antigone does operate, from the point of her subversion on, within the non-autonomous state of the living corpse, she is not so much the defeated, fearful or obedient slave that has just been described. She is proud and self-righteous; moreover, she is passively rebellious – and this is suspect. To borrow Butler's thought: 'Violence against those who are already not quite living, that is, living in a state of suspension between life and death, leaves a mark that is no mark.'[39] It is this ill-fittingness, this failure of sovereignty, which prompts a re-reading of the tragedy, this time, perhaps, suggesting that the death penalty may be better understood within the context of the struggle unto death.[40]

The 'living corpse' is such because it has introduced death into its existence without gaining recognition. Creon, the sovereign who was himself Hegel's living corpse before attaining recognition, resides once more within the struggle; no longer is he a self-conscious and recognized lord but an entity battling through his Desire. To adopt Kantorowicz's remark, here 'kingship itself comes to mean Death, and nothing but Death'.[41] Despite already being sovereign, Creon, through the death penalty, acts still as the consciousness that seeks the destruction of the other in order to be recognized as Lord, for '[w]ithout the power over life and death, the sovereign would be unable to define her/himself as sovereign'.[42] After all, if he allows Antigone her transgression, it would be her who 'decides on the exception'[43] – in the words of Jean Hyppolite, she would become the 'master of the master'.[44] Creon cannot accept Antigone's wilful subversion: 'pride is impossible for anyone who is another's slave', he proclaims, not recognizing that Antigone and himself have regressed back to the primal struggle, where he is no longer sovereign and she no longer slave. This is further demonstrated through his desperate efforts to seek her subjugation through the penalty, where everything is once more at stake. When Antigone asks if he wishes 'for anything more than to take [her] and kill [her]', Creon replies: 'Not I! When I have that, I have everything' (*A*, 47).

It might at first seem that Antigone, on her part, is not truly affected by the re-initiated struggle – indeed, she seems simply transposed from the living corpse which Hegel calls Slave to the living corpse that is here understood as Condemned. The crucial difference, however, is that through this transgressive 'crime' that instantly puts her under the death penalty, she no longer retains 'the discipline of service and obedience' or lives 'in terms of terror' (*PS*, 119; *LPS*, 27). The progression has been stopped; the cogs have stopped turning. A specifically anti-Hegelian definition of 'transgression' can here be advanced: it is to work *against* the master, rather than *for* one's progress (or the progress of History). In other words, Antigone is no longer allowed the position of a slave who can work towards liberation. Her transformative transgression is a provocation to Creon, and the proclamation of the death sentence is thus sovereignty's reactive and instantaneous re-initiation of the struggle, which recurs because 'the Master prefers death to slavish recognition of another's superiority' (*LPS*, 46). As Creon states: 'If we must perish, it is better to do so by the hand of a man, and then we cannot be called inferior to women' (*A*, 65–7). Hence, while Antigone is a living corpse by virtue of being condemned to death, Creon here starts to emerge as identically having reverted back to a living corpse engaged in the 'bloody Fight', re-introducing the possibility of death into his existence without having yet achieved his so-desired recognition from the slave (*LPS*, 56). As the drama continues, in fact, all recognition falls away subsequent to his insistence on condemnation; he is no longer recognized by Haemon, the Chorus, Tiresias or by his people. As the Messenger makes eminently clear, Creon, who 'once was enviable', can no longer be considered 'a living being, but an animated corpse' (*A*, 109–11).

Just as the ancient Near Eastern king, Creon must first die in order to truly have the possibility of becoming sovereign once again. As the play draws to a close, in fact, it is he who now describes himself as 'fraught with death', 'a dead man', 'no more than nothing' (*A*, 119, 121, 125). He has, by decreeing the penalty of death, once again made himself partake of the unexperienced experience of the *Kampf* – for Hegel is clear that the master must *not* kill the slave, and so this time there can be no recognition from a slave that has been condemned and thus already killed. As soon as the sovereign wields the sword of the death penalty, he deprives the slave of his future of work and potentiality (indeed, the sovereign transposes the condemned's death to the past), and at once the sovereign regresses to nothing once more, finding himself unable to be recognized by a dead thing that will always remain so. As Bradley writes, 'someone who exists outside of life and death can, after all, be neither killed by a master nor forced to live as a slave'.[45] By enacting the death penalty, sovereignty undoes its own dynamic, undoes itself.

Antigone thus enacts the *Kampf auf Leben und Tod* insofar as it is read as a literary work engaged with the mechanisms of the death penalty. It is important to clarify that what is here being stated is not that Creon is now himself a living corpse while Antigone has become lord. From the very beginning Creon justifies his sovereignty – his ability to decide the exception through the death sentence – as the thanatopolitical power of his 'kinship with the dead', through having introduced death into his existence (via the *Kampf*) and obtaining recognition (*A*, 19). Rather, the point being made here is that the provocation, initiation and enactment of the death penalty – which eradicates any possibilities for the bondsman's work and possible freedom – returns both Lord and Bondsman, sovereign and subject, to the first, necessary fight, one with a necessarily failed ending. As Kojève makes very clear, '[w]ithout the Slave's work, the "first" Fight would be reproduced indefinitely'. This is what happens in the death penalty. The Master, therefore, 'is fixed in his Mastery. [. . .]. He must conquer [. . .] or die'; the sovereign 'must kill the other in order not to be killed himself'. Nonetheless, the sovereign 'can be killed' (*LPS*, 51, 22). Indeed, when resolving to kill Antigone despite everything, Creon victoriously states that 'she no longer exists' – and his 'existential impasse' and unravelled sovereignty is fully revealed, for how can he himself exist as sovereign if his subject no longer exists (*A*, 57)? Understood in this way, then, the points that this study has made in relation to the ontological displacement of death are further clarified: through condemnation, both sovereign and condemned are consigned to the 'life without life' of the living dead.

The death penalty, therefore, not only constitutes sovereignty (and with it, human society), but also simultaneously and paradoxically undoes it. It is not transgression that threatens sovereignty but sovereignty's response to it. This is another reason as to why, as Derrida says, 'it will always be vain to conclude that the universal abolition of the death penalty [. . .] means the effective end of any death penalty'. Not only is it perennially there wherever there is sovereignty, but it is there also for the relation between sovereignty and subject to come into being. It troubles even the idea of the Heideggerian polis,[46] and what Butler writes of Antigone, therefore, rings true: 'as a figure for politics, she points somewhere else'.[47]

Earlier, 'the encounter of death with death' was read as affirming a relationality with the other that persists in the state of 'life without life', after one has been sentenced to death. Now emerges a further significance: it is the encounter of the condemned subject's death with the death of the sovereign, and this 'encounter' is also a violent one. Thus, it is not only the other and the self who maintain a relation in the state of living the relational death – like 'a corpse holding a corpse' – but it is also the case of a corpse fighting a corpse (*A*, 117). The *droit de glaive* that constitutes the thanatopolitical sovereign is thus always and necessarily double-edged: in condemning the slave, the sovereign kills himself all over again. Hence the dramatic irony of Creon's despair when he asks, pleadingly: 'Why has no one struck me to the heart with a two-edged sword?', and the pointedness of Tiresias's question: 'What is the bravery of killing a dead man all over again?' (*A*, 123, 97). Sovereign and condemned are, through the penalty, twinned. While not thinking specifically of the death penalty, Bradley sums up this mirroring perfectly:

> [T]he sovereign who is above all life finds his dark mirror image [. . .] in the unbearable life that is beneath life, a life that does not live or die, a life that is not. If the sovereign is able to decide not merely upon life and death but on what counts as life in the first place, in other words, it may not be because he is the highest form of life but, to borrow an intriguing hypothesis of Jean-Luc Nancy, because sovereignty itself logically occupies a kind of infinite or supreme void that is entirely excepted from, and incommensurate with, the life/death nexus over which it presides.[48]

Jean Paulhan, who is mentioned by name in *The Instant*, writes the following: 'a man, anticipating the violent blow that is about to strike him, already feels himself transformed into a corpse'.⁴⁹ However, with the violent provocation that is transgression, it is not only the condemned that is 'transformed into a corpse' but also the sovereign, who feels both provoked and threatened enough to condemn to death. In short: under the death penalty, death belongs to the condemned and the sovereign alike. Here, 'the rich polyvalence' of the name 'Antigone' becomes all the more appropriate – not only does 'Antigone' reveal, as Stathis Gourgouris and Richard Braun point out, kinship with the dead, 'an opposition of kinship to the polis' as well as 'an opposition to kinship' itself,⁵⁰ 'born to oppose',⁵¹ but it can also be understood as recalling 'antagonism', the Greek etymology of which signifies 'to struggle against'.⁵²

At this point, a few possible counterarguments must be addressed. First, that if Antigone transgressed she was never truly a slave. As Kojève makes clear, 'to serve a Master is to obey his laws', and this is exactly what Antigone does not do (*LPS*, 27). This leads us to a second contention – namely, that Antigone is indeed not a slave but a Greek citizen, markedly different from the historical slaves upon whose labour the Greek polis perpetuated itself.⁵³ If the death penalty can be taken as reducing the subject to a slave, a living corpse, then it is still not a reversion to the struggle unto death. Third, even if the above reading were to be taken in good faith, why can the Lord achieve recognition from the living corpse of the Slave, but not the sovereign from the living corpse of the condemned? Answers to these questions have all, to some extent, been implied earlier, but let us try again in reverse order.

In answer to the last two questions, one must remember that the Lord's achieving of recognition from the Slave is only illusory. The lord is 'recognised by someone whom he does not recognise', and as such the recognition by the slave is 'without value'; 'to be recognised by a slave is not to be recognised by a *man*'. This is the 'impasse' of lordship as Kojève situates it, and why 'a Master will never be satisfied'. The sovereign can never, then, be recognized by a living corpse, condemned or not. This is why it is not the lord who is on the road to the satisfaction of complete self-consciousness but the slave, and this through a 'dialectical overcoming' of his status through work. He is repressed consciousness labouring to transform itself to 'true autonomy', and this is the Hegelian progress of History, the way out of the Lord–Bondsman deadlock: 'History is the history of the working slave' (*LPS*, 19, 46, 20). This is the reason the death penalty proves to be so jarringly contra-temporal, a spanner in the machine of Hegelian progress: this dialectical work of overcoming is cut short, where, as Tiresias says, a dead man is killed all over again, where autonomy is irreparably denied, and where (the possibility for) autonomous life continues to be taken away. Just as there can be no future for one already dead, so too, in condemnation, there is no future for history.

Had not the slave's possibility of work and 'historical becoming' (the eventual quenching of Desire by Satisfaction) been placed into his past, this future would have gradually transfigured the Slave into the Citizen of the State. The latter is the true point from which the Slave 'realizes and reveals his freedom', and this 'long and painful' transformation is the fruit of his labour over time. To achieve this status, the slave must, according to Hegel, go through several steps – Stoicism, sceptical-nihilism, a breaking from Christian transcendence – with the first step being a recognition of the idea (and possibility) of freedom by the Slave itself, and the last being the 'dialectical overcoming': that is, an acceptance of mortality and the realization that absolute 'liberation without a bloody Fight [. . .] is metaphysically impossible'. Hence Hegel's identification of the final fight for liberation, the true and long-awaited exit from the impasse of Lord and Bondsman, with 'the Fight of the working Bourgeois' manifested as the French Revolution: 'it is only thanks to the Terror that this idea of the final synthesis, which definitively "satisfies" Man, is realized' (*LPS*, 22, 47, 57, 68–9).

Regrettably, not much more than a couple of paragraphs can here be devoted to the extremely pertinent problematic of the Revolution. Although many other studies have thoroughly examined it, it would have been worth revisiting the period through the angles presented here, from the precedent of the industrialization of death to the figure of Robespierre the Incorruptible himself, 'memorably described by one of his enemies as a "living cadaver" (*cadavre vivant*) who presided over a republic of the dead'.[54] Some related points, however, can still be raised in the key of reflection, especially since this is a time predominantly characterized by the penalty at its most naked and public form. In line with this, Rebecca Comay's astute Hegelian ruminations on the guillotine seem to coincide exactly with the arguments of this chapter:

> The guillotine retroactively retracts the minimal recognition it concedes its victim [. . .] in that it directs itself toward *an already annihilated nonentity*. By stripping death of its intensity and singularity it provides a practical demonstration of the object's nullity. [. . .]. *The cut effaces its own traces by offering a kind of 'ontological argument' for nonexistence*. This is perhaps why, at the limit, revolutionary justice needed to be applied even to cadavers. It was not enough that even before the blade fell, the victim on the scaffold was already lying prostrate. As if to prove the uncertainty of the distinction between the living and the dead, even corpses had to be killed. [. . .]. *The fall of the blade marks the transitionless transition from an already mortified existence to the*

posthumous mortality of a subject for whom the ontological difference between life and death has already been eroded.[55]

Comay's last sentence, describing the instant of death, maps perfectly onto the argument advanced thus far. It is this nullity of the condemned individual, already a corpse, existing posthumously, that thus initiates the struggle unto death once again. But is it really the case that, as Comay writes, this 'machine [of the death sentence] perfects the evacuation of alterity that Hegel locates at the origin of modern democratic [and biopolitical] sovereignty', when, along with the corpse of the condemned, we have seen a necessarily withheld relation, in living-relational-death, to the mirrored corpse of the sovereign? If the death penalty, as is argued here, transforms revolutionary regicide to a suicidal regicide, how can a revolution overthrow a king who has killed himself in the face of such revolution, when by his own hands, upon decreeing another's sentence, his head rolls, as Hegel describes, like 'a head of cabbage' (*PS*, 360)?[56] One thus wonders whether we are really in Hegel's 'political modernity' if the death penalty can never disappear. Moreover, one questions how Terror 'announces the heroic rebirth of the subject from the trauma of its own annihilation' if the subject was never buried alone and annihilation was never simply 'its own'.[57] When the king is dead the revolt is over before it begins, and the guillotine both progresses History as well as regresses it. The contra-temporal fall of the guillotine not only finally and traumatically cuts off modernity from antiquity but also conjoins the two. As the true symbol of the *droit de glaive*, sharper than the sword, the guillotine cleaves.

Let us return to the foregoing questions and not forget Antigone. Antigone, as a woman, occupies what Warren and Ann Lane call 'the politically marginal and *subordinate* position of women in the city-states'; she, for Hegel, is 'the paradigmatic figure of womanhood' (and 'we cannot be called inferior to women', Creon indignantly proclaims).[58] Antigone's femininity is not to be overlooked in a discussion that examines otherness as well as resistance (to totalitarianism, to the oppression of the subject to the point of nullity) from this same space of alterity.[59] Additionally, she cannot be considered as Bourgeois in still having a master to recognize. Nor, in having a master, can she be considered a citizen in the Hegelian sense: the master's subject can only be a slave, and this is why, as Warren and Ann Lane remark, Creon's 'subjects are all potential enemies'.[60] All must, as he himself demands, 'keep their necks beneath the yoke' (*A*, 31). Above all, Antigone is not a Citizen since she is barred from liberation (as the eventual culmination of labour) through the death penalty, and any progress towards liberation is in this manner thwarted. Her actions are the antithesis of the 'warlike action' of the Citizen; her burial of Polynices can in fact be understood as an attempt to undo the logic of war. Rather, she 'has accepted life granted [. . .] by another': as long as she is subject to the thanatopolitical sovereign, she is subject to the death penalty, and lives life only because the sovereign grants it. This is the very groundwork of the drama. Furthermore, mastery can be 'human or divine', and so Antigone's primary response-ability to the gods does not negate Creon but rather sustains an added level of mastery, the latter being at odds with the Master that is the sovereign (and, again, this conflict of interests is why *Antigone* is a tragedy) (*LPS*, 61–2).

Here is, then, an answer to the first and final question: Antigone's transgression is constituent of the historical progress of the Slave and may thus be better phrased, perhaps, as 'revolution'. She is neither 'reformer' nor 'conformer', and, in transgressing, she attempts the 'dialectical overcoming' of her status as Slave, which, Kojève elaborates, can be understood as a 'revolutionary overcoming'. It is because she has a Master who 'engenders the desire of revolutionary negation' that Antigone transgresses.[61] However, if the Master is, for Hegel, 'the catalyst of the historical, anthropogenetic process' because he incites revolt from the Slave, it certainly cannot be the case when the Master punishes such revolt with condemnation (*LPS*, 60, 16, 29, 25). What Hegel seems to neglect is this second attitude of Mastery, which is not simply a mediated pleasure that is ultimately inefficient, but a lordship that always grasps its sheathed sword. If, for Kojève, the slave can only revolt by becoming a master and taking the risk of life, then Antigone's revolt – as one killed and thus no longer able to be on the path of self-consciousness, with her self always already executed – comes from a different (thanato)political space. The problem of the death penalty, therefore, is in its halting of both future and history, where revolution is not left to progress the monarchy to republic, polis to State. Endlessly repeating upon itself, the death penalty is history's trauma.

Antigone's revolutionary, transgressive negation is a negation of the world as is, both politically and ontologically, and this is not simply an act of defiance but the only and necessary attempt at progress. As Kojève writes: 'The Master can never detach himself from the World in which he lives, and if this World perishes, he perishes with it. Only the Slave can transcend the given World (which is subjugated by the Master) and not perish' (*LPS*, 29). Transgression of the onto-political order is *what the living corpse does*, and, as with Antigone or Robespierre, 'the revolutionary assume[s] the sovereign position of a dead man'.[62]

Luce Irigaray points out how '[Creon's] fragile strength, as apt to be broken as to break, demands that he fear [...] the slaves' revolt'.[63] Antigone could transgress or revolt against the World as given by the sovereign *precisely because* she was a slave: 'slave' and 'revolt' are not mutually exclusive but rather necessarily inclusive terms. The death penalty, then, needs to be necessarily considered within (and as rethinking) the Lord–Bondsman dialectic, since, evidently, transgression does not only result in Hegel's idea of progress. The problem then, of course, is the impossibility of eventual reconciliation and synthesis. What *Antigone* thus reveals, seminally, and which will here have to be postponed until the next chapters for its deserved elaboration, is that the living corpse and its innate 'thingness' is a direct challenge to our concept of both *anthropogenesis* and *anthropos*, and which leads us towards a re-evaluation of this word – 'thing' – that not only does away with the term's dismissive connotations but also re-evaluates the passivity, or even archi-passivity, that has all too often been attributed to it, leading us instead to different (and *in*different) forms of resistance.

One thus returns to the relational death as that which *makes lived the death one has already died*. This is not only the death at the instant of condemnation and the ontologically modified *Langweile* of living on but also the struggle, that which excluded the slave from sovereignty and made her executable in the first place, which transforms the Slave-with-a-future into the Condemned-to-death-with-a-past. This death is not one through which the condemned lives on alone; with her, there is always, necessarily, the figure of the dead sovereign. This is why the question of death's property is seminal in this context: not only does it reveal death under the death sentence as relational (shared, mutual property, state of being; both condemned and sovereign struggling unto death), but the question of *property* also reveals the properties that characterize relational death.

This functioning of the death penalty, of course, is not restricted to *Antigone*. Let us very briefly return to Blanchot's narrative. While we are not given any details regarding the soldiers, we do know it was a time of war (as opposed to the post-war or *jus civile* of *Antigone*). This, if anything, magnifies the reading carried out above, for is not war a struggle on the wider, historical scale that Hegel conceives of? If the soldiers have the sovereign power to aim their guns and condemn to death, is it not because they (as the arms of sovereignty) are already at war, taking part in the struggle, risking their lives by introducing death into their existence? Is this perhaps why *The Instant* points us specifically, unashamedly, to Hegel? After all, the protagonist's chateau bore the inscription of 'the date 1807', that 'famous year of Jena, when Napoleon, on his small gray horse, passed under the windows of Hegel, who recognized in him the "spirit of the world'" (*ID*, 7).⁶⁴ Is this why (and here a cursory nod to the grey horse which suggests that the struggle unto death is undertaken on horseback) Derrida intimates that to understand the unexperienced experience one must look to Hegel (cf. *D*, 63)? And does Antigone move from 'the house of Creon' to the chateau of Hegel,⁶⁵ where the latter 'abolish[es] the distinction between military and civilian' and levels everything, especially when understood through these mechanisms of the death penalty (*D*, 88)?

And here, once again: what of the three sons of farmers, the third who interrupts the struggle?

Acknowledgement *contra* recognition

This chapter has continued to understand the idea of 'relational death'. First, it is the living death one lives on under the death sentence, where there is a temporal and persistently ontological relation to the death one has already died in an instant. Time here is full of *adieu*, beginning from the end rather than awaiting it, and in this way living death becomes the antipode of anxious, individuating Heideggerian existence. Moreover, relational death implies a relation to the other or third party, which has so far been mostly discussed in terms of sovereignty, which finds itself condemned along with the subject the moment a sentence is passed. However, there is also involved, as has already been intimated, the 'third party', to which this chapter now turns, and it is immediately clear why it is a 'third' and not a 'second': if the struggle unto death already implicates two (the subject and the sovereign), it can only be a third who interrupts it, who makes us miss our death, who comes to die with us or even in-stead.

This is not to say that the Third is always welcome. Ismene, for instance, whom 'Hegel fails even to mention [. . .] in his references to the play', tries her utmost to include herself within the struggle after having turned away from the possibility of transgression.⁶⁶ She claims that she is 'not ashamed to make [herself] a fellow voyager in [Antigone's] suffering', but her sister reprimands her for failing to revolt, for choosing life instead of death; bluntly, she tells her: 'Do not try to share my death' (*A*, 53). As regards *Mitsterben*, one can also think of Haemon, who refers to himself when exclaiming that 'by [Antigone's] death she will destroy another', or even Polynices, whom Antigone addresses on these same terms ('in your death you have destroyed my life') and who 'shared a common death' with Eteocles (*A*, 73, 85, 17). But these latter 'shared' deaths are closer to Stone's conception of the relational death; the closest relation to Antigone, on the lines of relational death as understood here, is perhaps neither her brother nor her betrothed, but the critically overlooked and nameless Guard.

After discovering the dust on Polynices, the Guard reports the crime to Creon because he has lost the drawing of lots. He is not a voluntary participant; when another guard demanded that the crime be reported, all 'bow[ed their] heads to the ground in terror', and so they drew lots. On his way to the sovereign, the Guard asks himself: 'Wretch, why are you going to a place where you will pay the penalty?'. Creon in fact quickly condemns him to death, assuring him that only '[i]f [he finds] the author of this burial and reveal him' will he be free of the 'heavy charge' (*A*, 29, 25, 31, 43). This is once more the Slave who is sentenced – only this time it is because of another's transgression.

The Guard is Sophocles' unseen living corpse, not only in the capacity of Hegelian and Hellenic Slave but also as one condemned. Here, however, after forcibly being made to substitute for Antigone (just as the sons of farmers involuntarily replace the protagonist's proper death with their own), the Guard reverses the substitution by bringing in Antigone. His remarks are revealing: 'to have escaped oneself from trouble is most pleasant, [although] to bring friends into danger is painful. But all this matters less to me than my own safety' (*A*, 43). The Guard does not interrupt the sovereign's *droit de glaive* but aids it.

The Third, then, can fail to appear *as* the Third. Ismene, who is rejected, becomes the *arrivant* who waited, and '[t]he third [only] arrives without waiting' – it is for this reason Antigone has the possibility of rejecting her. On the other hand, the Guard does not intend to arrive at all, but rather to depart. Upon learning of his simultaneous task and penalty, the Guard utters the following: 'Why, let [the criminal] be found by all means! But whether he is found or not, for that is something that fortune will decide, you will never see me coming here again!' (*A*, 35). Although he resolves to disappear, to continue living on under the death sentence but away from its *glaive*, the Guard does return, and his re-arrival only more acutely marks his failure to appear as one who interrupts the death penalty. For a brief time, both Antigone and the Guard were sentenced by Creon; in this case, however, the corpse has abandoned the corpse. What would it mean, then, for the Third to appear *as such* (for the Third, as Levinas writes, must always appear); that is, what would it mean for this figure to appear in a way that cannot be refused? In search of an answer, we now turn to three literary works which, apart from many other points of connection, reveal how an interruption of the death sentence through the Third would entail the latter's *acknowledgement* as opposed to its assimilation into the dialectics of *recognition*.

Much like his later novella 'The Third Man', Graham Greene's novel *The Tenth Man* foregrounds this disruptive thanatopolitical figure.[67] As with Blanchot's protagonist, Greene's Jean-Louis Chavel is also 'a man of property' and war prisoner of the Nazis (*TM*, 45). The herald of the death penalty arrives with the news, 'at three' in the afternoon, that there are three men to be condemned, and Chavel draws his losing scrap of paper when 'there were only three slips left' (*TM*, 39, 44). Like the Guard, Chavel is condemned to death because he lost the draw. Desperate to save his life, he offers to give everything he possessed in life (property and three hundred thousand francs) to whomever is willing to take his place at the morning executions. It is at this point that Janvier, the tenth man to have drawn his lot, interrupts the sovereign struggle between executioner and condemned by accepting Chavel's offer.

Earlier, we explored the idea that the death penalty hides away certain death, which occurs at the instant of condemnation, behind what is only a false or illusory certainty: the time of proper death that should befall the subject at the moment of execution. The Third, interrupting sovereignty and substituting itself for the condemned, arrives to fully disperse this illusion, undoing the imagined certainty of proper death and leaving behind a living corpse perennially condemned, living on in abeyance *outside the lawful structure of the death penalty* – just as with Blanchot's protagonist who has run to the heath and, subsequently, to Paris. The first chapter of *The Tenth Man*, in fact, immediately problematizes any certainty of time, where the incarcerated squabble over imprecise watches and clocks, having 'no means of telling the time exactly' (*TM*, 29).

With time so problematized, so too is the subject which experiences it. When Chavel offers his wealth to him who would take his death, feeling himself 'beside himself – almost literally beside himself', the acceptance of his offer indeed comes from the one who is beside him, able to step into the troubled borders of the non-autonomous living corpse (*TM*, 46). Janvier thus not only transforms himself from poor to 'a rich man', with Chavel's house suddenly becoming, for Janvier, 'my house', but Chavel's death too now becomes Janvier's (*TM*, 49, 51). The Third truly takes everything the condemned has, and even Chavel's proper death has now been 'outstripped'. This is not a matter of sacrifice, which would fall within Heideggerian *Jemeinigkeit*; Janvier's personal gain notwithstanding, it cannot be sacrifice because Chavel has already lost his life and can only live on instead of simply live; if it was so intended, Janvier's action comes too late to be considered as such. Greene's assertion that 'in the minds of the three men the future stood inalterably as birth' is consciously belied by the fact that one has taken another's death, and thus both time and subject are untethered (*TM*,

53). Crucially, too, this is not a giving of death, but a taking: as Chavel fills with hope, now ecstatic in a completely different manner, he asks the tenth man (or, in truth, now the third man): 'You'll take my place?' (*TM*, 48).

'How does one hand over everything one possesses?', Chavel asks himself (*TM*, 48). Being a lawyer (and a descendant of many generations of lawyers), he drafts a 'very odd document', signing everything away; just as a piece of paper confirms the identity of the condemned, another one undoes it (*TM*, 50). This may at first seem to firmly position the death penalty as subservient to law, but the inverse, as we have seen, is also true – law is unable to truly or fully outlaw the death penalty. Not only is there later revealed another law that undoes Chavel's document ('the Decree of the 17th [. . .] which makes illegal all change of property that took place during the German occupation' – one might add even the property that is death), where law undoes itself without being able to undo the death penalty, but also, more fundamentally, no matter the law (and its incarnation, the lawyer), the death sentence cannot be survived once proclaimed (*TM*, 134).

As such, when Chavel is released back to Paris, his taking up of the name of 'Charlot' is not only a manner of protective disguise, as if hiding his status as living dead. He is still Chavel – his 'face had altered somewhat, [. . .] but it was still, if carefully examined, the same face' – but he is also no longer himself (*TM*, 62).[68] There is now alterity inscribed into his face. Surveying 'his' house once more (now belonging to Janvier's family), he reflects how '[t]his landscape is not *his*, not anybody's home now', and this simultaneous lack and excess or doubling of identity is maintained to the very end (*TM*, 59). His last signature, as Chavel dies his proper death from a gunshot wound, 'reads[s] only Jean-Louis Ch . . . which stood of course as plainly for Charlot as for Chavel' (*TM*, 149). To be both more and less than what one should be is a fate, perhaps, worse than proper death; as Chavel laments: 'I didn't ask for two lives – only Janvier's' (*TM*, 91).

More can be said about *The Tenth Man*, of Janvier's sister and especially of the imposter Carosse, who turns up unexpectedly near the end of the novel and pretends to be Chavel, believing him far away and not the man 'Charlot' in front of him. This double of a double, which connotes an infinite configuration of Borgesian proportions, itself deserves a lengthy analysis: what role does the concept of the double *play* here (also in the sense of dramatic representation) when another doubles the condemned who, in the struggle, himself doubles the sovereign and is doubled by the Third? 'Charlot [. . .] watched not only Carosse – a mirror on the wardrobe door reflected both of their images', Greene writes (*TM*, 117). Does the Third hold up a mirror to the mirroring of desire, to the mirroring of the subject by the sovereign still entrenched within the *Kampf*?

On these lines, let us move forward to Charles Dickens in further sketching the elusive and doubling figure of the Third, which seems, by its very nature, to disappear all too quickly for analysis.

Dickens's *A Tale of Two Cities* returns us to the terrors of the French Revolution and, with its celebrated opening paragraph, recalls the contradictory and contra-temporal elements outlined in the above section.[69] Andrew Sanders, quoting a letter the author wrote to François-Joseph Régnier, writes that Dickens 'himself believed *A Tale of Two Cities* to be the best story he had ever written', and that here '[d]eath looms larger and more brutally than in any other of Dickens's novels, but [. . .] integrally linked to the idea of resurrection'.[70] The opening heading 'Recalled to Life', in fact, initiates the story of the 'Ghost' of Dr Manette who 'had been dug out' from his prison and exhumed into a world of living death, rife with Resurrection Men, condemned prisoners, the buried and nameless poor, and a noble class which holds mock-funerals and creates only 'fear and slavery' (*TC*, 28, 53, 128). The dance of the period is the Carmagnole, and one is required to keep time with it.[71] In short, the world outside Manette's solitary cell, in the throes of revolution, is not too dissimilar from the world inside, where the condemned revolts against sovereign tyranny merely by being the ghost, the living dead.

The central triad of Dr Manette, Charles Darnay and Sydney Carton (which revolves around Manette's daughter Lucie) is reconfigured when Charles Darnay is sentenced to death, whereupon the father figure of Manette is replaced by the sovereign, a 'king with a large [i.e. masculine] jaw', and the characters' desire becomes something much more Hegelian (*TC*, 5). The remarkable physical similarity between Darnay and Carton, who eventually takes Darnay's proper death, is made immediately obvious: when we first meet Darnay standing trial, Carton is recognized by all as his 'counterpart'; as for Carton, who also loves Lucie, he later tells himself that he could only get her attention were he to '[c]hange places with him' (*TC*, 86, 89). This sentiment, of course, comes to realization when Darnay is condemned to death in Paris, and where Carton, 'the idlest and most unpromising of men' who considers himself 'a worthless fellow [. . .] coming and going at odd times', indeed arrives wholly unexpectedly and sacrifices himself for Darnay (and Lucie) (*TC*, 90, 216).

This text does, then, seem concerned with the kind of moral and ethical sacrifice that Heidegger had in mind when declaring that the act of dying-for does not trouble the *Jemeinigkeit* of death, or which Levinas claims is the culmination of justice and morality. Darnay's oft-foreshadowed action, however, is not without its complications. Madame Defarge, Tricoteuse and ardent supporter of 'the

Republic of Liberty, Fraternity, Equality or Death', knits Darnay's name into the certainty of the penalty and the *Jemeinigkeit*: "'[Lucie's] husband's destiny [. . .] will take him where he is to go, and will *lead him to the end that is to end him*. That is all I know, she says'" (*TC*, 282, 191).[72] Darney believes that '[t]roubled as the future was, it was the unknown future, and *in its obscurity there was ignorant hope*'; however, the death sentence seems to illuminate the future to its fullest and most precise extent with its promise of the where and when of certain death (*TC*, 264).[73] Condemned and '[a]bsolutely Dead in Law', he is placed in La Force with fellow condemned men – that is, in the 'spectral [. . .] company of the dead' with 'eyes that were changed by the death they had died in coming there' (*TC*, 328, 265). And yet, although the unexperienced experience cannot be survived, the Third can nonetheless arrive and restore the future to stygian darkness, undoing the (supposed) certainty of the death sentence, returning finitude (but not mortality), and making room for 'ignorant hope' so long as it is indeed ignorant. Indeed, as Darnay writes his 'final' letter on the eve of his death, he 'never thought of Carton. His mind was so full of the others, that he never once thought of him' (*TC*, 362). As always 'issuing from that obscure corner from which he had never moved', the Third – here Carton – is not awaited (*TC*, 347).

Dickens's narrator reflects on the 'wonderful fact [. . .] that every human creature is constituted to be that profound secret and mystery to every other' (*TC*, 14). Carton emerges, arriving as the mysterious Third *as such*, one hour before Darnay's death (and 'the final hour was Three'), and takes his death forcefully, knocking the condemned man unconscious and telling his aid and spy to escort the man 'with whom [he had] exchanged' (*TC*, 363). 'For a few seconds', Darnay 'faintly struggles with the man who had come to lay down his life for him; but, within a minute or so, he was stretched insensible on the ground' (*TC*, 366–7). He cannot reject the Third who appears without waiting. In this mirroring of the Hegelian *Kampf*, this time fought between the Third and the condemned, sacrifice transforms, through the struggle, into something more theft than sacrifice, forfeit than gift, something that can indeed outstrip death. Darnay's act of resistance, even if a failed one, turns Carton's ethical dying-for into the irresponsible or demonic dying in-stead. In addition, we should note how Carton acts as the Third not only as the one who possibly dies in-stead but also the one who later dies-with (*Mitsterben*), this time with a young and nameless seamstress who asks this 'stranger' to hold her hand and to face their death '[e]ye to eye, voice to voice, hand to hand, heart to heart' (*TC*, 388).

The *Tale*, then, 'somehow evokes the [. . .] vast movements of history'; here, as Richard Maxwell appositely notes, 'History leaks into the everyday life'.[74]

Georg Lukács is, in part, right to claim that the Revolution 'becomes [in the novel] a [mere] romantic background' and that the 'turbulence of the times is used as a pretext for revealing human moral qualities'; however, as evidenced above, Dickens's work also meditates the nuances of the Guillotine up to its own undoing, to the extent that the Revolution is not just 'background' but rather the determinative characterization of the novel's conclusion.[75]

Before attempting to address the numerous questions already posed through these two texts, let us move to this chapter's third and final literary work: *The Last Day of a Condemned Man*. Of Victor Hugo, Libby Purves comments that while '[s]ome call him "The French Shakespeare"', he 'is far more of a Dickens: what marks his best work is a sort of furious, hectoring compassion, combined with a headlong Dickensian willingness to pull every emotional string in sight'.[76] Indeed, the breaking of Narcissistic subjectivity (through an awareness of alterity's implicit role within the death penalty) is something that Hugo also shares with Dickens, as can lucidly be seen in this particular work of his.

In Morisi's words, *The Last Day* presents us with 'the improbable considerations of a prematurely dead man almost until the moment of his killing'.[77] Like *A Tale of Two Cities*, Hugo's novella contains elements that, almost in the manner of the countertextual, are seemingly irrelevant to the sociopolitical argument that Hugo intended to advance. For instance, aside from reflecting his well-known abolitionism, this short work presents us with the elusive figure of the Third.[78]

Hugo's nameless narrator-protagonist is condemned to death (for an unknown crime) and, at the instant of condemnation, goes through the unexperienced experience, once more illustrating the (existential and ontological) difference between being condemned to death and condemned to die: 'Before hearing my death sentence I was aware that my lungs breathed, that my heart beat, and that my body lived in the community of other men; now I plainly saw that a barrier had sprung up between them and me. Nothing was the same as before' (*LD*, 29).

The protagonist's lungs and heart have stopped working, and in the mind of the living corpse 'it seems that there is room for none but thoughts of death'; here, there is no more possibility for work, future or coming self-consciousness – only a consciousness of one's own, present death (*LD*, 75). In the six weeks of his condemnation, 'this six-week death agony' of constant 'final spasms', clocks chime constantly and precisely up to the moment when '[t]he clock struck three, and they came to tell [him] it was time' (he is executed, however, at four o'clock) (*LD*, 77, 85). In this case, unlike the populated cell of the tenth man, the protagonist is trapped in solitary confinement and seems that much surer of both certitude and solitude. He understands the absolute power of the 'monstrous framework' of the penalty, which is both above the law – 'the question of life and death' is 'not in the hands of the judge but in the executioner's', he writes – and beyond even the force of the Revolution: 'the scaffold is the only construction that revolutions do not demolish', he wryly notes, reflecting the inability of transgression to undo the foundation of social existence marked by punishment (*LD*, 66, 4, 6). Revolutionary transgressions, in fact, only construct the scaffold; any attempt to overthrow sovereignty's power of the exception establishes it.[79] However, and despite the fact that his 'glance never strays to the square peephole [of his cell] without meeting [the guard's] two wide, staring eyes', the panoptic sovereign is not the singular fated companion in his living death (*LD*, 36).

Through the other opening in his cell – a barred window – the intrusion of another alterity is repeatedly intimated. He not only hears the girl who sings of 'the struggle between the felon and the constabulary' (an unwitting echo of the *Kampf*) but also observes the chain gang being led away to their forced labour (*LD*, 51). 'Once you are bolted to this chain', the protagonist observes, 'you are no more than a fraction of the hideous entity called the chain-gang, that moves as one man. Your intelligence must surrender, condemned to death by the collar of the convict station' (*LD*, 46). Despite this 'fraternity' in death (to use a contextually apposite term for *Mitsterben*), the protagonist also sees 'each man [. . .] abandoned to himself'; he remarks that 'each man bears his chain by himself, side by side with a stranger' (*LD*, 42). The two descriptions of the chain-gang seem to be at odds with one another – one eradicates subjectivity while the other reinforces it – and this can be understood, perhaps, on the basis of the protagonist's fear of self-surrender. While 'ignorant hope' is needed for the Third to appear *as such*, the protagonist has no hope: 'If I were pardoned? Pardoned! but by whom? on what grounds? and how? There is no way that I could be pardoned' (*LD*, 48). He is open to no one but the sovereign, rejecting anyone else who could stand beside his self. 'Everything around me is a prison; I find the prison in every shape and form, *in human guise* as in the bars or in the bolts' (*LD*, 53).[80] Here, there is no space left for an acknowledgement of the Third.

This failure of acknowledgement is in fact twice repeated. In the governor's office, another condemned man (of whom the protagonist is scared) joins him with 'sudden raucous laughter'; he joins him both literally, in the office, and, as this other condemned man sardonically notes, ontologically, in the 'bleeding *limbo*' of condemnation (*LD*, 61). The protagonist admits to horror when faced with this double: when he 'tried to take my hand. I drew back in horror' (*LD*, 63). The laughing murderer openly offers the possibility of dying-with, but is rejected.

'I've a good mind not to appeal, if they'll top me today along with you. The same priest will do for both of us; I don't mind eating off your plate. You can't say fairer than that. Aren't I a good mate to you? Is it a deal, eh, pal?'

He took another step, drawing nearer to me.

'Sir,' I replied, pushing him away, 'I thank you, but no'. (*LD*, 63)

This rejection leads to a very different outcome than that seen in *A Tale*. Carton and Darnay end up exchanging clothes – boots, cravat, ribbon and coat – and there is a similar exchange that happens here: the protagonist and the murderer exchange coats; or, rather, just as in the *Tale*, the protagonist's coat is taken from him. The crucial difference, though, is that while Darnay's ignorant hope lies in losing the struggle, Hugo's protagonist knowingly accepts this loss. 'It was not out of indifference or a feeling of charity that I let him take [my coat]. No, but because he was stronger than I was. If I had refused, he could have beaten me to a pulp' (*LD*, 64).

Whereas Darnay could not reject the *arrivant*, Hugo's protagonist could do so on two counts: not only does he retreat from this struggle against the Third but also on count of the 'sizing up' of the other (in terms of physical prowess), a moment of recognition from which Darnay clearly omits Carton. The sovereign demands all recognition; for the Third, then, there is to be left simply acknowledgement. Although he recognizes condemnation as that which no longer leaves solitude to the self (here and in the *Tale* demarcated with clothing: 'my trembling hands groped vainly for my clothes', as Hugo's protagonist writes of his instant of condemnation), Hugo's condemned man can acknowledge no other double but the mirrored consciousness of the sovereign, involved only in the battle for recognition (*LD*, 27). Indeed, he thinks of the sovereign only in terms of himself: 'In this very city, at this very hour, and not very far from here, there lives in another palace a man who also has guards on every door, a man set aside like you from the common herd' (*LD*, 78).

Despite having earlier understood that the only possibility of escape lay in the exchange of clothes – consequently, a literal (out-)stripping of subjectivity and one's ownmost death, as, for instance, when he contemplates escaping while wearing the prison gardeners' 'old blue smock embroidered in red' – the protagonist recognizes and thus fails to acknowledge the irruptive potential of this other condemned man (*LD*, 52). Here is recognition that functions as the erasure of alterity; in Levinas's words: 'To know [that is, recognition] amounts to grasping being out of nothing or reducing it to nothing, removing from it its alterity' and making of philosophy 'an egology'.[81] The protagonist refuses the telling sign of the Third, who wears an 'open shirt', and begs this Third to 'leave [him] alone'. This he seems to realize later and tries to reverse his mistake: when a superstitious gendarme is willing to do anything for the protagonist if only he promised to visit him in a dream (after having been executed, so that he could relay to the gendarme the winning lottery numbers), the condemned regains 'crazy hope' and promises to do so only if they 'will change clothes'. The guard, at first without hesitation, begins to acquiesce to this request, but falters upon realizing that this was only a ruse: 'you have to be dead', he conclusively tells the sentenced man (*LD*, 63–4). Here, like *Antigone*'s Guard, the Third rejects the condemned: proper death cannot be given, only taken, outstripped, unexpected. Even the priest, whom the protagonist had earlier acknowledged as 'the only human being to me', and so the only one allowed the possibilities of the Third, is eventually dismissed as an extension of sovereignty and subsequently refused; the protagonist concludes that there can be 'nothing given him by me' (*LD*, 68–9).

The dynamics of the exchange of clothes, standing for an exchange of subjectivity and its proper death (dying in-stead), allows for an alternative to recognition – that is, *acknowledgement*: the non-positive affirmation of the Third *as such*. This principle of disguise already points towards an impossibility of recognition; it is an old gesture and a surprisingly common motif. We see something similar, for instance, in *The Merchant of Venice*, when Antonio is taken out of the dialectics of condemnation by a disguised Third, and something identical happens in the ritual of the substitute king, where the commoner is made to dress in the king's regalia.[82] In living the relational death, proper death is something that can be taken from the subject, 'like a coat', as Sartre notes, 'which I leave [the Other] after my disappearance'.[83]

The fact that all three narratives of condemnation are situated in Paris, the birthplace of the guillotine, is the first step in understanding the roles of the players in the drama of the death penalty. The condemned subject is – through transgression – both the constructor and victim of his own scaffold, and thus lives on through a *Langweile* of killing time, awaiting proper death – a death mine by property – as delivered by the guillotine. With him, the dead figure of the sovereign, who kills both the slave and himself, troubles not only assumed political structures but also any idea of Heideggerian solitude in or 'property' of death. The struggle moves towards the chimes of three o'clock; however, Donne's bell tolls backwards, too. In Catherine Malabou's words we are shown that, as with the chronological troubling of *The Instant*, under the death sentence, '[t]ime is not what it is. It *turns*, and by its very concept is susceptible to revolution'.[84] The supposedly inviolable certitude of the time of proper death, following the prior certitude at the instant of one's ontological death, is interrupted and indefinitely suspended by the revolutionary entrance of the Third.

While the condemned can do nothing but wait, the Third cannot wait. There is no *Langweile* for he who interrupts; his death is not in abeyance. Upon his unexpected arrival, death is outstripped, and with this loss of proper death, we see another nail in the coffin of Narcissistic subjectivity. Proper death is taken from the future of the condemned just as it had been promised him by the sovereign, and the living corpse must go on living on. Thus, the interruption is, in its very gestures, not an act of mercy or salvation, and neither is it the ethical sacrifice or gift, but rather the prolongation of the death penalty, where its 'monstrous framework' is transported back into the human society to which the condemned both belong and return. This is the demonically irresponsible action that Derrida concludes must take place in the absence of sacrifice: for, after all, if the *arrivant* renders indeterminate '*all the distinctive signs of prior identity*', with this must be erased the firm ipseity of 'my' death and the responsibility that is the property of mortality. The salvation by the Third may, in its own way, simply be another form of condemnation; as Louis-Sébastien Mercier writes in his *Tableau de Paris*: 'It is not death which is terrible. It is to die last of all.'[85] Living on, one misses and yearns for proper death. E. M. Forster drolly notes, in fact, that one must '"[m]istrust all enterprises that require new clothes"'.[86]

In the condemned's past, then, there is only death; in his future, there is also only death. But the Third's irruptive arrival suspends all future certitude, all sense of timeliness, and this contra-temporality is, furthermore, fully inherent to condemnation itself – revolution is, by its very nature, and as indicated by the term itself, contra-temporal. Comay notes how 'the machine [the guillotine, the revolution] turns against itself', and 'terror inevitably comes to terrify even itself, to denounce and purge itself'. Just as the guillotine produces the modern subject, it executes it, demonstrating the death penalty's 'illogical inability to sustain itself', doing and undoing itself in a 'repeated short-circuiting of the Revolution [back] to prerevolutionary positions': that of the persistently thanatopolitical living corpse. Comay asserts that Hegel does see 'the spectre of repetition at the heart of revolutionary regeneration'; what this study adds is that, through the death penalty, there can be nothing other than the contra-temporal and eternal repetition of consciousness-not-yet-self, the 'I' without self-unity, both lacking and exceeding in selfhood, and History has not and can never come to an end or culminate into autonomous subjectivity when all it has to stand on is the trapdoor of the scaffold.[87]

If condemned, then, one is truly beyond the *Langweile* in which one is 'enchained within the mere present' of mortality;[88] after all, Heideggerian *Being* is the 'privileging [of] the present tense'.[89] In contrast, contra-temporality is the revolutionary time of the relational death, a limbo full of itself. It cannot be the case that, in the absence of a future, one returns to the past: in revolution, time cannot be concretized – one need only recall the failure of the Republic Calendar, or the symbolic failure of the Revolution to execute Dickens's fifty-two prisoners, 'in number as the weeks of the year' (*TC*, 360).[90] The condemned no longer has a past: he has not survived the death penalty, and who he was has been killed. Charlot cannot become Chavel once more, and it is the same with all the others. Moreover, the future is not so much absent as it is in excess: the question of 'when will death ever come', a death missed in all senses, is an open-ended one. The figure of the Third incarnates the death penalty's undoing of itself – after all, the Third can only appear *as such* if there is a death penalty – and that is why, in addition to the suspension of futurity, its entrance is contra-temporal (or, for Levinas, 'diachronic'). An important rephrasing, therefore, is necessary: the entrance of the *arrivant* is not irruptive, but rather eruptive. The Third breaks the tyranny of the Carmagnole, but his entrance is one more step of the dance that is intrinsic, and not extrinsic, to the death penalty itself. This is the double-double, for the condemned is not only doubled by the sovereign, but also by the third. Chavel is doubled by Janvier (later by Carosse), Darnay by Carton, Hugo's protagonist by the other convict and later almost again by the gendarme. Blanchot's narrator, through the levelling *exécuté*, is mirrored by the farmers' sons. This is the doubling necessary in the revolution – like two cogs working against each other – because it connotes not only simultaneity but also asynchrony; double time is also when History progresses and regresses simultaneously, when three o'clock approaches and recedes, where one's death has already been died and yet is taken away. This is the time of the relational death, founded on an eternal instant. Contrary to Georges Danton's assumption, then, the verb 'to guillotine' can indeed be conjugated in all tenses, including 'I have been guillotined'.[91]

Let us turn, in coming to a conclusion, to Malabou's reading of Hegelian temporality, where she makes evident how, for Hegel, the future of subjectivity is not determined in advance but, rather, finds form through plasticity. Malabou's (and Hegel's) concerns remain within the confines of the progress of *self-knowledge* through the 'three great movements of self-determination – the Greek, the modern [or, one can say, French], and that of Absolute Knowledge', these being sites 'where identity is retained within difference and difference preserved within identity'.⁹² In this light, how can one hold the view that the death penalty unworks work and bars self-consciousness, outstripping the future (and, along with it, ownmost death), when the Third doubles the condemned, when the Third comes from *within* the system to open up finitude into infinity, and when difference explicitly wears both the face and the coat of identity?

Indeed, the cleaving guillotine perhaps demonstrates Hegel's understanding of 'the openness to the future, the openness to the event' in contrast with the Heideggerian certainty of the train's scheduled arrival.⁹³ The certainty of the time of proper death is displaced by the Third, and in this sense renders the future 'plastic', an 'excess of the future over the future' where the condemned's future regains all possibilities taken away by condemnation.⁹⁴ The Third thus plays its cleaving role in 'the "becoming essential of the accident" in the Greek moment of subjectivity, or the "becoming accidental of essence" in the modern moment'.⁹⁵ If the machinery of the death penalty is interrupted by its own mechanisms, and the relationship between subjectivity and alterity is only 'the recto and verso of the same event', then subjectivity is not suspended but rather reinforced by a Third as phenomenon which 'at once suddenly arises [. . .] and just as suddenly disappears'.⁹⁶ After becoming essential, the accidental phenomenon becomes accidental once more. Malabou writes: 'The phenomenon, *qua* moment, is always a manifestation of something other than itself. And this relation to alterity is a twofold one. The phenomenon, like the "now" that passes by, implies a relation to a new "now", *to another instant*'.⁹⁷

However, Malabou is here making the Third into Hegelian '"phantasmatic alterity"', an act of kenosis which (rather hubristically) brings death to death itself.⁹⁸ While 'to posit the future as "plasticity" amounts to *displacing* the established definition of the future as a *moment of time*', it is, in Hegelian thought, never to displace the Self; the dialectical process is in fact, at core, 'the movement of self-determination'.⁹⁹ If the future is plastic and thus an '*anticipatory structure*' which names this kind of future as '"to see (what is) coming" (*le "voir venir"*)' – that is, 'of both "being sure of what is coming" [. . .] and of "not knowing what is coming"' – it is only a future where subjectivity projects *itself* in advance of *itself*, and thereby participates in the process of its own determination.¹⁰⁰ For Hegelian subjectivity, all difference is '*a difference within itself*'.¹⁰¹ It is never a future where alterity undoes subjectivity; *that* would truly be what cannot be seen coming, the *tout autre*, the absolute difference which cannot be synthesized. Indeed, while the Third returns the uncertain future of finitude to the condemned subject it has replaced, it does not return the life lost at the instant of death – that is, it does not return mortality.

Malabou writes that 'habit brings [self-]becoming to life', but the figure of the Third, as a mechanism of the death penalty, breaks both the habit of death and that of life. Death is taken away, but life cannot be granted again (for one does not survive the death penalty). Alterity dissolves subjectivity to the point where 'it finds itself dispossessed of itself, to the point of becoming truly mad' (and to this Malabou adds the dimensions of disease and derangement).[102]

If, as Malabou writes, '[t]he route to recovery [from madness, disease] is the work of habit' – and only from there emerges 'the possibility of a Self', a synthesis of spirit and nature – then the most ontologically destabilizing aspect of the death penalty is that it bars the condemned from work and habit and, therefore, from *selfhood*.[103] This is its diabolical nature (in the Derridean sense), which maintains the living corpse in a state of disease or derangement – or, as shall be forwarded in the following chapter, a state of *decomposition*. After all, the 'habit' is also simply another item of clothing, to be stripped and taken away from the condemned subject.

Hugo's narrator, the one who retreats from the figure of the Third out of fear, is perhaps the most astute of our condemned men: the Third is terrible and to be feared. Summarizing, Malabou concludes that '[i]t would be futile to want to determine some ontological priority of essence over accident, or accident over essence, for their co-implication is primary' – and this might seem, in the death penalty, true.[104] But the Third is one who forcibly takes priority because it does not wait. In outstripping the *Jemeinigkeit* of death, there is enacted an ontological precedence, and the condemned, even if he is allowed 'release', can never be the 'pure and absolute autonomy' he could have been without condemnation, without having gone through ontological death.[105] The Third thus undoes the Cartesian *cogito* as taken up by Hegel to signify the certainty of the 'I=I of pure self-consciousness'.[106]

Having explored at some length, too, the relationality of death in terms of alterity – the sovereign, the Third – we must now ask: what of the condemned, now escaped, who lives on as a living corpse, a revenant, back in the world of those not condemned but nonetheless living under the penalty of death? What about the one whose future is in excess, whose face is irrevocably marked by alterity? The protagonist of *The Last Day* asks pertinent questions: 'if these dead return, in what form do they return? What do they keep of their incomplete and mutilated body? What do they choose? Does the head or the body turn into a ghost?' (*LD*, 79). For this escaped living dead, is there still a head, still a sovereign? Or is there a body without a head, a postsovereign subject, a Slave without a Master (but one, like Antigone, who is not Bourgeois)? And what of the ghostly body – is this the decomposing subject, who, living the relational death, undergoes some sort of ontological decomposition? Is this the other side of the Hegelian becoming-subject – that is, the un-becoming-subject?

And to which community, exactly, do they return? If there is a relation withheld in the contra-temporality of death, then there is also a community; as Levinas writes, '[t]here would be no separated being if the time of the One could fall into the time of the other', as seen in the instant(-)aneity of dying-with, which makes ontological selfhood impossible.[107] Might the members of such a community belong to some modern polis (an obvious antithesis), and is this necessarily a place to be in-habit-ed? Gourgouris writes of how '[t]he drama of Antigone performs in exemplary fashion the perils of singularity and death-driven thought'; in the above reading of the permeation of singularity by alterity, where even Being-towards-death is 'altered' in all senses of the word, might we find the plurality of the polis that is both modern and Greek, as cleaved by the death penalty? Let us keep in mind Heidegger's *polis*, which, as Gourgouris reminds us, 'comes at the cost of forgetting that the polis signifies neither city nor place, strictly speaking, and certainly not mere spatial designation, even metaphorically or philosophically', but which is, rather, 'linked to a differential autonomous plurality, the ensemble of *polites*'.[108]

We can thus finally situate the mechanisms of the death penalty, and its enactors, beyond both the Narcissism of the *Jemeinigkeit* and the egoity of Hegel's 'I am'.[109] This is a death that is not proper to me; rather, it is a 'we' that is the property of death. What this 'more-than-I' ensemble of living corpses is, each with more than one life, doubled and doubling, and where they assemble, shall be discussed in the next chapters. In particular, several questions shall be explored. Is this site of assemblage an 'abyssal', even stygian, place where '[self-]creation *coincides* with alterity' rather than synthesizes it? What is the action of the living thing who, like Antigone, as Gourgouris writes, acts 'against singularity but in a singular fashion'?[110] Does the literary figure of the condemned, excluded by his very nature, nonetheless allow us to rethink the state of *anthropos*, *demos* and *polis*, reconceived as a polis of death – a home for thanatopolitics, the *necropolis* – where there persists in death the relational par excellence? And is this why, at the end of all this, one finds the autothanatographical, living through relational death and 'speak[ing] in the name of death' without having necessarily been condemned to it?

4

After death, anonymity

Angels and demons

When Derrida heard his angel speak, he heard only the voice of the demonic. When the angel prophesized the idea of a deconstruction of death, a doing away with death, these were the whispers of a demonic Other. Against the ethical death epitomized by self-sacrifice, this Other who forcefully strips our death and dies in-stead does away with any such notions of responsibility, irreplaceability or ethics and its individuation. It puts under erasure the very category of subjectivity itself. The face of the Other who dies in-stead expresses not the command 'Thou shalt not kill' but rather 'Thou shalt not die'.

In light of this radical rephrasing of the ethical command, Levinas's thought shall here be considered so that we may continue our attempt at understanding what lies beyond the confines of the *Jemeinigkeit* of Heideggerian ontology. While Levinas never directly discusses the death sentence, it is nonetheless through his thought that the death penalty, as understood both philosophically and literally, will here be further revealed as that which questions the very *being* of human *beings*. This does not mean, however, that one needs necessarily arrive at the same conclusions as Levinas; indeed, the question of the death penalty and its workings repurposes some of the basic tenets of Levinasian thought, whereby the modality of the human is understood otherwise on the basis of relational death.

The Third arrives unexpectedly. Carton entered Darnay's cell and 'stood before him face to face, quiet, intent upon him' (*TC*, 363). This face-to-face encounter, for Levinas, is beyond ontology: it is the realm of the ethical. Returning once more to the angel, this time not a demon in disguise, Richard Cohen reminds us that Levinas takes the concept of the face-to-face 'from Genesis 32:31, where, after having fought an angel all night, it is written: "And Jacob called the name of the place Peniel: for I have seen God face to face, and my life is preserved"'.¹ The face, for Levinas, stands for the Other whom Narcissistic ontology firmly places in the stratum of the ontic. While Heidegger stresses that *Mitsein* is an essential part of the *being-there* of Dasein, Levinas recognizes that Heidegger's conception of alterity – following René Descartes, Kant, Fichte, Hegel and Edmund Husserl – is ultimately only self-contained, merely existentiell, whereby alterity amounts to *das Man* and its Saying merely distracting chatter [*das Gerede*]; this is here encapsulated in the term Narcissism.² Authenticity is thus, for Heidegger, to be found solely in the understanding of *being* refracted through the 'substantive and substantial identity of the *I*', and finding it in the anxiety of being-toward-death has neither a need for a relation to the other nor acknowledges in the other's death anything more than a corpse, a thing.³

Levinas's radical contribution to this discussion comes in defining the other as '[t]he *there* of *being-there*', shifting gravity away from the totality of *being*.⁴ The face of the Other demands from us that we prioritize its life and needs over ours, calling for justice, piercing through the autonomy of the self and, in so doing, individualizing the irreplaceable self who beholds, from below, the face of alterity. Its primary command, Levinas says, is 'thou shalt not kill'.⁵ This face-to-face encounter and the subsequent ethical demands reveal the self's asymmetrical relation to the other – one of *acknowledgement* and not *recognition*, a 'relation without relation' – which in turn conceives the self as inseparable from the *there-ness* of Dasein as well as going beyond ontology in its account of ethics.⁶ Finally, this intersubjective 'relation' with non-present alterity and the consequent demand for justice are that which, as Cohen writes, 'inform the whole of social life and constitute the very humanity of the human'.⁷ It is not *my* mortality that makes me human, *contra* Heidegger – it is the other's. 'My solitude', as Levinas states, 'is thus not confirmed by death but broken by it'.⁸

The figure of the Other as read here, as one who interrupts the death penalty from within and dies in-stead, may to a certain extent be read in accordance with Levinas's broader understandings of alterity. As we have seen, the Third can only be acknowledged, and its time is indeed diachronic; the time of the other, writes Levinas, is that which 'does not gather into re-*present*ation' (as opposed to 'synchrony as *being* in its egological gathering').⁹ As has been argued, this is analogous to (or perhaps even deeper than) the gestures of the Revolution's Carmagnole, where the Third emerges as a figure that undoes the temporal certainty of the death penalty from within, rendering the future completely and creatively novel once more, stygian, or what Levinas calls 'pure future'.¹⁰ If, as Heidegger writes, '[d]ying is something that every Dasein itself must take upon itself *at the time*', there is not always only an(-)other self, but also an(-)other time (*BT*, 284).[11]

However, the literary works discussed here point to a different understanding of both 'my death' and that of the other, and, with this, of sociality, justice, and the time of death and life in general. To briefly introduce the argument expounded in this chapter, the relational death which includes within it the Third dying in-stead deeply challenges Levinas's account of death as one always necessarily in the future and one always mine, and thus also bears a different testimony to social being. Levinas does briefly question this characterization of death, the 'mine every time', but ultimately answers in the affirmative, seeing in death a necessary part of the freedom that 'is not found in autonomy but responsibility, responsibility in the face of the other person'.[12] He writes:

> But the death thus announced as other, as the alienation of my existence, is it still *my* death? If it opens a way out of solitude, does it not simply come to crush this solitude, to crush subjectivity itself? [. . .] The problem does not consist in rescuing an eternity from the jaws of death, but in allowing it to be welcomed, keeping for the ego – in the midst of an existence where an event happens to it – the freedom acquired by hypostasis.[13]

This freedom is at core social, responsible and moral – a 'difficult freedom' found not in the subject, as for instance Sartre would claim (the 'for-itself'), but in the other.[14] On the other hand, as we have seen, at the core of the very notion of human society itself one finds only the death penalty, and, with this, relational death. Death is not only no longer mine but also no longer able to 'happen', no longer an event *à-venir* in the *avenir*. In this relational death-made-present and past, it is not life, as Jacob proclaims in Genesis, but death which is preserved, and the freedom for subjectivity to avoid being condemned, or 'crushed' in Levinas's words, is brought starkly into question.

On this, as we shall see, the figures of the angel and the demon, so often bound to an afterlife strictly demarcated by proper death, simultaneously recede from and manifest in our living of the relational death.

The unbecoming subject

After death begins decomposition. The corpse is certainly unbecoming, for most a visceral affront to all vital senses. For some, however, it is beautiful, as Lacan says of Antigone, or has a naturalist aesthetic, as explored in Jim Crace's *Being*

Dead, or is even 'exquisite', as Maria Torok calls the corpse.[15] Beautiful or not, does the one who *lives on* also *decompose*? Of course, without proper death, there can be no proper decomposition (except in the cases of certain illnesses), but living death as the unexperienced experience can perhaps be understood as an existential, ontological, and even ethical decomposition, a rotting away or shedding of what *life* and *being* are, of what makes *being* be.

This is to a certain extent touched on by Malabou when she speaks of the disease and derangement that would grip the ego were habit not capable of leading to the notion of Self, the becoming subject – but habit is indeed stripped in the death penalty. What shall be made clear in this section is that the 'unbecoming subject', whatever that is, is first and foremost not a process leading from state *a* to *b*, but a permanent condition of the human – or, more precisely, a constant process with no true beginning or end. 'Unbecoming', this adjective-*cum*-gerund, may be understood similarly, not only grammatically but also conceptually, to how Derrida speaks of the crypt as '[t]o crypt'.[16]

As previously discussed, the condemned man is a dead man walking, a 'living corpse' as Mbembe and Kojève would say. Though both these thinkers have helped elucidate the complex matrices on which the death penalty operates, neither refers to the penalty specifically, nor thinks of the primary 'activity' of the corpse – that is, decomposition. What, then, is the unbecoming corpse, this thing that, in this reading, every human emerges as being? How is the one who is not condemned to death, such as ourselves, also to be understood as the corpse living on, living the relational death, living the death one has already died?

Some answers may be found through Sartre's 'The Wall', a short story set during the Spanish civil war where the protagonist Pablo Ibbieta, along with two other men (Juan Mirbal and Tom Steinbock), is condemned to death by firing squad by a Falangist tribunal.[17] After their sentence, the three cellmates spend their last night accompanied by a Belgian doctor. As in the other works examined here, these prisoners, described as 'three bloodless shadows', have gone through the instant of death, the unexperienced experience, becoming the living corpses of those condemned, easily doubling one another in their lack of identity (*TW*, 62). As night turns to the dawn of their execution, Pablo thinks of their miserable state: 'grey and sweating: we were alike and worse than mirrors of each other', with 'bodies dying in agony while yet alive'. Tom, the more vocal of his cellmates and who 'wore death on his face', doubles (in death) both the thoughts that run through Pablo's mind and his expression: 'now we looked as much alike as twin brothers, simply because we were going to die together'. He tells Pablo: 'I can feel the wounds already; I've had pains in my head and in my neck for the past hour. Not real pains. Worse. [. . .] I see my corpse; that's not hard but *I'm* the one who sees it, with *my* eyes' (*TW*, 60–1).[18]

Together, they watch the doctor – 'the Belgian, the living' – who watches them with 'false solicitude' (*TW*, 60, 62):

> All three of us watched him because he was alive. He had the motions of a living human being, the cares of a living human being; he shivered in the cellar the way the living are supposed to shiver; he had an obedient, well-fed body. The rest of us hardly felt ours – not in the same way anyhow. (*TW*, 62)

The three are living corpses, no longer human beings; they are decomposing, grey, with strange, detaching and unbecoming bodies. But does not their distance from the Belgian doctor – an uncrossable distance between life and death, ironically personified by a man of medicine just like Hippocrates – only reinforce the idea that the state of the living corpse is one limited to death row, to where the condemned is trapped in the night between the experience of ontological death and proper death, 'between what is going to arrive and what has already arrived'?

The narrative also points to just the opposite being true. Aside from the shared mortality on the faces of Pablo and his cellmates – a dying-with (*Mitsterben*) signified by the mirrored Hippocratic face – there is also the death of Ramon Gris, the man whom Pablo is accused of having hidden in his house for a short time. After having killed Juan and Tom, his two cellmates, the militia offer Pablo a deal: if he tells them where Gris was hiding, he could have his life back. Knowing fully that Gris was hiding out with his cousins, Pablo plays to the absurdity of the situation, wanting to laugh but keeping a straight face, and feeds them the lie that Gris 'is hidden in the cemetery. In a vault or in the gravediggers' shack' (*TW*, 72). After a period of time, an officer informs him that he is being transferred to a courtyard to be with other prisoners; confused as to why he was not instead being led to his execution, he asks and finds out that the officers had found Gris exactly where he had told them he would be, and killed him.

The deal made between Pablo and the officers, 'his life against yours', is not an exchange of life – it is an exchange of death. 'You can have yours if you tell us where he is', an officer tells him; except, clearly, one does not survive the death penalty, and one cannot regain life or be fully resurrected (*TW*, 70). Ibbieta is now condemned to live on, outside the matrices of the penalty – just as Darnay, Chavel and Blanchot's protagonist – and at this knowledge he 'laughed so hard [he] cried' (*TW*, 74). This is not to say that he was not previously aware that this would be the case had he somehow managed to survive another way, or if he were pardoned. He was always to remain a living corpse, as he admits:

> In the state I was in, if someone had come and told me I could go home quietly, that they would leave me my life whole, it would have left me cold: several hours or several years of waiting is all the same when you have lost the illusion of being eternal. I clung to nothing, in a way I was calm. But it was a horrible calm – because of my body; my body, I saw with its eyes, I heard with its ears; but it was no longer me; it sweated and trembled by itself and I didn't recognise it any more. I had to touch it and look at it to find out what was happening, as if it were the body of someone else. (*TW*, 66)

Already one can see the power of the death penalty, the ability of the sovereign's *droit de glaive* to extend beyond cells and sentences, killing those on the outside of the decreed or 'lawful' condemnation. Pablo can imagine what living on is like, as a living corpse; moreover, this indeed is what happens to him. Ibbieta has been outstripped of his death, something he assuredly did not want ('I would rather die than give up Gris', he had resolved), and his death has been exchanged by Gris, who died in-stead (*TW*, 71). There is no voluntary or ethical sacrifice at play here; Gris has served as the 'lightning rod' just like the three sons of farmers or the commoner substitutes of the ancient king. What is here most revealing of the foundational nature of the death penalty, therefore, and what now needs close discussion, is not Pablo's living on but Gris's very incorporation and death.

What Derrida (with Kant) stresses in the two volumes of *The Death Penalty* must not be forgotten. Being 'at the origin of the social contract or the contract of the nation-state, at the origin of any sovereignty, any community, or any genealogy, any people', that which kills us is what lets us live. Hence, there can be no law, nor society, without punishment as epitomized by the principle of the death penalty; the death penalty is not only what is proper to law – 'the right to law [*le droit au droit*], the right to the violence of law' – but also what goes beyond it (*DPII*, 48). In its position as the foundation and birth of every law, every society, it is also outside such laws and societies. It persists throughout both peace and wartime – however difficult it is to properly distinguish between the two. Social justice, then, is not what employs the death penalty, but rather it is the other way around.

Such a reading of justice is extremely jarring when set alongside Levinas's. It is immediately apparent that 'thou shalt not kill' is diametrically opposed to a relation or sociality made possible only through the death penalty. While to discuss in detail Levinas's idea of sociality and justice would be to unavoidably recapitulate the whole of Levinas – such is his argument structured across his entire philosophical trajectory – let us quickly go over some important points before moving forward.

As briefly mentioned earlier, for Levinas, 'the responsibility for the others, the relationship with the non-ego, precedes any relationship of the ego with itself'.[19] The individuation of the Self, therefore, is constituted only through alterity, and this is what primarily obligates us to the other. This is why Levinas speaks of the self being obsessed, persecuted or taken hostage by the other, and why the self, in its responsibility and obligation, is unique and irreplaceable. Subjectivity can thus be characterized as 'the other in the same', and alterity is therefore both inalienable from and foundational of the 'I' that apprehends it.[20]

However, in it being completely *other* to the self, alterity also brings the subject into question. This same infinite responsibility posits the self as elected *for the other* and as charged with 'the possibility of putting oneself in the place of the Other', being responsible for the Other in the name of the Other, and dying *for* the Other in the manner of self-sacrifice.[21] For Levinas, subjectivity is, as Cohen writes, 'being beholden to the other beyond one's own being', and this intersubjectivity never allows for self-certainty or self-enclosure, being always asymmetrical in the prioritization of the Other.[22] In this way, ethics comes before any deliberation, choice or freedom, and, while starting inexorably from the self, is universalizable and made infinite beyond it.

In Levinas's later works, '*l'Autre* and *Autrui* [here "other" and "Other"] play a less important role, being largely replaced by *le prochain* (the neighbour)'.[23] This is the one whom I face, face-to-face, who discloses my unique responsibility (in religious terms, to 'love thy neighbour as thyself') and who can only be acknowledged as non-presence, non-Same – in sum, as 'the face of a neighbour, ambiguously him *before whom* (or *to whom*, without any paternalism) and him *for whom* I answer'.[24] Levinas, however, clearly understands the dangers of an intersubjectivity limited to two interlocutors; because the relation between self and Other is the Saying, response-ability, language as 'the dynamics of question and answer',[25] then this dyad 'would complete one another in a system visible from the outside'.[26] To transpose what he writes seven years later: 'As soon as two are involved, everything is in danger.'[27] Against this danger, Levinas acknowledges a third, *the third* [*le tiers*], who is always 'present at the encounter': '[t]he third party looks at me in the eyes of the Other' in the face-to-face, and through this break in an otherwise looped dialogue 'the epiphany of the face qua face opens humanity'.[28] In Levinas's opening up of the self's relation to the Other to a relation with the world, we see, writes Colin Davis, how '[t]he exposure to the Other brings the subject into existence as it also puts it into question; [and also how] the presence of the third party in turn raises questions about my relationship with the Other'.[29]

And what is in question? The foundations of sociality, justice. 'This means', Levinas says, 'that justice is not a legality regulating human masses, from which a technique of social equilibrium is drawn [. . .]. Justice, society, the State and its institutions, exchanges and work are comprehensible out of [that is, on the basis] of proximity' (to *le tiers*); thus '[t]he judge is not outside the conflict', and 'nothing is outside of the control of the responsibility of the one for the other'. He goes on: 'But justice can be established only if I [. . .] can become an other like the others'[30] – and this is what *le tiers* allows us to realize: 'a collectivity that is not a communion', that is not a sameness.'[31] The third, then, not only opens up our eyes to the obligations of justice but also makes the very concept of justice and world (as society) possible.

As Davis notes, 'Levinas concedes that his thought has a utopian aspect' and 'rejects the view that conflict is essential to human relations; instead, he derives the outlines of a social theory from his notion of exposure to the Other as pacific'.[32] In appealing for society to become more just, because and not in spite of humanity's violent history (hence why 'it is difficult to be good' and free, this violence being epitomized by the Holocaust),[33] Levinas sees morality and religion as the 'pacific imperatives' through which a just society may be achieved, the antithesis of the warlike actions wrought by Narcissistic or totalitarian thinking against alterity.[34] With the aim of justice being an anxiety not in relation to my own death but to the other's, Levinas reveals how mortality comes to us only through sociality, a mortality that cannot be separated from morality.[35] Ultimately, for Levinas, to be ethically just is to work towards the transcendence that is God: *illeity*, 'alterity at the furthest remove', further from any neighbour, at an *infinite* distance.[36] This is why Levinas understands religion as being an aspect of ethics, and not the other way around, as a means towards utopian justice enabled only through the ethical beyond ontology.

Essentially, when juxtaposed against each other, the ethical society and the society that has always and irremediably the death penalty at its core – the utopia and the necropolis – are incompatible.[37] Both are located beyond ontology in their intersubjectivity and relationality respectively, but each struggles against the other in defining the 'very humanity of human beings', diametrically opposed both in significance and in consequence: in Levinasian alterity, subjectivity is constituted; in relational death, while similarly emptied of *being*, subjectivity is condemned. Of which polis are we the citizens?

More useful, perhaps, than the scientific theory that the human face took its present features in response to the human fist, is Sartre's Pablo Ibbieta.[38] Looking at Juan as he weeps for the life taken from him, he says: 'I felt inhuman: I could pity neither the others nor myself' (*TW*, 67). Neither does he feel fear: 'it wasn't fear that made me sweat'; 'I felt myself crushed under an enormous weight. It was not the thought of death, or fear; it was nameless' (*TW*, 58, 56). This absence of pity and fear – the absence of the tragic, of catharsis – shall be further commented on in the next chapter, but we may already start to understand how, in death, *because* it is death, subjectivity is indeed 'crushed' (a word used by both Sartre and Levinas),[39] condemned under the anonymous or the 'nameless' – that is, beyond any definition of the humanity of the human: the 'inhuman'. In death made now, in the lived unexperienced experience and the decomposition of the unbecoming subject, ethics dies too.

What, then, is still to be determined is whether a society founded on the death penalty is only possible in the first place through the ethical, hence Levinas's insistence on ethics as first philosophy. The answer would be in the affirmative were the penalty of death simply a sentence one can utter, an action that one can take or be subjected to, as subject to the subject (phenomenologically) or subject of the sovereign (thanatopolitically). This would be, however, to consider the death penalty as law, spectacle, machine, retribution, vengeance and deterrent – important yet ultimately secondary terms. On the other hand, as we have seen through Derrida and shall here continue to explore, the 'justice' of the death penalty is the very way through which one can act in the first place, what makes every action, including the category of action itself, possible in the first place. It is prior to self-consciousness (as Hegel's *Kampf* goes some way in revealing), and it is both found through and founding of the very dynamic of the 'inter-' between any notions of subjectivity and alterity. In short, it might perhaps serve best to consider death as first philosophy.

In this last phrase we might once again hear the echoes of the *meletē thanatou*, but, simultaneously, in death, there is also the *im*possibility of any meaningful Saying when the only thing that matters is one Sentence, one that kills both interlocutors. In the death penalty being *before* the ontological or the ethical subject, creating the grounds for any and all of their relations, the relational death is *there-before*-being, 'what has already arrived'. Indeed, we here recall once more the question of birth, of whether one can be *born* in-stead, of the beinglessness before one is born or given a name. Is this the beinglessness or anonymity which Ibbieta speaks of when he utters the name of the 'nameless'? A response to this may be approximated still through Levinas's radical thought and 'the disturbance it provokes within philosophical discourse', suggesting a beyond or *before* ontology: the *il y a*.[40] Before getting to this in the following section, let us delve deeper into why subjectivity is so 'crushed' under death and does not find itself open to the *à-venir* of death.

The quick answer is that we are all Ramon Gris. We are alive but already in a crypt, a vault or the gravediggers' shack, hiding from the death penalty which kills us anyway. To be alive in a crypt, buried alive like Antigone, is to live in a society made society only because of the death penalty (further eroding any distinction to be made between 'making die' and 'letting live', as drawn by Foucault). One need not be condemned to be subject to the death penalty; one need only exist.

Ibbieta does not seem to realize that this is the case: 'Sometimes I had the impression I was missing something and began to look around for my coat and then suddenly remembered they hadn't given me a coat' (*TW*, 52). The coat, the symbol of the Sartrean other as previously mentioned, seems nowhere to be found within the matrices of the death penalty, the private and egological struggle unto death where (the) habit is stripped away. And yet alterity is always-already there, the coat is taken, for Gris does indeed die in-stead.

Once again, then, the third dying in-stead can be read in much the same way as the third party, in Levinas, disrupts what could become a systematic relation of the face-to-face and which subsequently unfolds society as a whole. In other words, the strict transposition of Hegel's *Kampf* onto the death penalty is unable to remain an untroubled and self-enclosed relation between sovereign and condemned, providing the self- and temporal-certainty of one's ownmost death. The Third steps in, not only questioning 'self' and 'temporality' but also unveiling the whole of society enmeshed in the penalty, disrupting – or rather *interrupting* – what is in Levinasian terms a 'dialectic that tears the ego apart [but which] ends by a synthesis and system whereby a tear is no longer seen'.[41] As such, the third withheld in relational death, who outstrips the *Jemeinigkeit*, reveals that sociality, society as a whole and at its basis, is where all of us are condemned to death no matter where we hide – if hiding is even a possibility at all – and we cannot escape the matrices of the death penalty. Even utterly outside its legal enactment, Gris, as an outlaw, is nonetheless made to exchange his death with one of the condemned.

In other words, literature reveals how we are all, like Ramon Gris, living corpses, and with this idea of the relational death, deeper significance is added to the thanatopolitical nuances of 'living corpses' in Mbembe and Kojève, as well as to the 'human' as understood by, for instance, Hegel or Heidegger. As all of us are living corpses, always-already a part of this necropolis, then we must face the *impossibility of living* at all, and we are thus turned away from the very core of Levinas's ethical and utopian ideas of sociality and justice, foreclosed at the very beginning.

In a sociality founded on the death penalty, but where sociality – because it is sociality, that which is more than an enclosed system of two – interrupts the dual struggle of the death penalty, the third is thus always-already there, having always-already interrupted sovereignty and died in-stead. Because we are not contained in egoity, then in this society made possible through the death penalty the third must have already stepped in. Phrased more simply, we are alive, socially, because someone else has already died in consequence of this sociality. This is the basis of understanding the necropolis, or, in other words, thanatopolitical sociality. This is why the command of the face is 'thou shalt not die': death has always-already been exchanged for our lives, and because this exchange of death is only possible through a society founded through the death penalty, it is not really life that is granted us, but only *living on*, a *living on with death*: the relational death.

This line of thinking, where one never begins to become a corpse but is rather always unbecoming – that is to say, the very impossibility of life itself – carries with it serious implications that must be addressed. First, it troubles the distinction earlier set up so rigorously between *condemned to death* and *condemned to die*. Derrida himself revisits this distinction by way of the 'paradigm of the *fatwa* [such as the one unleashed on Salman Rushdie] [which] complicates all the more the question' of distinguishing between the two (is it a death sentence if there is no specified time of death? Is any sovereign decree that is only partially recognized sovereign at all? etc.) (*DPII*, 197). To this, one can add the more commonplace example of death-row inmates who spend years on death row (this in the United States especially), always uncertain of whether natural death or execution will come first, and whose time of death is endlessly deferred.[42] As the epiphany of the third reveals, we understand how sociality *is* condemnation, and that we are all condemned to death and none condemned to die. This is the condition of the 'very humanity of human beings' that the present literary works espouse.

We have seen how the third can never save us from the death penalty because sociality is itself the death penalty; we can only survive without surviving. The third cannot wait, but, in its sociality, one founded through condemnation, it always arrives too late. None of the literary figures explored here, who are 'saved' from the death penalty, is ontologically resurrected. This, therefore, is why the Other is demonic, because the act of dying in-stead reveals to us that we have never lived without death; this, ironically, despite the soteriological undertones in the Saying 'thou shalt not die'. We see also how this phrase hides underneath it the impossibility of life: 'thou shalt not live'. It certainly seems a terrible situation; according to Dylan Thomas, echoing Mercutio's dying words, we should 'rage against the dying of the light' and not 'go gently into that good night'.[43]

It is, though, always-already night-time, and, as evidenced in 'The Wall', it is not a 'good' night at all. We seem to be truly in the realm of the diabolic, where the gift of death is no longer secret but *public* and thus stripped of the responsibility that can only come with my death's individuation; in other words, stripped of life. The Other, with its mirroring and Hippocratic face, is not the neighbour, who can move away, but the cellmate, condemned to die with and in-stead, sharing our cell on death row; moreover, the Third who reveals society beyond our cell reveals only that the death penalty is there too. In the incompatibility of the necropolis and the utopia, one is led to understand the necropolis as dystopic.

Simultaneously, however, we are in the realm of the angelic, where the 'radically impossible' has been done, where the border between death and life is made so permeable that death and life find themselves deconstructed, as if by a miracle, which, as Derrida points out (following Schmitt), is just another name for the exception: 'The exceptional situation, that is, the criterion of sovereignty [...] is the same thing as what are called miracles in religion' (*DPII*, 249). In this light, one reads the exception of the Third miraculously dying in-stead as one that interrupts not a pacific relation with the Other but a struggle unto death, the sovereign sentence, and in turn brings sovereignty, tyranny and totalitarianism into question through its contra-temporal, diachronic irruption.[44] Dying in-stead, then, is the act of both the demonic and the angelic.

Being 'both' and 'neither', this is the afterlife that is limbo. And we are indeed now in the world of angels and demons, here called so not only because these are Derrida's own terms but also in light of the Other's transcendental aspect – one must keep in mind how, apart from the Other's proximity and immanence, as the neighbour, the Other is simultaneously transcendent, beyond the self's grasp. Thus, one finds not only the Christian dictum 'love thy neighbour', but also infinite distance, as also found in the Bible through Jesus's parable of Lazarus and the rich man, who have gone to heaven and hell, respectively: 'between us and you a great chasm has been set in place, so that those who want to go from here to you cannot, nor can anyone cross over from there to us.'[45]

Hence the necropolis is also neither angelic nor demonic, neither utopic nor dystopic: it is merely the manifestation of a sociality founded, without alternative, on the death penalty. As intimated earlier, it is not the home or space of the tragic. The retention of these religious and figurative archetypes here serves a further purpose: being after death, we are, like the angel and the demon, also immortal. Certainly, many literary explorations of immortality – such as the myth of Tithonus, Oscar Wilde's *The Picture of Dorian Gray*, Virginia Woolf's *Orlando*, Simone de Beauvoir's *All Men Are Mortal* or Mary Shelley's *Frankenstein* and the countless other works of science fiction it has inspired – could here be read through the idea of relational death. Most relevant of all, however, that always inchoate line from *The Instant of My Death*: 'Mort-immortel'.

The impossibility of life, or, better, the *impossibility of mortality*: this is a Blanchovian idea, and not a Levinasian one.[46] For Levinas, in line with Epicurus as Cohen points out, 'death is never now, is always to come, always remains future', *à-venir*; 'it is always in the "meantime" [. . .] that human life is lived', and the impossibility of death comes from 'this interval between death and myself', where self and death can never collide.[47] Life is thus, for Levinas, '[t]he [eternal] postponement of death'.[48] This stands in direct opposition to what is narrated in *The Instant*, along with the idea of autothanatography in general and with the 'meanwhile', *die Langweile*, of waiting for the already departed train, where self and death do indeed collide.

If one accepts or least thinks the impossibility of mortality, life is not the eternal postponement of death, but rather *life is death lived in postponement*, or 'abeyance' [*toujours en instance*], where one waits for the instant of death one has already died. One is 'freed from life' (*ID*, 7). Death is no longer, as Cohen explains, 'forever future, and hence exterior to the self-presence it constitutes'; death is within the self already, and subjectivity must be declared dead if we are not to put the concept of death to death.[49]

The 'I', as defined by Levinas, 'is the being whose existing consists in identifying itself, in recovering its identity throughout all that happens to it. It is the primal identity, the primordial work of identification'.[50] It is the continually becoming subject. Moreover, we can acknowledge the infinity of the other only from the position of the 'I': the expression of the Face, that is, takes one beyond the self 'and yet maintains the I who welcomes it'.[51] The present conundrum, so to speak, can be put as follows: if the 'I' is, in our literary case studies, revealed as that which cannot recover from death (for that would not be death at all) – and thus finds itself always-already crushed in the primacy of death, always unbecoming rather than becoming – then how is alterity to be acknowledged? Moreover, how can there even be maintained, in the collapse of the Same, any notion of the Other? If we are not to put death to death, we must continue to interrogate this paradox of living death – in other words, this 'relation' in relational death.

We have already seen Levinas's answers to these questions – or, rather, seen that he would say that these are not the right questions at all, for death is in a future that never comes. Let us, then, continue to elucidate the concept of relational death, since what is at stake here is an ever deeper understanding of the unbecoming subject, the subject under erasure, of what it means to *be* without *being*. In short, alterity, as shall be argued, is actually best acknowledged by this subject under erasure; except that here it is not the erasure of the same when faced with alterity, but the erasure of subjectivity by what alterity necessarily brings with it: death. On this note, let us go back to *Hamlet* – and one may already see where this is heading.

'To be, or not to be: that is the question', and this is indeed the question to end all questions, a question about ends so eloquently phrased without a subject, and where the subject, standing yet before the choice of being or not being, is neither being nor non-being.[52] Levinas addresses Hamlet's monologue, reading it as a contemplation of suicide, and asks: 'Does not the hero of tragedy assume death?'[53] Levinas concludes, typically, that death is 'never assumed, it comes', and adds this crucial passage: '*Hamlet* is precisely a lengthy testimony to this impossibility of assuming death. Nothingness is impossible. It is nothingness that would have left humankind the possibility of assuming death and snatching a supreme mastery from out of the servitude of existence. "To be or not be" is a sudden awareness of this impossibility of annihilating oneself'.[54]

Levinas will later put aside this question, writing some thirty-five years later: 'To be or not to be – this is probably not the question par excellence'.[55] As mentioned, the previous passage has Levinas focus on suicide specifically: likening the desire for death to insomnia, Levinas explains how, just as in insomnia we are 'without possible recourse to sleep', so too 'this impossibility of nothingness deprives suicide, which is the final mastery one can have over being, of its function of mastery'. Life is 'an immortality from which there is no escape', and, he concludes, '[t]he notion of irremissible being, without exit, constitutes the fundamental absurdity of being'.[56] However, the relational death is not a death that can be assumed; it is one given, decreed by the sovereign and simultaneously taken by the third. For Levinas, death cannot be assumed because it lies eternally in the future; here, however, in death made past, there is nothing to do but live on – not because death never comes, but rather because it 'has already arrived'. Hamlet's question, then, is not to be understood as the futile hypothetical that Levinas makes it out to be. In being already dead yet living on, we have indeed both *being* and *not being* behind us. If the question is futile, it is not because we – as citizens of the necropolis – can only and irremissibly *be*, but because we can *neither be nor not be*.

Ibbieta's laughter at the end of 'The Wall' may reflect the 'absurdity of being' that Levinas describes – a being one cannot escape – and indeed this would be more in line with what Sartre's philosophy expounds.[57] While it would derail the present argument were we to delve into Sartre on freedom, absurdity, self, alterity, the human, or being and nothingness, suffice it to say it would be incredibly pertinent.[58] 'The Wall', though, is here read as evincing ideas that Sartre seems not to entertain, which may explain why '[m]any readers of Sartre, both admirers and detractors, view the ending of his short story [. . .] as a flaw',[59] and why Alexander Argyros writes that 'the "ironical twist" at the end belongs to a tradition of fiction which Sartre specifically repudiates'.[60] The Third seems, then, to betray 'a defect in Sartrean existentialism', though Argyros goes on to say, somewhat bafflingly, that 'the internal logic of existentialism and the internal logic of literary prose are in fact incompatible', seeing in Ibbieta's behaviour only an example of bad faith because he 'lives as if he were already dead'.[61] Likewise, Kevin Sweeney sees Ibbieta attempting to disengage from his past as an act of bad faith, 'deceiving himself with his project of disengagement' – as if he were not forced to 'disengage' by being cut off from life, quite literally, by the sovereign's *glaive*.[62] The 'calm' Ibbieta feels is not the result of 'disengagement' but rather the 'feeling of extraordinary lightness, a sort of beatitude (nothing happy, however)' that Blanchot's protagonist feels after being freed from life (see *TW*, 54; *ID*, 5).

'The Wall' itself, however, also posits a different absurdity, for, after all, Ibbieta has already escaped *being*, as made clear through his numerous reflections on his own corpse and his certainty that, even in leaving the matrices of the 'legal' enactment of the death penalty, neither would he have survived nor would he be resurrected. He laughs at the absence of choice, that much is true – in Bataille's words, this is 'laughter [as] the sign of aversion, of horror' – but this is not only the horror of the eternal impossibility of *non-being* but also that of the impossibility of *being*, or *being-once-more*.[63] One must not forget how Ibbieta's laughter is simultaneously a weeping, an understanding of how he 'misses' death in all its senses. His 'relation without relation' to Gris, the third, exposes only what can be phrased, in Blanchovian terms, as 'being without being'.[64]

Though likewise 'irremissible' and constituting 'an immortality from which there is no escape', the Blanchovian condition of 'being without being' cannot be relegated, as happens in Levinas, to *human life* or *the human being*. Note that

Pablo is overcome by the wall against which he will be shot: "'I'll see eight rifles looking at me. I'll think how I'd like to get inside the wall. I'll push against it with my back . . . with every ounce of strength I have, but the wall will stay, like in a nightmare'" (*TW*, 59). In contrast, utopia, according to Levinas, has no walls: 'The openness of space as an openness of self without a world, without a place, *utopia, the not being walled in*, inspiration to the end, even to expiration, is proximity of the other which is possible only as responsibility' – and, thus, Ibbieta is not in utopia but within the necropolis.[65]

To take the death penalty as constitutive of the human, therefore, is to find oneself unable to escape. When beyond *being* and *non-being*, one is trapped with their back against a wall.

The human thing

The *impossibility of living*, the *impossibility of being*. One is back to 'the viewpoint of common sense', the primary antagonist to this line of thought – for even when everything is stripped away, in the starkest solipsistic moment, is not the one certainty that you *are*? Even language struggles: 'being beyond being', the previous section expounds, floundering. To doubt these claims is only the human thing to do. However, any troubling of the *Jemeinigkeit* leads us to question the boundaries between being and non-being. A response may be impossible. One recalls one of the inscriptions in Cincinnatus's cell, the protagonist of Nabokov's *Invitation to a Beheading*: "'Measure me while I live – after, it will be too late'" (*IB*, 14).

In Derrida's 'Foreword' to *The Wolf Man's Magic Word*, he reminds us that, between the self and the other, '[t]he dividing wall is *real*'. This recalls the earlier unanswered problematic of how relationality can be maintained when, in death, subjectivity is crushed. How is the wall breached, and where does the Third come from, always too late to save us from the death penalty, if subjectivity is no longer (having been condemned) and there is thus neither *totality* nor *infinity*, where both self and other are already dead? In being beyond *being* and *non-being*, one is in the realm of the 'nameless' and 'inhuman', before ethics or ontology. Is this the anonymous existence that is the *il y a*?

It is only natural, in this context, to turn to one of Levinas's earliest concepts as expounded in *Existence and Existents* and *Time and the Other*, containing what he describes around thirty years later as 'insights that remain at best preparatory' and which precede the development of notions such as *le visage*, ethics, language, sociality and God.[66] In the decomposition of the unbecoming subject, revealing the extent of death-in life (or being without being) as that which troubles even the alterity of the Other (as a consequence of condemning the subject), one is returned to an existence lacking existents, without faces or words.

The *il y a* may be translated as the 'there is . . . ': the anonymous, silent, absolutely indeterminate night 'empty even of void', where there are no longer subjects or objects, a 'paradoxical existence' where there is neither *being* nor *non-being* ('void'), but simply 'the presence of absence' (*EE*, 59–60). The world (as understood in the Heideggerian sense) is absent, and there is neither 'I' nor 'You'. The *il y a*, writes Levinas, 'transcends inwardness as well as exteriority; it does not even make it possible to distinguish these'; it 'submerges every subject, person, or thing', 'the I is itself [. . .] invaded, depersonalized', and, here, '[t]he disappearance of all things and of the I leaves what cannot disappear, the sheer fact of being in which *one* participates, whether one wants to or not, without having taken the initiative, anonymously', even though this is, however, 'no longer an existence of the one' (*EE*, 52–3, 56).

Levinas is here responding to Heidegger's condition of being-toward-death: the problem, Levinas argues, is that one is horrified not by the nothingness of death but by the 'condemnation' that is a Being which cannot be exited (where to live is to be immortal, death forever postponed to a future that never comes), and it is noteworthy that the defining *Stimmung* of the *il y a* is horror and not anxiety. This is, writes Levinas, 'the seriousness of eternity, that is condemnation', where the self discovers the 'impossibility of disengaging itself from the eternity upon which it has opened' (*EE*, 23). As Levinas asks: 'Is not anxiety over Being – horror of Being – just as primal as anxiety over death? [. . .] It is perhaps even more so, for the former may account for the latter' (*EE*, 5). Through being-in-the-world, one realizes how '[t]he I does not turn to existence; it is enthralled by it. One possesses existence, but is also possessed by it' (*EE*, 39). Inversely, there is also possible 'an interval in existing' (through fatigue and world-weariness, for instance) where we can glimpse the *il y a*, for '[i]t is not by being in the world that we can say what the world is' (*EE*, 39, 43, 34).[67]

In this primordial and 'antecedent' night, we find articulated the very condition of the living corpse (*EE*, 8). One no longer *is*; *there is* no being: the self is depersonalized and made anonymous, 'nameless' and 'inhuman', a being without Being; and in this anonymity one finds that alterity can, likewise, neither be distinguished nor acknowledged (not even as transcendent). There is also no *non-being*, no nothingness: as Levinas writes, 'this nothing [of the *il y a*] is not that of pure nothingness. There is no longer *this* or *that*; there is not "something"', and 'this universal absence is in its turn a presence, an absolutely unavoidable presence', one 'full of the nothingness of everything' (*EE*, 52–3). To experience this 'plenitude of the void' is to live on through the cleaving paradox of the unexperienced experience, the unbecoming subject shedding *subjectivity* and *being* but remaining *there*, and this 'whether one wants to or not': the condemnation to death that is impossible to be willed, the paradox of 'living death' or 'dead man walking', where the third steps in to die in-stead without waiting for permission.[68] In the necropolis, through which Narcissus floats on a ferry, the landscape is truly stygian.

For Levinas, this night is terrifying: '[t]he rustling of the *there is* . . . is horror'. In the undetermined existence that is *il y a*, horror is 'a movement which will strip consciousness of its very "subjectivity"', where '[t]he participation of one term in another does not consist in sharing an attribute; one term *is the other*'. Levinas once more stresses how this horror 'is nowise an anxiety about death', but the horror of 'the subjectivity of the subject, his particularity qua *entity*, [turned] inside out': a fear of Being. This is, crucially, epitomized for Levinas by the figure of the corpse: 'A corpse is horrible; it already bears its own phantom, it presages its return. The haunting spectre, the phantom, constitutes the very element of horror' (*EE*, 55–6).

Levinas's corpse returns because, for him, one cannot dwell in the necropolis that is the *il y a*. One returns to *being*, and this is done in an *instant*. The 'instant', for Levinas, is precisely that moment where the anonymous existent takes up existence, where '*to be* means *to take up being*' (*EE*, 25). This is what Levinas terms the 'hypostasis', where being accomplishes its into-Being in an instant, where and when 'anonymous being loses its *there is* character' and signals 'the apparition of a substantive' of an 'I' or 'Other' now chained to a self (*EE*, 83). This instant of becoming subject or 'event occurs at every moment', a continual 'struggle for life' where '[t]o act is to take on a present' and where 'effort [and "effort" may here be read as quasi-synonymous with Hegelian work and habit] is the very effecting of an instant' (*EE*, 8, 10, 15, 23). This is, for Levinas, the way out of the *il y a*, which is continually exited in favour of Being without exit: a moment of instantaneous action through which the subject emerges, where '[t]he "present", the "I" and an "instant" are moments of one and the same event', that is, a birth, beginning or becoming, the taking up of and taking position from existence (*EE*, 80). From this instant, Simon Critchley notes, there is 'the establishment of the ethical relation as the basis of sociality' (*VA*, 65).

Levinas notes, in support of his argument, that Blanchot's *Thomas l'Obscure* 'opens with a description of the *there is* . . .'; however, Levinas would have found a very different version of the *il y a* had he been able to foresee *The Instant of My Death* (or any other later work of Blanchot's, especially *Madness of the Day* or *Death Sentence*, the latter published only a year after *Existence and Existents*) (*EE*, 58). There is only one change, but the change is radical. In *The Instant*, as in the other literary works examined so far, the 'instant' is not when Being is taken up and an 'I' is born, but, diametrically inverse, where subjectivity is divested of its being, returned to the *il y a* and reminded of the impossibility of life. It is not Being which has no exit, but the *il y a* itself. This is the (thanato-)literature of death as first philosophy.

To put this another way, 'condemnation' is revealed to be not *being* but the *il y a*, where to be condemned to death is to occupy the unbecoming state of the living corpse as neither *being* nor *non-being*. For Levinas, the subject *becomes*; however, in its perennial existence under the death penalty, the subject in truth *un-becomes*. In the instant which happens continually, one is not condemned to life but to death – to live under a time that kills, where no 'effort' or 'struggle for life' is possible – and the corpse, if it returns, returns only *as* a corpse. 'To "realize" the concept of nothingness', Levinas writes, 'is not to see nothingness, but to die': for Levinas, just as dying is impossible, so too is the realization of this nothingness (*EE*, 60).

To *become being*, when one takes up a name and a self, is to lose anonymity: 'existence in the world always has a centre; it is never anonymous' (*EE*, 29). One thus recognizes here how the *il y a* is also a deconstructive space, a decentralization of existence and subjectivity, fulfilling the prophecy of Derrida's angel. Indeed, the necropolis, as the thanatopolitical realization of the *il y a*, might be read very much in line with the Derridean space of the *chora*.

The *chora* (or *khôra*, as Derrida and his translators prefer) is originally a Platonic concept presented in *Timaeus* which Derrida reads, beyond Plato, as both 'place' and the placelessness from which the very possibility for place arises, where place *takes place*.[69] *Chora* is thus, as Brandon Wocke writes, 'unable to be assimilated into the dualistic Platonic schema precisely in so far as it is a *third* form, oscillating between two poles of being'.[70] It is what Yvonne Sherwood and John D. Caputo call 'the place of nongift, that which ungives, [. . .] closer to the French *il y a* rather than *Es Gibt*' – here a resonant echo of what has earlier been argued, that the gift can no longer be apprehended or anticipated, a 'dissolution' where 'death is all in all'.[71]

The *chora* is not the middle-ground, or *no man's land*, that in some way synthesizes being and non-being. And this is why dwelling in the *il y a* is never to be understood as being *between* being and non-being, but rather as being *before*, *beyond, without,* or *at the limit of* being and non-being.⁷² It is 'the very invisibility [or anonymity] of visibility' that shines with 'nocturnal light', 'prior to all naming', where there is only 'existence of the most extreme abstraction [. . .] prior to all social or political determination, prior to all intersubjectivity'. The *chora*, that is, does 'not [allow] itself to be dominated by any theological, ontological, or anthropological instance, without age, without history, and more "ancient" than all oppositions'; it is 'nothing (no being, nothing present), but not the Nothing which in *Dasein* would still open the question of being'; in sum, it is 'the very place of an infinite resistance, of an infinitely impassable persistence [. . .]: an utterly faceless other'.⁷³ The fiction of the death penalty, then, foregrounds an element central to autothanatography: not only the *impossibility* but also the *impersonality* of life, life without *a name*, life that cannot be called life – *faceless* life, as shall be further explored in the following chapter.

Before moving on, it is important to take further note of Levinas's reference to Blanchot's fiction; on this, Critchley provides additional insight. While he observes considerable differences between Blanchot and Levinas in their respective estimation of literature and ethics, he sees much in common in their view of death – particularly, the impossibility of death, and our 'being riveted to an existence without exit'; 'this experience of the night', Critchley writes, 'is the experience of a dying stronger than death' (*VA*, 36; see 68). The *il y a*, as Critchley observes, is something fundamental to both Levinas and Blanchot, and he supports Levinas's sense that this is shared in *Thomas the Obscure*, citing a convincing passage from the novel as a chapter epigraph and furthermore bringing in *The Instant of My Death* to this discussion. 'My claim', writes Critchley, 'has been that the *il y a* – this vertiginous knowledge of finitude – is the secret of Blanchot's work' (*VA*, 76; see 35).

However, one cannot read in *The Instant* an apprehension of the *il y a* that is identical to Levinas's, if only because one cannot find the idea of the impossible death and immortal life in a text where the condemned protagonist is explicitly 'freed from life' and comprehends 'the happiness of not being immortal or eternal' (*ID*, 5). While death is for the protagonist 'forever in abeyance', this is not the immortal life forever postponing death, as the last sentence reminds us: '"I am alive. No, you are dead"'. 'Mort-immortel' – the sequence, like Shakespeare's 'exits and [. . .] entrances', is important: the young protagonist is not immortal because he never dies, but because he has already died; what is immortalized is not mortality but finitude.⁷⁴

The Instant, therefore, reveals not only 'the experience of a dying stronger than death' but also the experience of death itself, the paradoxical unexperienced experience where to live is *to live on with (relational) death*, where one has always died already. 'In the *il y a*, death is impossible, which is the most horrible of thoughts', Critchley goes on; however, in the *il y a* revealed in *The Instant* – the instant not of hypostasis but of the condemnation of subjectivity – it is also life which is impossible (*VA*, 77). Whether this thought is horrible or not shall be discussed further on, but already, in the absence of the tragic, where one may find 'a sort of beatitude' or 'calm', an answer may be intimated.

As is clear, then, Blanchot's '*other* or *essential* night' is one 'in which one cannot find a position, where the body refuses to lie still'; it is, indeed, 'the spectral night [. . .] of phantoms, of ghosts', and reading Blanchot is to be 'drawn from daylight into an experience of the night' (*VA*, 36). In this *il y a*, however, just as the transcendence of alterity is erased, so is the futurity and impossibility of death. Critchley writes how 'the only relation that the living can maintain with death is through a representation, an image, a picture of death, whether visual or verbal', and where 'the relation with death is always a relation with *my* death' (*VA*, 86–7). The death penalty, however, makes that relation with death far more than mere representation: rather, it is the lived (unexperienced) experience of all of us condemned to death through the sociality created by the death penalty, where one finds the 'Isaianic paradox', as pointed out by Sherwood and Caputo, where 'the people have achieved the impossible and "made a covenant with death"'.[75] In the *il y a* that disables all possible distinction and eradicates the 'I' as the 'one', there can be no such thing as 'my' death.

One can agree with Critchley, on the other hand, when he says that, for him, 'what opens in the relation to the other is not, as Levinas would have it, the trace of the divine, but rather the trauma of the *il y a*' (which Critchley terms 'atheist transcendence') (*VA*, 40). In finding ourselves reading Levinas backwards – bringing to bear on Heideggerian ontology not Levinas's ethics but his *il y a* as pre-ontology, simultaneously sloughing off and putting into question ethics, alterity, language and so on through the state of decomposition or *unbecoming* – we may, with Critchley, convincingly doubt whether the *il y a*, like the 'revenant that returns [. . .] again and again to the moment of nonsense, neutrality and ambiguity', is 'ever surmounted in Levinas's work' (*VA*, 92, 90).

In a move echoing Levinas's reworking of Heidegger's title *Being and Time* into *Time and the Other* (shifting away from Narcissism to altruism), one might refer to this neutral, ambiguous, and nameless existence of the unbecoming subject as, not the *human being*, but the *human thing*. Mirroring Levinas's substitution of 'Being' with 'Other', here the 'being' of 'human being' is replaced with 'thing', reflecting how death is no longer eternally in the future but rather in the now, where one is the living corpse. As Blanchot writes, in part echoing Silenus, 'death is the greatest hope of human beings, their only hope of being human'.[76] With death no longer a hope or impossible possibility, the dead body that is the corpse is, as Heidegger emphasizes, no longer a person or a human being: it is 'a *lifeless* material Thing [. . .] something *unalive*, which has lost its life'.

The etymological roots of 'thing' – which incorporate not only the idea of an inanimate object (without *anima*, Heidegger's corpse) but also 'entity', 'creature', 'event', 'appointed time', 'stretch or extent of time', 'draw[ing] out or [drawing] together', 'assembly', 'law court' and 'legal case' – all are important to this discussion.[77] All of these notions, sketching the figure of the non-theological, non-ontological and non-anthropological human thing, are in play here.

In this study, the 'thing' was first mentioned vis-à-vis Kant's justification of the death sentence, which argues that the condemned man, through crime punishable by death, 'turns himself into a thing', like an animal or something perhaps even 'below the beasts'. This is the *homo phenomenon*, the 'man' who is just a body and nothing more, whom Derrida describes as 'nothing and nobody, in a certain way' – in other words, anonymous – where what is killed by the sovereign's *glaive* is no longer human, no longer a person. Schopenhauer's notion of bestiality echoes Kant here – bestiality being 'a condition in which, quite literally, there is nothing which elevates the human being above the animal' (and this he views negatively).[78] One almost hears Cassio's lamentation, too, when he cries: 'I have lost the immortal part of myself and what remains is bestial'.[79] Indeed, the living corpse seems to bridge the gap between contrasting and dichotomous yet anthropocentric definitions of human and animal, whose being is excluded from Heideggerian ontology – or even between human and plant.[80] Other previous points converge in this notion of 'thing', too; however, not very lengthy discussion can be afforded in attempting to name the nameless as understood here. One might, though, think of the Lacanian concept of *Das Ding*,[81] for instance, or the Hegelian slave (at least its historical aspect, which Alain Badiou accuses Hegel of neglecting) that is the attempt to '*identify the slave with a thing*. The real slave is not simply he who can work the thing to offer it to the master; he is himself thing-ified, treated like, sold as, bought as a thing'.[82]

Leaving for the next chapter the last set of associations with the word 'thing' – as 'legal case', 'law court' or, in Lacan's words, 'a proceeding, deliberation, or legal debate' – let us begin to move towards the last literary work of this chapter, keeping in mind the idea of 'thing' as 'assembly', as the aggregation of a multitude, as congregation or coalescence rather than as political assembly.[83]

In the *il y a*, '[t]he participation of one term in another', writes Levinas, 'does not consist in sharing an attribute; one term *is the other*' – and this is, clearly, the exact opposite of the sociality enabled by the third, the 'collectivity that is not a communion'. With Agamben already ringing in our ears, here one becomes so intimate with another that an 'I' or 'You' is no longer discernible. The idea of sex, of course, presents itself plainly here, and sex should never be kept at a distance from any understanding of death. Indeed, the *relational death* may also be understood as a *sexual relation*, which would return us to the discussion of both clothing and the act of taking off one's coat.[84]

And so we return, for the last time, to the question: if we are indeed, as humankind, best understood as living corpses, and this state, in its paradoxical nature, finds a home only in homelessness, the (non-)place that is *chora* or *il y a* without exit, then how is there a sovereign who condemns, or a third who dies in-stead? While we remain outside Narcisstic egoity because the human *being* has been killed, what kind of relation can exist when both life and death are impossible?

One answer is found in understanding the *chora*, as Derrida does, as the originary place of 'the faceless other'. While Levinasian thought exits the impasse through the instant of hypostasis, it would be worthwhile to further think the faceless other. In Levinasian thought, this would be impossible – the Face *is* the Other; the Other without a face would be the Same. In Derridean thought, it is impossible to properly think this at all, just as the *chora* can be neither realized nor adopted as a dwelling or a place of residence, for the notion of the Other in the Same is still housed in notions of living subjectivity. In the literary texts examined here, however, this thought – of the Other that is the Same, where one term *is* another – is possible through the twin face.[85]

When a face gazes upon its twin, that is, something which is *both* Other and Same as well as *neither*, it sees the doubled face, the excess of identity which is also its lack, the faceless. This is the doubled Hippocratic face of the condemned men in 'The Wall', who in living death 'looked as much alike as twin brothers'. This is Darnay's face, Carton's 'counterpart': the two already looked very much like each other, and, upon Carton's removal of his wig, 'the likeness became much more remarkable' (*TC*, 77).[86] This is Chavel's face, whose 'face had *altered* somewhat, [. . .] but it was still, if carefully examined, *the same* face'.[87] This is Hugo's protagonist, nameless and faceless, a '(counter)sketch' of generic anatomy that 'suspends the sense of an individual humanity'.[88] The Face is, of course, more than the physical face: the twin face is also, then, the excess of doubled identities ('Charlot [. . .] watched not only Carosse – a mirror on the wardrobe door reflected both of their images') and doubled names ('Jean-Louis Ch. . . [. . .] stood of course as plainly for Charlot as for Chavel'). This is the disguise of alterity as ipseity, when the Other takes one's coat and wears it as their own; it is the *making same* of execution, which is at once assassination and slaughter. In this living death, the human thing as the human assembly is equivalent to the chain-gang, as condemned men assembled together where 'each man bears his chain by himself, side by side with a stranger' and yet is 'no more than a fraction of the hideous entity called the chain-gang, that moves as one man' (*LD*, 46). This is the 'absolute *arrivant*' who annihilates or renders indeterminate '*all the distinctive signs of a prior identity*'.

The question, then, follows: Why does the Other who dies in-stead die with my own face?

While not ignoring Nabokov's rich and purposefully indeterminate ideas in *Invitation to a Beheading*, such as his stated intention of revealing the limits of fiction and literature itself, the novel's situation – that of a death sentence – opens a way towards answering this question, especially when reading the novel as being, 'in essence, a poetic paraphrasing of Plato's *Timaeus*', where one first finds the notion of *chora* in the first place.[89]

The novel may at first seem to posit the Levinasian concept of death, self and hypostasis. Note how Cincinnatus C., the protagonist condemned to death, describes himself: 'I issue from such a burning blackness [. . .] that to this day I occasionally feel (sometimes during sleep [. . .]) that primordial palpitation of mine, that first branding contract, the mainspring of my 'I'. How I wriggled out, slippery, naked! Yes, from a realm forbidden and inaccessible to others' (*IB*, 67). Is this not exactly the emergence of the 'I' from the 'primordial' and 'forbidden' night or 'blackness' that is the *il y a*? And is this not exactly what we have seen should be impossible under the death penalty, where the 'I' of Cincinnatus, in being made to collide with death, is affirmed rather than condemned to anonymity? However, if this is indeed the case of hypostasis, then why can Cincinnatus not find the Other, the alterity that necessarily constitutes and precedes the 'I'?

After all, everyone around him is *recognized* not as other but merely as 'indistinct figures' or '"dolls"': '"I am surrounded by some sort of wretched spectres, not by people"', he cries (*IB*, 40, 86, 21). To his mother, he says: '"I can see perfectly well that you are just as much of a parody as everybody and everything else"', and in a letter to his wife, he writes: 'understand that they are murdering me, that we are surrounded by dummies, and that you are a dummy yourself' (*IB*, 102, 111). Despite the apparent hypostasis, then, Cincinnatus can find no trace of the other, just more of the same. In sum, there is no Face for him to behold: 'This cold ochre [of his cell] smelled of the grave [. . .], yet his gaze still persisted in selecting and correlating the necessary little protuberances – so starved he was for even a vague semblance of a human face' (*IB*, 96).

The Third, furthermore, does not here die in-stead. In fact, Cincinnatus is presented with two 'thirds'. The first, a twelve-year-old girl named Emmie, the prison director's daughter, promises to help him escape – but when Cincinnatus follows her outside the jail, she only leads him back inside. The second one, M'sieur Pierre, is described as the protagonist's 'fate-mate' and presents himself as the other condemned man, claiming that he 'was accused of attempting to help [Cincinnatus] escape from here', and tells him: 'I ended up here because of you. And I'll tell you more: we shall mount the scaffold together, too' (*IB*, 83–5). This is no lie – as M'sieur Pierre says, he does not lie, and we are further duped because both Cincinnatus and Pierre are thirty years old, as twins would be – but he is later un-disguised as Pyotr, Cincinnatus's would-be executioner, for whom meeting the condemned 'face to face only at the last instant before the sacrament itself' is 'the barbarity of long-bygone days', and so he wanted to spend some time with the condemned (*IB*, 138). Here is the third who does not step in at the last instant to die in-stead, the third who does not face: the other is here faceless.

Moreover, the world Cincinnatus inhabits' is itself not real – '"But what if this is only deception, a fold of the fabric mimicking a human face . . .'", he wonders (*IB*, 87). This is only heightened as the novel progresses, culminating at the end where other characters, as if actors, inexplicably change their roles and appearance completely, and the world starts disintegrating, like a stage falling apart: the spider that had occupied his cell is revealed as being only a plush copy, trees are two dimensional with amateur shading, and the back rows of the crowd gathered to see him beheaded are 'really quite badly daubed on the backdrop'; by the end, Cincinnatus 'knows perfectly well that the entire masquerade is staged in his own brain' (*IB*, 177, 172).

Let us leave to one side a reading of the theatricality (or even technology) of the death penalty through Nabokov. What is one to make of this Cincinnatus who is the only real human, and who can acknowledge 'beings akin to him' only in the last line of the novel, when the world has quite literally fallen apart (*IB*, 180)? And what is this fake world?

This world must here be read as 'world' in the ontological sense, to which Cincinnatus does not belong; he is, in fact, condemned to death because of his very non-being. This is the illusory world of mortality and being as Being-towards-death. As the novel's epigraph highlights: 'As a fool thinks himself God, we think ourselves mortal.'⁹⁰ This sentiment is directly linked to the reason for Cincinnatus's condemnation. He is condemned because he is 'opaque', 'pitch-black [...] as if he had been cut from a cord-size block of night', and in his stygian form 'there was expressed the suggestion of Cincinnatus's basic illegality' (*IB*, 12–13, 17). The tests he is forced to go through make him 'enact everyday scenes', testing him for life through small talk, illnesses, or trades, but he is ultimately accused of 'gnostical turpitude, so rare and unutterable that it was necessary to use circumlocutions like "impenetrability", "opacity", "occlusion"' (*IB*, 17, 51). The crime he is charged with, as James Porter puts it, is a 'crime against reality itself', the 'reality' of mortality.⁹¹

The 'I' of Cincinnatus emerged from 'primordial' and 'burning blackness', and yet he is still archaically opaque, anonymous, a state which in the novel can be described only through 'a strange, almost forgotten word' that is foreign to the world of mortality (*IB*, 18). He is not mortal, like those around him – but neither is he the immortal self of Levinas. As evidenced by the false world in which he resides, he has never left the blackness, the *chora* or *il y a* without exit, and neither can he acknowledge nor be acknowledged by the other.

He is, then, the living corpse, the decomposing and unbecoming subject. He sheds, that is, not only his body parts ('He took off his head like a toupee, took off his collarbones like shoulder straps, took off his ribcage like a hauberk' – *IB*, 19) but also his ontological *being*: 'I had a strange sensation last night – and it was not the first time – I am taking off layer after layer, until at last . . . I do not know how to describe it, but I know this: through the process of gradual divestment I reach the final, indivisible, firm, radiant point, and this point says: I am!' (*IB*, 66).

As he dis-assembles and 'divests' himself of being (removes the *vestis*, garment or clothing), he knows only that he *is*. As previously stated, the human thing *is*, but *how* it is – Heidegger's question – remains, like Cincinnatus himself, opaque and inarticulate. The death sentence 'strikes at the very ontological root of his being', and his 'I am', as Porter goes on to argue, is by no means Cartesian in that it cannot find itself at home in the world of the here and now.⁹² In this way one can understand Cincinnatus's strikingly incomplete sentence, a reflection of his perennially incomplete and decomposing being: 'I am comparatively' (*IB*, 2).

'All the world's a stage' because one can see, through *Invitation*, that the idea of mortality is merely assumed, just as one would take on a role in a theatre production.⁹³ In this context, the *il y a* that comes before being may be likened by analogy to the originary Platonic Form, which is why Cincinnatus cries, referring to the 'world' around him, that 'there must be an original of the clumsy copy' (*IB*, 69–70). There is, however, no exit from Plato's dark cave into the light – like Antigone, one is caved in.

For Cincinnatus, proper death is 'forever in abeyance' – he is never told the hour of his death, and, when the execution is about to happen, he simply walks away; equally in abeyance, therefore, is 'proper life'. Cincinnatus can only live on through the impossibility of life, forever condemned. The impossible statement 'I am dead', as is echoed in *Invitation* and our other literary case studies, paradoxically retains both the 'I am' and the non-Levinasian collision or assemblage of the 'I' and death, where death cannot be mine because subjectivity has been killed. This entity or thing, for it is no longer a being, can only be housed without recourse in the necropolis, the *il y a* or *chora* that is anonymous.

Indeed, it is only through the death penalty which, as sociality, encompasses the entire world (a 'world' fooled, as the epigraph claims, into thinking itself mortal), that Cincinnatus realizes his namelessness. What he is, as quoted earlier, can neither be measured nor expressed through language, and while he believes he has a name, this is quickly contradicted: '*That which does not have a name does not exist*. Unfortunately, everything had a name. "Nameless existence, intangible substance," Cincinnatus read on the wall where the door [of his cell] covered it when open' (*IB*, 13). It is only when the door of the cell is closed – when one is condemned to death – and Cincinnatus is able to read the inscription, that he can realize how, as a condemned man, he is himself the '"[n]ameless existence, intangible substance"' that is anonymity. One cannot find here what Davis describes as the 'ethical utopianism' that 'characterizes the distinctive *humanism* of Levinas's writing'.[94] The 'I am' collapses further – the 'I' has no name or tangibility; it merely lives on as an immeasurable, anonymous remnant; here is no anthropology, ethics or ontology.

Therefore, while Cincinnatus understands he is immortal because he is not mortal, his immortality can only come through the death penalty's unexperienced experience, where 'death' and 'self' have met already, where death has already arrived and is in the past, and where there is withheld a relation to death in the other-less *il y a*. A crucial passage from *Invitation* has Cincinnatus writing in his diary: '"death", he wrote on it, continuing his sentence, but he immediately crossed out that word; he must say it differently', after which he 'walked away from the table, leaving on it the blank sheet with only the one solitary word on it, and that one crossed out' (*IB*, 165). Here is ~~death~~, death under erasure, here and not yet here, the state of the living corpse. Life, then, is under erasure too – the previous page of his diary he writes: 'I have discovered the little crack in life, here [in the perennial state of being condemned to death] it broke off, where it had once been soldered to something else, something genuinely alive, important and vast [. . .]. Within this irreparable little crack decay has set in' (*IB*, 164).

Because the crack is 'irreparable', and already 'decay has set in', it is not only death which is 'forever in abeyance' but also life. ~~Life~~ and ~~death~~, the time of the living and decomposing corpse.

The 'hypostasis' of Cincinnatus is the instant of death which returns him, continually, to the necropolis. In the world of mortality, time is not allowed to be stygian but rather meticulously re-presented: the prison clock's dial, for instance, '"is blank; however, every hour the watchman washes off the old hand and daubs on a new one – and that's how we live, by tarbrush time"' (*IB*, 104). On the other hand, Cincinnatus, the human thing, lives on through the series of dead instants. Speaking of the time he saw a man move and who, for a second, left behind his shadow, Cincinnatus says this: 'here is what I want to express; between this movement and the movement of the laggard shadow – that second, that syncope – there is the rare kind of time in which I live – the pause, the hiatus, when the heart is like a feather' (*IB*, 35). This is the instant of death, the duration and *Langweile* of the abeyance of both life and death, a limbo when the heart is too light ('a feeling of extraordinary lightness') to beat.

Upon the full realization of this time of/in abeyance, as the world collapses, Cincinnatus goes on to join those 'akin to him'. By the end, 'the cell, no longer needed, was quite obviously disintegrating'; the whole world, the 'real' world, is now with Cincinnatus condemned to death, now living on in his time (*IB*, 169). This multiplicity in the *il y a* is where one finds the other as kin, the faceless others who look back with your own face, with more than family resemblance. Cincinnatus has foreseen this 'real world' of the *chora*, where 'one term *is the other*' and yet, crucially, there is more than one term. After death, there are relations. He thinks of himself on the executioner's block:

> with my shoulders drawn back, showing my heels to the headsman and straining my goose neck [. . .] [a]nd afterwards – perhaps most of all *afterwards* – [. . .] then perhaps we shall somehow fit together, you and I, and turn ourselves in such a way that we form one pattern, and solve the puzzle: draw a line from point A to point B. . . without looking, or, without lifting the pencil [. . .] we shall connect the points, draw the line, and you and I shall form that unique design for which I yearn. (*IB*, 41)

This assembly of humans, where different terms are connected and drawn together in the duration of the instant drawn out (keeping in mind that 'assembly' means also to 'draw out or draw together'), is the excess of the Same that allows the third to step in and die in-stead. One observes here the intimation that Cincinnatus C. stands only for Cincinnatus Cincinnatus. This excess is redoubled with the presence of 'an additional Cincinnatus', who throughout the novel accompanies Cincinnatus but does different things (*IB*, 4). For instance: 'Cincinnatus did not crumple the motley newspapers, did not hurl them, as his double did (the double, the gangrel, that accompanies each of us – you, and me, and him over there – doing what we would like to do at that very moment, but cannot. . .)' (*IB*, 12). Here, then, is the Same that is doubled, that which is the same yet different, the twin face that renders alterity faceless. Where everyone has the same face, there is, *il y a*, anonymity.

By thinking the human thing not only as 'corpse' but 'assembly', we are beginning also to think of a plurality in anonymity, and this shall be pursued in the following chapter. Alongside our previous authors, what Sartre and Nabokov here put forward is a death that puts under erasure the infinity of the self (contra Epicurean and Levinasian thought, where 'death' and 'self' never collide), and, with this, a death which necessarily places the infinity of infinity under erasure too, the infinity that is alterity, and thus, in consequence, also sovereignty and the possibility of totalitarianism, seeing as how we are not total beings but merely anonymous things, remnants, remains or, in Hugo's words, remainders. Hugo's description of the corpse is in fact most pertinent:

> To be naught but a remainder! Such a thing is beyond the power of language to express. To exist no more, but to persist; to be in the abyss, yet out of it; to reappear above death as if indissoluble. There is a certain amount of impossibility mixed with such reality. Thence comes the inexpressible. This being – was it a being? This black witness was a remainder, and an awful remainder – a remainder of what? Of nature first, and then of society. Naught, and yet total.[95]

Hugo is here describing the remains of a hanged man – or, rather, 'the *thing* which had once been a man' – which engenders nothing but horror without catharsis and which, persistently, remains.[96] Decomposing, like this hanged man, like Cincinnatus, we are 'fleshy incompleteness' (*IB*, 92). To live on through death, in this non-Heideggerian context, is not to possess the possibility of no-longer-being-I, and neither is it the Levinasian horror of being-forever-I. Rather, it is the non-tragic experience of revelation, prophesized by the Other who is both demonic and angelic, that I was never 'I' to begin with.

The next chapter, then, shall read how the anonymity or impersonality that comes after the 'person' (i.e. posthumously) – an anonymity which is nonetheless manifold, for the crypt in which we hide, like Ramon Gris's, 'must necessarily incorporate more than one'; as Derrida writes, its 'secret [. . .] must be shared, at least with a "third"' – and this is the space of postsovereignty, the absence of the totalitarian tyrant that is not the utopia but the necropolis, the space of the thanatopolitical.[97]

5

The death of no one

Who? What?

Let us start with a thought experiment. Imagine a man condemned to death. The Division Director for Offender Operations has chosen the execution team members. He has also appropriately planned all pre-execution, execution and post-execution activities and has documented approval of everything. Yesterday afternoon, the condemned man's telephone and visitation privileges were terminated, and now he is taken to the execution room, secured to the execution table and injected with a lethal dose of pentobarbital. One full set of syringes is used. The man dies. After he is pronounced clinically dead, the backup set is deemed unneeded, witnesses are escorted out of the building and the media briefing takes place in the Press Room. Meanwhile, under the Warden's supervision, the corpse is taken out of the execution room and carried to some other room, temporarily, while personnel trained in disease-preventative practices take the necessary precautions. In this other room, where the dead man lies alone for a few minutes, there is the rustle of sheets and the dead man rises again due to what doctors later describe to frenzied journalists as the Lazarus phenomenon, a known scientific occurrence.[1] The resurrected man is then discovered and there follows a commotion.

Though not entirely impossible, this would be a remarkable, exceptional event. In cases where this has happened (mostly in non-death penalty scenarios), the formerly deceased simply pick up their lives as they left them, whether in hospital beds or outside them.[2] Already, however, many problematic thoughts race through the mind. After death, does this Lazarus have one 'I' or two? If so, do they have the same name, identity, presence? Are they still the same person? Is it even a person at all? Still thornier questions are that of justice, law fulfilment and retribution. The man condemned to death has paid the penalty and died. What power does the sovereign of condemnation have over him now? The condemned has paid in full, with his life, and yet he still walks, living. Having been politically eradicated, is this revenant now, finally and epilogically, beyond the monopoly of sovereign exception?

He walks around, looking for those who are like him, but no one understands what he is saying. They seem not even able to hear him.

Anonymous voices

At the very end of *Invitation to a Beheading* we read that 'Cincinnatus made his way in that direction where, to judge by the voices, stood beings akin to him' (*IB*, 180). Despite the protagonist's decomposition and subsequent understanding that there was never a 'world' (as 'being-towards-death') at all, what is suggested in this last line of the novel is that there remains, even in this worldless, postmortem space, the possibility of a voice. The voice, much more particular than the name, denotes a self in possession of what Cavarero calls a 'personal identity [which in turn] postulates an *other* as necessary'.[3] Problematically, this idea of the personal voice runs directly counter to where Cincinnatus finds himself after the literal collapse of his world: a space here termed *chora* or the impassable *il y a*, where being indeed *is* but *is* only *in general*, a condition of plural anonymity, of placelessness and facelessness, and where neither the voice of subjectivity nor alterity should be heard.

How, then, can there still be a voice, 'here' in this no-world space that is the necropolis? And, indeed, whom does the voice address? In living with death, as has been examined in the previous chapter, there is no longer an Other who speaks to you in the manner of Levinasian *Saying* (after all, the Other's face is only one's own), and so there is no 'ear of the other [which] says me to me and constitutes the *autos* of my autobiography'.[4]

This paradox of the subjectless or anonymous voice is yet one more way of thinking the human as the living-dead human thing, which foils any attempt at definition in its very anonymity. To categorically define or name the human thing would be the Orphean attempt of looking back at Eurydice, who always recedes because she has 'living in her', writes Blanchot, 'the plenitude of her death', and thus cannot be *recognized* in her anonymity no matter how furtively one looks.[5] The understanding of the human as explored here is not, then, to be taken as some re-definition; rather, the human has always been the incomplete, the fragmentary, 'sensible insensible, living dead, spectral' – in short, more quasi-concept than concept (*BSI*, 187). In Derrida's words, the quasi-concept is 'an indecision or an indeterminacy between a determinacy and an indeterminacy' – and this what ironically emerges, here, in the decree of the state of exception, at the point of the ultimate decision (*BSI*, 173).

In this indeterminacy, the question of *how* and *what* the voice speaks presents itself. If autobiography is necropolitically impossible – for death kills the *autos*, and no interlocutor 'says me to me' – it might be best now to turn, finally, to the genre of autothanatography.

'Clearly', as Ivan Callus writes, '(auto)biography cannot uncannily go beyond or proceed from the tomb, where it is (auto)thanatography that would be – impossibly – at home'.[6] In this light (or lack thereof, seeing as how we are shut in with Antigone), autothanatography may be taken as a literary genre that makes overt the human condition: a state not of non-being or beinglessness, but of being-in-the-necropolis – that is, being-without-an-I.

To call 'autothanatography' a genre is perhaps to already presume too much. Due to its very nature, as Callus also points out, it is 'resistant to classification', and even attempting to discern prevalent themes or mulling over the possibilities of developing a poetics of the autothanatographical is likely to conjoin the impossibility of death's narration with its categorization.[7] However, as has been intimated from this book's first chapter through Blanchot's *The Instant* – which has here been taken as an urtext of sorts, both of autothanatography and of the fiction of the death penalty – the very term 'autothanatography' must be questioned (even if in light of its generic quasi-nonexistence), and this in terms of the *autos* as well as the *thanatos*.

If subjective being-in-the-world can be understood, as Jean-Luc Nancy broadly sums up, as '*place* – site, situation, disposition', 'the coming into space of a time, in a spacing that allows that something *come* into presence', where '[p]resence takes place' from 'where there was nothing (and not even a "there")' – in Levinasian terms, the instant of hypostasis, the emergence from the *il y a* and towards the state of becoming subject – then autothanatography, where one bides in nothingness, marks the human condition as placelessness itself, as 'being' in this place that is 'not even a "there"'.[8] As Derrida notes, 'the true way of speaking about nonbeing [. . .] always remains "strange", inhabitual', and this last descriptor emphasizes not the place of non-being but rather the non-place of being-without-habitat (which also recalls being-without-*habit*, in the Hegelian sense) (*BSII*, 284). Autothanatography may be appropriately described, therefore, not as the genre of subjective disappearance, a retreat or return back into nothingness, but rather the literary realization of never having left this nothingness in the first place.

Nonetheless, in the necropolis, persistently and (im)possibly, one hears voices from beyond the grave. Indeed, if, as Peter Brooks writes, '[w]hat we seek in narrative fiction is that knowledge of death which is denied to us in our own lives', then autothanatography both addresses this need and challenges the assumption that death is something denied to us in life.[9]

Without going over, once again, the ideas discussed earlier, it suffices here to say that what the literature of the death penalty puts forward is the paradoxical human condition of living death, one that is not limited to prison cells but which spills over into sociality. None of the literary works discussed in this book, save for *The Instant of My Death*, are traditionally considered to be autothanatographical works (indeed, the word 'traditionally' is here itself debatable). However, insofar as death penalty literature examines the human relation to death as something that indeed *is*, then there is common ground from which we may look at how 'death is not merely the end of being but hides within life as its necessary condition'.[10] As intimated in the introductory discussion of the possibility of speaking in the name of death, literature may thus be understood as the site of the death penalty, where death speaks in its own name, as itself – which is to say, never in the first person. Insofar as these dead men walking are also dead men talking, the fiction of death penalty and autothanatography exhume similar thoughts.

Autothanatography, then, challenges the Heideggerian idea of the non-relational death, where 'being' and 'death' must always be separated by a 'towards'. If the autothanatographical 'subject' is dead yet still alive, then the human condition can no longer be ontologically summed up as 'I am because I *will* die'. Furthermore, this relation with death, in its very annihilation of the subject, breaks the *autos* of the syntagm '*my* death', revealing the possibilities of dying in-stead and putting under erasure the category of subjectivity itself – and, with it, alterity. A lived experience of death, in eliminating the 'I', cannot be subjective.

Something of this paradox is touched upon by Bede Rundle when commenting on the strangeness of the grammatical 'I' in general:

> We, anticipated by Descartes, are struck by the fact that someone's utterance of 'I' cannot but identify the speaker, but we had to *suppose* that there was a speaker – a person to whom the utterance could be referred and a person making a genuine use of language. Without this assumption the utterance would not have had the same significance: 'I' *somehow produced from the mouth of a dead man* or by an electronic device is not the basis for any such inference.[11]

The 'I', therefore, can no longer be assumed when talking of, specifically, the condemned prisoner, or, more broadly, a decomposing subjectivity defined by a sociality founded through the death penalty. Certainly, the paradoxical term 'autothanatography' seems to be very much in line with the present, constantly revolutionary thought of the human thing; however, perhaps a more appropriate response to the anonymity or impersonality of the dead 'I' might be, instead of the *autos*, the concept of the Neuter.

While Blanchot and Levinas share similar views on death – such as its inherent impossibility and the failure of suicide – there is in Blanchot a stress on the possibility of a very real and profound human relation with death that is greatly at odds with Levinas's notion of eternal postponement. Blanchot's is a view that is extrapolated throughout his oeuvre, often quite literally in fragments. Consequently, his writings on death have been read as both anti-Heideggerian (Levinas's own opinion, and as Blanchot is in fact read here)[12] as well as wholly compatible with Heidegger's idea of being-towards-death, where, in Blanchot's own words, 'man knows death only because he is man, and he is man only because he is death in the process of becoming' (*LRD*, 337). As Blanchot writes elsewhere, death 'is not a given [. . .] [but] must be achieved' through 'a task, one which we take up actively' (*Angst*), and thus 'man *is*, starting from *his* death' (*Jemeinigkeit*).[13] Indeed, Blanchot himself here refers the reader to Heidegger – despite his next claim, momentous and drastically non-Heideggerian, which is that this taking on of death would offer man the possibility 'to be without being'.[14]

But what is it 'to be without being'? This question is what has here been pursued throughout. For Blanchot, it is the act of literature. Following Franz Kafka, Blanchot describes the writer as one who writes not in order to survive (in the Derridean sense) or transcend history (in the Hegelian sense) but in order 'to establish with death a relation of freedom' – that is, to be able to die.[15] For Blanchot, literature 'speak[s] in order to say nothing', to 'attain negation in itself and to make everything of nothing', and this (as has also been mentioned in the introduction) because language destroys the very thing it names (*LRD*, 324). To participate in the act of language, then, is essentially to murder and divest of being, and this is especially relevant in the context of the death penalty, where the inverse is also true: to kill is to speak a sentence, naming the condemned. The act of condemnation is itself the execution, and so, recalling what has been said in the first chapter, perhaps the word 'execution' would here be more apt than Blanchot's own description of language as 'deferred assassination' (*LRD*, 323).

For Blanchot, language kills the person and is thus impersonal. Unlike everyday language (which in this context is not to be equated with *das Gerede*), the very act of language – as that which does not express meaning but both creates and destroys it – is 'impersonal' in that, for Blanchot, it 'does not imply anyone who expresses it, or anyone who hears it: it speaks *itself* and writes *itself*.'[16] This is the impersonal or anonymous voice of the 'I', one 'somehow produced from the mouth of a dead man', which speaks into no ear and denotes no 'I' at all. For Blanchot, as Rustam Singh elucidates, 'language – and this is an important point – is subjectless', and it is from this basis, Singh continues, that one can 'see here the beginnings of Neuter or the neutral, a notion that is central to Blanchot's work'.[17]

There is, therefore, what can be described as a lack or absence at the heart of the concept of the Neuter, one which 'free[s] us from what is' – and, recalling the previously discussed undoing of the cogito at the hands of the Third, from the necessity of the 'is' in the first place.[18] As Garth Gillan remarks to Levinas in an interview, recalling *Thomas the Obscure*, '"I think therefore I do not exist" [. . .] can be understood as "I speak therefore I do not exist"'. Levinas's response is still more illuminating: 'The Neuter or this Excluded Third Term is neither the affirmation, nor the pure negation of being. For affirmation and negation are within Order [. . .]. Yet, nevertheless, the insistent character of this Neuter contains an indeterminate negative.'[19] The writer is able to die, therefore, because the work of literature requires that '[he ceases] to be linked to Others and to himself by the decision which makes him an "I"', and so it is that 'he becomes *the empty place* [chora, *il y a*] where the impersonal affirmation emerges'.[20] By its very nature, no words can be heaped upon this absence of the 'I', and language is thus, as Walter Brogan appositely describes it, the 'unsubjected' 'nullification of oneself'.[21] Being emptied of subject and object, the Neuter neither affirms nor denies; it is that which hollows out the space between dichotomies and reveals a space beyond them. To invoke T. S. Eliot, this is the space of us hollow men, the nameless 'shape[s] without form' in 'this hollow valley' of death.[22]

As Singh writes: '[The Neuter] turn[s] a thing into something about which we cannot say: it *is* or it *is not*; it is *here* or it is *there*. The only way we would be able to describe this thing is this: *it neither is nor is not; it is neither here nor there*.'[23] This is the very (non-)being of the human *thing* that persists as something that '*neither is nor is not*', and the choral placelessness where it resides is '*neither here nor there*'.[24] Living in the necropolis – this paradoxical 'empty place', empty not of contents but of 'place' itself, a 'space infinitely empty' and empty of the infinity of alterity[25] – one sees how '[d]eath exists not only

[. . .] at the moment of death; [but that] at all times we are its contemporaries'.[26] 'Here' is the impassable *il y a* (and the transcendence of the 'there' in 'there is' is thus put under erasure) and the 'very experience of ambiguity' that leaves us unable to describe any(-)thing, for doing so would be an affirmation of presence that forgets the negation at its core (*EE*, 59). The Neuter is that 'something "radically exterior" which Blanchot had named the Outside (*le dehors*), a space corresponding to [Levinas's] *il y a*' in which the (non-)subject impossibly dwells.[27]

In fact, not only does Blanchot himself equate the two concepts – '[t]he *il y a*, because neutral, mocks the questions that bear upon it', he writes – but Levinas too.[28] 'One does not', he writes, 'associate with [the Neuter] – it is the "frightening" par excellence'.[29] The latter comment, of course, recalls the horror of Being and the rustle of the night, and perhaps most interesting is the concordance between the two. If these two concepts should thus be read as not only similarly inchoate but also inchoate in similar ways, then we are returned to the idea of the impassable *il y a* that negates the *autos*.

At this junction, where the concepts of the Neuter, the Third, *chora* and *il y a* seem to have melded, an important point must be made. The Neuter – that which is the 'incessant, interminable and indeterminable voice that reverberates outside of all intimacy, disposing the "I" and delivering it over to a nameless outside', as Critchley describes it – is 'a *literary* experience'.[30] What Blanchot denotes when he speaks of the impersonal voice is primarily a *narrative* voice, which 'speaks as one vast, continuous buzzing [or rustling], [. . .] an unqualifiable murmur, an impersonal whining'.[31] In this study, however, the voice of the Neuter that is beyond 'the very structure of being and non-being, the "is" and "is not"', seems to have been transposed to the condition of the human itself, speaking in the name of all of us, dead or alive.[32]

It would not be too trite to remark that if for Blanchot the writer can 'become', 'inhabit' or, at least, understand themselves as 'the empty place [of] impersonal affirmation', so too can all of us. After all, death has traditionally been viewed as the end of life's narrative – where 'death retroactively gives narrative shape to my life', as we have seen previously through Stone, Cavarero and Butler – and thus insofar as the 'I' can be viewed as 'the author', the dispossession of one's self need not be confined to the scene of writing.[33] In light of all that has been said on the impossibility of life and the inherent impossibility of writing autothanatographically, it might be apt to recall Gary Saul Morson's claim that, '[t]o understand one's situation, it is often helpful to imagine the rest of [one's] life *as if* it were an epilogue'.[34]

While this remark, especially with its emphasis on the careful conditional 'as if', seems only to uphold the idea of the necessary presence of the cogito, it does succeed in rebutting the idea that death ends all narratives. To put this more directly, the human condition may be read as more than analogous to the Neuter in that, through the epilogic nature (i.e. of and like an epilogue) of the literary works read here, there is revealed a human experience that lies beyond the dichotomy of the 'is' and 'is not' – a human experience that is beyond produced and productive narrative (*poiesis*) and instead lies within the epilogue which, necessarily, comes after the narrative. Derrida asks: 'How can one accord the phantasmatic or the fantastic with the narrative, with narrative fiction, or even with fantastic literature, with stories that accord time and future to the dead person?' (*BSII*, 162). The answer might be to look beyond the idea of narrative itself. In a manner that is autothanatographical, the literature of the death penalty goes beyond the ontological account of the human in reminding us that 'the presence of absence is not pure negation',[35] all the while asserting that, like an epilogue which somehow comes before a narrative, '"I" die before being born'.[36]

If writing is, as Blanchot argues, 'the approach to that point where nothing reveals itself' – which means not that nothing is revealed, but that what is revealed is Nothing – then the Neuter of literary language reveals the nothing that is the human.[37] To believe that the 'I am' of the human is fully present in narrativized Being is to ignore the non-productive experience of the epilogue, to exclude the epitaphic. As Morson writes, 'epilogues are typically narrated at a distance', and it is from this distance of a yet-maintained relation to death, this place beyond place, that we might begin to understand the human.[38]

As such, if the spaces of the Third and the Neutral are more than similar – and one should perhaps refrain from saying 'identical', despite Levinas's and Blanchot's own comments, because of the concepts' respective roles in the philosophers' trajectories – then just as the Third is necessary in understanding and 'open[ing] humanity', so too the Neuter. The neutral, therefore, is not just bound to the act of literature but also to that of language, in which we all partake. The human thing, that is, speaks only neutrally; its language is that which 'does not belong to the living [nor] to the language the dead do not speak'.[39]

The Neuter opens up to us in terms of our relation to death and its instantaneous time in different ways. First, this death maintained by the anonymous voice is likewise anonymous, a death in general. Discussing Rainer Maria Rilke's *The Notebooks of Malte Laurids Brigge*, Blanchot writes of 'anonymous death' as the anguish of those 'already dead of an unwitting death never to be achieved', where one is 'cast into the insecurity of a space where he cannot live or die "himself"', and where 'the idea of a human nature, of a human world in which we could take shelter collapses'.⁴⁰ In this we read once more Cincinnatus's sympathetic scribble, whose world has collapsed and where the human being is no longer: ~~life~~.

However, Malte's 'anguish of the "They die" and the hope for an "I die"' is the pain through which subjectivity 'retrenches', a 'perspective [which] suffers the obsession of the "I" that wants to die without ceasing to be "I"'.⁴¹ This is to see the instant of *my* death as *mine*, as one's *ownmost* affirmation, rather than as the common death here discussed, the anonymous death shared with three sons of farmers. This is why Blanchot powerfully reworks Rilke's prayer that God might 'grant to each his own death' as:

> Grant me the death which is not mine, the death of no one, [. . .] where I am not called upon to die, which is not an event – an event that would be proper to me, which would happen to me alone – but the unreality and the absence where nothing happens, where neither love nor meaning nor distress accompanies me, but the pure abandon of all that.⁴²

This absence of the 'distress' that can only come with 'my death' echoes what was earlier intimated as the absence of tragedy in this condition of the living corpse, the no one that dies the anonymous death. It was not pity or fear that made Pablo Ibbieta sweat but his inability to be reconciled with the 'nameless'; Cincinnatus's main anguish was not belonging to no world but believing he should indeed belong; the tragedy of *Antigone* is not that Antigone is no one but that Creon attempts to make her into someone he could kill. And so on. While this shall be further addressed in the following section, and while multiple theories of tragedy have to be left to one side, suffice it to say that the tragic finds no home in the indifference of impersonality.

The second way in which the Neuter opens up to us in terms of our relation to death is time. The diachronic time of the Third, that is, 'does not gather into re-*present*ation'; similarly, the time of the Neuter is that which is beyond the not-yet and the no-longer of death as pure negation. Its time is that of limbo, where the 'meanwhile' of the death penalty maintains the human beyond the 'is' and 'is not' of the world. In Foucault's words, recalling the thanatopolitical sovereign power that leads us to this understanding: 'the subject is, by rights, neither dead nor alive. From the point of view of life and death, the subject is neutral (*neutre*)'.⁴³ The inability of the condemned to participate in the ontological dichotomy of absence and presence (indeed, *this banishment is precisely what condemnation is*) is what allows one to go through the unexperienced experience of the instant of death. As Blanchot explains:

> Wherever we turn away, there is death, and what we call the moment of dying is only the crook of the turn, the extreme of its curvature [...]. [I]f we are somehow stolen from death it is because *without even perceiving it we pass the instant of dying*, having gone too far, inattentive and as if distracted, neglecting what we would have to have done to die (be afraid, hold onto the world, want to *do* something[, be present]). And in this negligence death has become forgetfulness; we have forgotten to die.[44]

If, for Levinas, the instant is where one 'take[s] up being' and becomes an 'I' inhabiting a present, then inversely, for Blanchot, the instant is the very moment where the 'I' ceases to be and decomposes its participation in presence and absence. Perceiving the instant of death is revealed as a remembrance of death, a remembrance of the 'I' from an epilogic distance. This is the distance of the condemned man, who can no longer participate in the making present of himself while, simultaneously, remaining 'here', talking as a dead man from beyond the grave. This is the human thing that is radically exterior to the human being of ontological presence and identity, '*neither here nor there*', neither totality nor infinity, a mere *fragment* of what we call the human being.

Indeed, as a quasi-concept, the fragment is indissoluble from the Neuter. It is, for Blanchot, 'the work of the absence of work' (the lack of *habit*), 'an affirmation without duration, a freedom without realization, [...] pure consciousness of the moment' (a consciousness that is not *slave* on the way to *self*-consciousness).[45] This is the time of the Neuter, a presence that is not made present. The fragment is 'the outside of time in time'; it is what interrupts history itself.[46] Speaking of German Romanticism, Blanchot writes that it seeks, in part, to 'be everything, but without content or with a content that is almost indifferent ["the pure abandon of all that"], and thus at the same time affirm[s] the absolute and the fragmentary', thus producing a work which 'does not realize the whole, but signifies it by suspending it, even breaking it'.[47]

The present absence inherent in the state of condemnation can be, as Singh astutely notes, this same breaking, '[f]or, lack means a break, too – that is, a crack or a gap. It is something that divides a thing into fragments, for example, a thing like discourse; or something that breaks a narrative, even breaks it down'.[48] From its vantage point outside of law and society, the death penalty lucidly reminds us that the idea of life as a narration that ends in death fails to recognize how, if life is indeed narrated, it can be narrated only in fragments, a plurality and polyphony of voices which interrupt any holistic presentation – and preservation – of the ego and its Other. Ipseity and alterity are thus fragments which do not complete one another; there is neither totality nor infinity. It is thus that 'death sentence', as a phrase, is revealed as a grave misnomer – it is never a 'sentence' at all, for this is not the language of Saying, belonging to the 'dynamic of question and answer'. It would be more apt to think of the 'death sentence' as the 'death rustle', 'death murmur' or 'death fragment'.

This is not an alternative phrasing or narration, for the fragment does 'not represent the real but replace it'; Derrida's dividing wall between self and other is shattered into pieces, and the fragment's unworking of the work shall be returned to in the coming section.[49] At this point, then, let us arrive at a response to the questioning of autothanatography.

The paradoxical equivalence of *autos* and *thanatos* – an impossible feat – is certainly one useful way of inflecting this book's main concern, the corpse living-relational-death. Indeed, it might be especially appropriate in that, as mentioned in the first chapter, 'autothanatographical' seemed to Derrida to be the truest way of describing *The Instant of My Death*.

However, death cannot be taken lightly – it eradicates all that it touches. To think of autothantography is to think of a self that is somehow balanced with and preserved in death. While indeed there is still a voice that speaks from the necropolis, understanding that voice as belonging to an 'I' that is a self implies that two wholes are kept in equilibrium: death and the ego, negation and presence. Rather, it is the case that, as we have seen, there was never an *autos* to begin with ('"I" die before being born') and that, because of this very relation to death, what lives on is only a *fragment* and not the whole. Crucially, the Neuter does not imply 'both this and that' but rather 'without this or that' or, better yet, '*neither this nor that*'. A relation to death, therefore, is never a relation between being and non-being, but rather a relation before, beyond, without, or at the limit of (non-)being itself.

Autothanatography, as Callus remarks, 'exceeds even the undead, who can and do die', and so the living corpse is 'living' only insofar as one understands that it is impossible to live.[50] Whereas 'literature', writes Blanchot, '*begins* with the *end*', autothanatography attests that the end has not eradicated the beginning which it precedes, and thus seemingly participates in *poiesis* through death (*LRD*, 336). The *autos* in autothanatography thus needs to be, if not replaced, at least rethought: it testifies to a self eternally present despite it never having really been 'here' but rather always 'nowhere', always fragmented and under erasure, unbecoming.

In sum, the literature of the death penalty allows us to view ourselves as subjectless things. But then how is the death penalty, even in its space outside of sociality, possible at all? If the sovereign without subjects is no sovereign at all, how are we condemned to death in the first place when death is always already the first place?

Sovereign (without) subjects

Let us recall our earlier thought experiment. Having already died and now living 'the death of no one', the risen man is no longer a subject 'called upon to die'; he simply *is* no longer. Blanchot's prayer has been answered, and we encounter the mere fragment of a subject – alive and thus inside the law but also dead and so outside of it. Is this what one might call the realm of the postsovereign? The questions to be addressed in this last section of this book, then, are as follows: Who is the exception, and is 'who' even the right pronoun? What is the topology of the exception? Is it possible to think of politics without the rule of the exception, and can the exception become the rule while somehow remaining, simultaneously, an exception? Does the fiction of the death penalty, along with ('auto')thanatography and the literary more broadly, allow us to envision or even extend such a thanatopolitical condition, a lawless space beyond the sovereign figure that creates its very possibility?

Barring the last, these are not novel questions. Starting with the first, one notes how Blanchot critiques the pronoun 'who' when it comes to the exception that is the subjectless human. The fact that an alternative to subjectivity remains a 'who' and not a 'what', he writes, 'postulates the beginning of an answer or a limitation of the question', where he 'would be expected to know that what comes after is some*one* and not some*thing*, not even something neutral'.[51] Derrida would later echo this, writing that 'death [. . .] always risks coming back from who to what, to reduce who to what, or to reveal the "what" of "who". Is to die not to become "what" again? A "what" that anybody will always have been' (*BSI*, 137).

The 'one', or 'who', in sovereignty, is up against the 'thing', 'anybody' or 'what': the individual and subjected being as opposed to the being-in-general of the living corpse. It is, though, only the latter which unveils the true mechanisms of sovereignty. One recalls what Blanchot writes in *The Madness of the Day*: 'As nobody, I was sovereign', or what he writes over twenty years later, of how, in the non-experience and 'extraordinary lightness' of death, he felt what he could only describe as 'sovereign elation' (*ID*, 5).[52] Sovereignty is, for Blanchot, defined via finitude, and vice versa: one achieves death only by understanding oneself as 'sovereignly, extremely mortal'.[53] Sade, Blanchot writes in 'Literature and the Right to Death', is indeed the 'writer par excellence' because of his realization that 'death is sovereign, that freedom is death', and that the 'work of negation' is, in itself, 'absolute sovereignty' (*LRD*, 321).

This is both the negative work of language, as discussed earlier – of how 'writing aims to reach the point of powerlessness', requiring 'what Blanchot calls the nullification of oneself' – and of our own condition within sovereignty, we who consider ourselves, at least to some degree, non-fictional.[54] Negativity is to be divested of subjectivity while also unsubjected. This is to a great extent discussed also in Bataille's oeuvre, who exclaims, vehemently, that '[s]overeignty is NOTHING'.[55] Bataille means the opposite of saying that nothing is sovereign, while at the same time, as Blanchot reads it, there could yet be hidden in this claim that which escapes it.

> Pronounced thus the word 'nothing' does not only imply the ruin of sovereignty, for sovereign ruin could still be a way for sovereignty to affirm itself by elevating and glorifying nothingness. [. . .]. But it may be that nothing is not at work here. Perhaps in its ostentatious trenchant form, it only hides what is hidden in what cannot be named [only voiced], the neutral – the neutral which always neutralizes itself and which has about it nothing sovereign that has not already surrendered in advance.[56]

The most important question being begged here, then, follows: Is the nothingness of the exception only another form of sovereignty, one which lays bare its full extent, or might it transport us outside the schema of sovereignty? In terms of sovereignty, how does one attempt to describe the impossible contradiction of the human thing? There are some possible answers to be found in Bataille – after all, for him the subject 'becomes *sovereign* in ceasing to be',[57] and, '[i]n order for Man to reveal himself ultimately to himself, he would have to die, but he would have to do it while living – watching himself ceasing to be'.[58] However, perhaps more so than even Bataille, it is Agamben who might help us pursue the matter further.[59]

In *Homo Sacer*, Agamben thinks of these same questions, although his idea of the death penalty remains at best ambiguous and at worst misrepresentative, and will be taken into account shortly. Crucial here are his thoughts on the topology of the exception. Building on the works of Schmitt, Foucault and Arendt, Agamben considers the ancient figure of the *homo sacer*, a figure from Roman law who '*may be killed and yet not sacrificed*' (and in many ways this finds its earlier analogue in the substitute king). This figure may offer, to a certain extent, another glimpse of the citizen of the necropolis (*HS*, 8).

Let us, though, work up to this last statement. As Agamben points out, the exception is what is excluded from the rule of law but which, simultaneously, can only exist within law, in a relation – albeit suspended – with the law which excludes it: '*The rule applies to the exception in no longer applying, in withdrawing from it*' (*HS*, 18). The exception, therefore, is not outside the reach of the *droit de glaive* but, rather, *is* the realm of sovereignty itself. The sovereign, like the exception it creates and which creates it, is both inside and outside the juridical order; in not needing law to create it, and 'having the legal power to suspend the validity of the law, [the sovereign] legally places himself outside the law', enabling him to declare that '"there is nothing outside the law"' (*HS*, 15). This logic of the inside/out applies also to Agamben's (and of course Benjamin's) thinking of violence as that which both establishes the law and demolishes it: 'the sovereign', writes Agamben, 'is the point of indistinction between violence and law, the threshold on which violence passes over into law and law passes over into violence' (*HS*, 32).

Thus, for Agamben, sovereignty 'does not limit itself to distinguishing what is inside from what is outside but instead traces a threshold (the state of exception) between the two', a topological 'ordering' that is 'above all a "taking of the outside", an exception', and which is thus 'essentially unlocalizable', a 'fundamental ambiguity [. . .] that [. . .] necessarily acts against [the law] as a principle of its infinite dislocation' (*HS*, 19–20). As such, 'Law is made of nothing but what it manages to capture inside itself through the inclusive exclusion of the *exceptio*' (*HS*, 27).

Agamben describes this inclusive exclusion as an abandonment or *ban*, 'the pure form of reference to something in general, which is to say, the simple positing of relation with the nonrelational' – or, at least, 'to something *presupposed* as nonrelational' – and its infinite dislocation, he argues, reflects 'the originary structure in which law refers to life and includes it in itself by suspending it' (*HS*, 28, 109–10, 29). This banned, banished or suspended life – beyond both political *bios* and natural *zoē* – is the bare life of the *homo sacer*, 'the originary figure of life taken into the sovereign ban', a life that can only be described as 'bare, *anonymous* life', the life of a corpse (*HS*, 83, 124).[60] As Agamben writes, 'the production of bare life is the originary activity of sovereignty', and '[t]he sacredness of life, which is invoked today as an absolutely fundamental right in opposition to sovereign power, in fact originally expresses both life's subjection to a power over death and life's irreparable exposure in the relation of abandonment' (*HS*, 83). It is thus '*[n]ot simple natural life, but life exposed to death (bare or sacred life) [that] is the originary political element*' (*HS*, 88).

In sum:

> Sovereignty [. . .] presents itself as an incorporation of the state of nature in society, or, if one prefers, as a state of indistinction between nature [*zoē*] and culture [*bios*], between violence and law [. . .]. The state of exception is thus not so much a spatiotemporal suspension as a complex topological figure in which not only the exception and the rule but also the state of nature and law, outside and inside, pass through one another. (*HS*, 35–7)

The act of the sovereign *nomos* is, then, this: in always taking inside what is outside, it 'always already contains its own virtual rupture', and its topology is never settled (*HS*, 37). In other words, it is that which 'achieves the paradoxical union of these opposites' – most fundamentally, life and death – necessitating them to persist through paradox without synthesis (*HS*, 31).

But, Agamben asks, '[w]hat is the status of the living body that seems no longer to belong to the world of the living?' (*HS*, 97). The resurrected man of our thought experiment – he who lives a suspended life inside and outside law, who having been executed is thus banned from both life and death – is then a prime exemplification of Agamben's answer to the question, which he terms *subiectus superaneus*: 'he who will appear later [. . .], according to a curious oxymoron, as the new sovereign subject (*subiectus superaneus*, in other words, what is below and, at the same time, most *elevated*) can only be constituted as such through the repetition of the sovereign exception and the isolation of *corpus*, bare life, in himself' (*HS*, 124).[61]

This returns us to *The Instant*'s 'sovereign *elation*', where bare life – as anonymous being, being-in-general – is, most lucidly, the life of sovereignty itself. Indeed, the term 'sovereign subject' conjoins (without equating) the undying *homo sacer* with sovereignty, the clearest feature of which being 'its perpetual nature'; one here sees, therefore, 'the body of the sovereign and the body of *homo sacer* enter into a zone of indistinction in which they can no longer be told apart', just as with the corpses of Antigone and Creon (*HS*, 94, 96). This paradox of the sovereign subject – the subject as sovereign, the sovereign as subject – may also be inverted, as perhaps was intimated by Hugo's nameless protagonist when he asks: 'if these dead return, in what form do they return? [. . .] Does the head or the body turn into a ghost?'. This possible inversion is noteworthy. In this land of the dead, is it also the case of the body (subject) *without* its head (sovereign), and the head *without* its body?

We will soon return to the possibilities of this inversion within the pressing context of the death penalty, but one last point must here be made in relation to Agamben's figure as one more archetypal than archaic. Indeed, one might note how, in Agamben's conception of sovereignty, it is not that the exception creates the rule but, rather, that the exception *is* the rule, a figuration that is more the exceptionalization of the norm than the normalization of the exception. The exception of the human thing defines the rule of the human in general; as Howells observes, '[t]he truth, then, always resides with the exception, never with the rule'.[62] With the mechanisms of sovereignty being the very operations of sociality, 'human life', writes Agamben, 'is thus included in the political order in being exposed to an unconditional capacity to be killed' (*HS*, 85). By its very nature, he continues, 'the "juridically empty" space of the exception [. . .] has transgressed its spatiotemporal boundaries and now, overflowing outside them, is starting to coincide with the normal order'; as he goes on to say, '[e]verywhere on Earth men live today in the ban of a law [. . .]. But this is precisely the structure of the sovereign relation', and thus '[b]are life [. . .] now dwells in the biological body of every living being' (*HS*, 38, 51, 140). Our 'mere "capacity to be killed"' is therefore what leads Agamben to state that, ultimately, 'we are all virtually *homines sacri*', and that 'biopolitics necessarily turns into thanatopolitics' (*HS*, 114–15, 142).[63]

From what we have recapitulated of Agamben thus far, the figure that has here been termed the 'human thing' seems to map perfectly onto that of the *homo sacer*, and this on several points. The simultaneous immortality and shared death of bare life and political sovereign, for instance, is both the murder of the abattoir (the commoners were not animals, *zoē*, but, being slaughtered, were not killed as citizens either) as well as assassination – which as we have seen, when they happen simultaneously, collapse into the idea of execution. What survives (without surviving) in this shared death is, writes Agamben, 'a paradoxical being, who, while seeming to lead a normal life, in fact exists on a threshold that belongs neither to the world of the living nor to the world of the dead: he is a living dead man', one 'belonging to the world of the deceased' and thus 'a living pledge to his subjection to a power of death'. His death is 'a *missing* death', in abeyance, with all the resonances discussed earlier.[64] It is a condition 'incompatible with the human world', and, '[i]n every case, sacred life [living death] cannot dwell in the city of men' (*HS*, 99–101). This is no longer the *polis* but 'the no-man's-land between the home and the city'; in other words, the necropolis (*HS*, 90).

Furthermore, this necropolis which we all inhabit – in all of us being condemned at the mark of sociality, in all of us being virtually *homines sacri*, dead as we are born – is the death penalty's overflowing of its spatiotemporal boundaries, maintaining us in our unexperienced experience of death. With death, it is not the case that there can be no relation, but rather that there is a relationality in the form of a ban, an acknowledged 'relation with the nonrelational' that brings out only 'some*thing* in general' – that is, anonymous being. The topology of this relation, like the position of the fragmented Neuter, is neither inside nor outside but 'radically exterior', and the neutral interruption of the Third, who dies in-stead within the anonymous topography of the impassable *il y a* or *chora*, is the 'virtual rupture' that is a necessary part of the contradictive mechanisms of the death penalty; 'the machine turns against itself', and its movements are always contra-temporal. Even language, argues Agamben, 'holds man in its ban' (*HS*, 50). 'Language', he states, 'is the sovereign who, in a permanent state of exception, declares that there is nothing outside language and that language is always beyond itself' (*HS*, 21).

The anonymous and pluralized choral topology of the always-exceptionalized rule – being 'essentially unlocalizable' and infinitely dislocated – thus displaces any level of certainty imbued in the preposition 'towards' (as in, being-*towards*-death) and the either/or of 'here' or 'there' (as in, *Da*-sein). In turn, this presence of absence that is not pure negation, but rather the neutral, is an excess of identity, one that exceeds the being-mortal of the human (the Da-*sein*). This is also identity's complete lack: where the condemned is doubled – that is, exceeded and eradicated – not only through the sovereign (as in the *Kampf*, or as in *subiectus superaneus*) but also through the Third who dies in-stead (outstripping the 'I', the 'my' of 'my death'). What remains from all this is the fundamental ambiguity of *remainder*, the human thing as human remains: fragments of dead men walking, living corpses, living the relational death.

Putting to one side our suspicion that Agamben has read Blanchot much more closely than he lets on, we must ask ourselves whether all that has been said so far necessarily or solely culminates in Agamben's own vision of sovereignty, a vision which ultimately endorses Heidegger's Dasein as well as suggests that an escape from sovereignty is unthinkable. An answer contradicting these tenets may here be proffered by examining more closely what Agamben says of the death penalty proper, and from this we may begin, finally, to determine the post-sovereign gestures of the literature of the death penalty.

In this connection we must first note that, for Agamben, the ultimate 'zone of irreducible indistinction' is not death row but the camp (*HS*, 9). The camp, according to him, is 'the pure, absolute, and impassable biopolitical space [which in Agamben's use of the term means *thanatopolitical* space] (insofar as it is founded solely on the state of exception)', and appears 'as the hidden paradigm of the political space of modernity' (*HS*, 123). It is where 'bare life and the juridical rule enter into a threshold of indistinction', a 'place' which 'decisively signals the political space of modernity itself', 'the new biopolitical *nomos* of the planet' (*HS*, 174, 176).

While it is clear that Agamben tries to separate those condemned to death from '[t]he bare life into which the camp's inhabitants were transformed', it is not so clear as to where the line of separation is (*HS*, 171). For the most part, the state of the condemned man can be read alongside the figure of the *homo sacer*. Similarly to what has been done here, Agamben differentiates the camp from the prison based on the state of exception, and, when talking of VPs (*Versuchspersonen* or human guinea pigs), he describes them as 'persons sentenced to death or detained in a camp, the entry into which meant the definitive exclusion from the political community', and thus 'situated in a limit zone between life and death, inside and outside, in which they were no longer anything but bare life' (*HS*, 159; see *HS* 20). He goes on:

> Those who are sentenced to death and those who dwelt in the camps are thus in some way unconsciously assimilated to *homines sacres*, to a life that may be killed without the commission of homicide. Like the fence in the camp, *the interval* [the limbo, abeyance] *between the death sentence and execution delimits an extratemporal and extraterritorial threshold in which the human body is separated from its normal political status and abandoned, in a state of exception, to the most extreme misfortunes.* (*HS*, 159)[65]

The camp/death sentence equivalence clearly at work here is elsewhere refuted by Agamben on the basis that the *homo sacer* is that which cannot be sacrificed. Despite saying, *contra* Bataille, that '[t]he dimension of bare life that constitutes the immediate referent of sovereign violence is more original than the opposition of the sacrificeable and the unsacrificeable', the killing of *homo sacer*, Agamben states explicitly, 'constitutes [. . .] neither capital punishment nor a sacrifice, but simply the actualization of a mere "capacity to be killed"' (*HS*, 113–14). Indeed, when discussing the neomort – 'an extreme embodiment of the *homo sacer*' – he says that 'what is at stake is, once again, the definition of a life that may be killed without the commission of homicide', and which is, 'like the *homo sacer*, "unsacrificeable", in the sense that it obviously could not be put to death following a death sentence' (*HS*, 165).

Agamben also invokes the figure of the werewolf as 'a monstrous hybrid of human and animal, divided between the forest and the city', which 'corresponds perfectly to the state of the exception' (*HS*, 105, 107).[66] Here is echoed Kant's declaration that the condemned man 'turns himself into a thing' and 'can be treated by others as an animal or a thing; he can be dealt with like a horse or a dog, for he is no longer a man'. These sentiments of Kant, though, go unnoticed, despite Agamben's frequent reliance on Kant in an effort to exceptionalize the topology of the camp beyond all else. In sum, in Agamben's thoughts, sovereignty and condemnation seem to be to some degree separated due to the unsacrificeability of the *homo sacer*: 'sacred life', he states, 'may be killed by anyone without committing homicide, but never submitted to sanctioned forms of execution' (*HS*, 103).

It is not the present intention to replace the inchoate space of the camp with that of death row, ascribing some hierarchy of disaster. Rather, what is being argued here is that, in allowing the death penalty its revelation of bare life that is not named *homo sacer*, one might be led deeper into the non-ontological topography of humanity than the *homo sacer* allows. It also puts into question Agamben's support of Heideggerian Dasein despite thinking a relation with death, which Heidegger categorically says is intolerable. This is, therefore, why the term 'human thing' is here retained in favour of Agamben's figure: it allows us to put into question the order of *being* itself. In short, the human thing, unlike the *homo sacer*, affords a conceptual space where the human can indeed be separated from sovereignty, which, in Agamben, is what is proper and inalienable to man.

Agamben is most clear regarding ontology when responding to Antonio Negri's *Insurgencies: Constituent Power and the Modern State*, of which he writes how '[t]he problem [of sovereignty and the state of exception] is [there] moved from political philosophy to first philosophy (or, if one likes, politics is returned to its ontological position)' (*HS*, 44). Only through such a move, he continues, may we begin to think the impossible impossibility.

> [Re-viewing politics through ontology creates the possibility of thinking] a constituting power wholly released from the sovereign ban. Until a new and coherent ontology of potentiality (beyond the steps that have been made in this direction by Spinoza, Nietzsche, and Heidegger) has replaced the ontology founded on the primacy of actuality and its relation to potentiality, a political theory freed from the aporias of sovereignty remains unthinkable. (*HS*, 44)

So, does the literature of the death penalty think the unthinkable, that is, a post- or non-ontology? This question may, by its very wording, be unanswerable, for to think the unthinkable would be to make present its impossibility. It may also be too presumptuous to state that we have already arrived at a space of freedom from aporetic sovereignty, for the unthinkable, here, would be 'a completely new politics – that is, a politics no longer founded on the *exceptio* of 'bare life', an end of the exception that is not the route of the exceptionalization of the norm (*HS*, 11). As such, our discussion of the fact that we are all condemned at the point of sociality and that the sovereign is himself a living corpse, would in this manner only reinforce sovereignty rather than pushing towards some thing postsovereign. 'Only if it is possible', Agamben continues, 'to think the Being of abandonment beyond every idea of law [. . .] will we have moved out of the paradox of sovereignty toward a politics freed from every ban', and this would imply 'nothing less than thinking ontology and politics beyond every figure of relation, beyond even the limit relation that is the sovereign ban' (*HS*, 47, 59). In this vein, he ends on a cautious note: 'only if we understand the theoretical implications of bare life will we be able to solve the enigma of ontology' (*HS*, 183).

This 'Being of abandonment beyond every idea or law' has here been named the living corpse of the necropolis, and in this naming there has indeed been an investigation into its 'theoretical implications'. Cue Foucault: 'If Man is dead, everything is possible!' – and that includes a thinking of postsovereignty that does not merely either reaffirm sovereignty or reconfigure its superficial aspects.[67] It is interesting that one of the figures Agamben specifies as (nearly) discharging the power of sovereignty, and thinking beyond it, is Melville's Bartleby, who, through his indifference, 'push[es] the aporia of sovereignty to the limit' despite not 'completely freeing [himself] from its ban' (*HS*, 48). Keeping this in mind, we might thus be able to give a different inflection to an earlier concept of Agamben's as explored in *The Coming Community*: that of the 'whatever being'.

The relation between 'whatever being' and *homo sacer* converges and diverges at several key moments. While Bartleby is, for example, used in the same context here as in *Homo Sacer* (i.e. contextualized by Aristotelian actuality and potential to be and to not-be, vis-à-vis thinking beyond Being), the two works diverge significantly: for instance, on the fact that limbo (later the 'interval' of the camp fence or the time between condemnation and execution), with its 'impassable' bodies, would only be a persistence of 'natural joy'; the lack of distinction between the example and the exception; his notions of good and evil, the demonic, the ethical, ease and the 'whatever being's' lovability as opposed to its total destitution.[68]

'Whatever being' is, above all, what is neither general nor particular. Being the 'matheme of singularity', prior to the *principium individuationis* (which may be read on the lines of Levinasian hypostasis), it is where 'pure singularities communicate only in the empty space [*chora*] of the example, without being tied by any common property, by any identity'.⁶⁹ The communication of these pure singularities, like the voices Cincinnatus hears after the collapse of life and world, does not, though, constitute presence. Rather, 'here is the idea', writes Agamben, 'of an *inessential* commonality, a solidarity that in no way concerns an essence. *Taking-place, the communication of singularities in the attribute of extension, does not unite them in essence, but scatters them in existence*'.⁷⁰ The whatever being that populates this community is, then, '[n]either generic nor individual, neither an image of the divinity nor an animal form'.⁷¹ This community of 'whatever being' – which gains additional nuances of indifference when translated into English, ones which are not present in the original *essere qualunque* – clearly relates to all that has been said so far, in particular: the 'undecided, or, in a very rigorous sense, "*vague*"' condition of living on;⁷² Kant's paradoxical 'animal society'; the chain-gang and the notion of bestiality; the hollow men who are standing alone yet 'leaning together' and 'grop[ing] together'; and so on.⁷³ While this may also return us to the werewolf, Agamben argues, crucially, that death is 'the ultimate frustration of individuality' and reveals life 'in all its nakedness':

> [I]f instead of continuing to search for a proper identity in the already improper and senseless form of individuality, humans were to succeed in belonging to the impropriety as such, in making of the proper being-thus not an identity and an individual property but a singularity without identity, a common and absolutely exposed singularity – if humans could, that is, not be-thus in this or that particular biography, but be only *the* thus, their singular exteriority and their face, then they would for the first time enter into a community without presuppositions and without subjects, into a communication without the incommunicable.⁷⁴

Here, it seems, Agamben desires the impropriety of death, the divestment of individuality, the anonymous and multiple face (in effect, facelessness) – which is by no means a desire for the Jewish prisoner of the camp, the anonymous *homo sacer* who knows only sovereignty. And this lack of 'particular biography', allowing us to hear the rustles of autothanatography, is certainly different from what Agamben intimates is the tragic inescapability of sovereignty. What he gives us, then, is a community that is 'incommunicable' rather than 'unthinkable', a community 'without presuppositions and without subjects', communal but nonetheless non-social and thus also without sovereign. As Blanchot writes in *The Unavowable Community*, '[t]his community is not the place of Sovereignty'.⁷⁵

Here is the neither/nor – neither head nor body, inside nor outside, here nor there, being nor non-being. On this Agamben would say: 'negative (or mystical) theology, with its "neither... nor..." [...] is not outside theology and can actually be shown to function as the principle grounding the possibility in general of anything like a theology' (*HS*, 17). It is with this logic, too, that Agamben accepts Heidegger's Dasein with its potentiality not to be.[76] To this, one may respond with the indifference of the instant, that which reads also as the instance, the example, 'an instance (without stance, a "without" without negativity)'.[77]

Indifference is the manner of whatever being. This indifferent being 'is not, in terms of the division that dominates Western ontology, either an essence or an existence, but a *manner of rising forth*; not a being that is *in* this or that mode, but a being that is *its* mode of being'.[78] Here we have, as Leslie Hill writes, a '"we" without a "we", inassimilable into any communal "us"'.[79] Or, as Mark C. Taylor writes with reference to Blanchot's unavowable community: 'In the cemetery, *we are together as alone in a community without community*'.[80] Or else, Levinas's *le tiers* as a 'collectivity that is not communion'; Derrida's marionettes, or the crypt as what 'must necessarily incorporate more than one'; or, indeed, the etymology of 'thing' as 'assembly'. Whatever being is 'purely linguistic being' – that is, neutral – and its position is only the example, never the exemplary.[81] Its being is perfectly common, and here one can only have a death equally as common, irreparably unworking the syntagm of 'my death'.[82] It is, for Agamben, an 'empty and indeterminate totality [...] indeterminable to a concept', a quasi-concept; it is, moreover, 'a singularity plus an empty space', which allows for substitution – dying in-stead – to reveal the human as living with death itself.[83]

In whatever being we find a state analogous to the *homo sacer* but which has shed or sloughed off one if its presumed essential features, its political mode, by means of its sheer indifference to and lack of individual identity within it. That is to say, in the death which is not mine, 'the pure abandon of all that' abandons even the ban. Although the Agamben of *Homo Sacer* would disagree with this interpretation (claiming indifference is not quite enough) – and perhaps even the Agamben of *The Coming Community*, who identifies a culmination of whatever being in the *homo sacer* – we nonetheless see Agamben return to this disastrous indifference, at the end of *Homo Sacer*, with the figure of the *Muselmann*. This is a figure whose instincts, Agamben writes, 'are cancelled along with his reason', and who moves 'in absolute indistinction' with a manner 'which does not register any difference' and 'might perhaps be a silent form of resistance' (*HS*, 185).

In 'whatever being' we see, therefore, a more accurate (non-)localization of the condition of the human thing – and its ontological topography – than that afforded by the *homo sacer*. Despite their disparate contexts, 'whatever being' emerges as yet another synonym for the neutrality that is the irremissible *il y a* or *chora*, here presented under the umbrella term of 'necropolis'.[84] Whatever being, divested of its properties, is what Blanchot would describe as 'to be without being'. In its characterization through the manner of indifference, we see here all relationality decompose (except that of the (non-)relation with death, which creates and necessitates such indifference). Whether the law withdraws or not from the state of exception, whether it claims for inside itself that which was outside, thus rendering it radically exterior – it is neither here nor there. Such indifference is perhaps the only manner of resistance to the oeuvre of sovereignty, a passive resistance that does not come from anywhere – neither inside, outside, nor at the threshold, trembling through the negative relation of the neither/nor – because it comes from death. From this non-place of 'infinite resistance' there comes an *indifferent resistance*, a resistance that does not care how or whether it resists because it is already dead.[85] Indifference is, though, neither actual nor potential; an indifferent resistance neither works nor wears the habit in its inhabituality and lack of habitat. There is no tragedy here, for there is neither identification nor identity; only the disaster of the unidentifiable.[86] This is what the tragic *homo sacer* is incapable of, for it is immersed only in the *polis*, but not the human thing, the citizen of the necropolis.

This resistance is not laborious resistance, neither positive nor negative, for its domain is not (Hegelian) work, impossible within the trauma of the death penalty, which strips us of our very future, but (Blanchovian) unworking, *désoeuvrement*.[87] The neutral voice of the human thing has thus always spoken in the key of resistance, an 'affirmative powerlessness or non-power', the work of death that is always an unworking.[88] Its language is not meaningful – while the citizen of the necropolis lives '*the life that endures death and maintains itself in it*' (*LRD*, 336), its voice does not, as Agamben rightly reads Hegel's dialectic, '[have] the "magical power" that "converts the negative into being"'.[89] The voice of neuter-thanatography is not Saying anything at all. This is not the subjective 'power of the negative', the historical life that, as Critchley writes, 'consists in the emergence of new, true objects for consciousness through the labour of negation'.[90] In being unworked, this resistance is always disastrous: it is a resistance that is 'the interruption of history and destiny [. . .], which is what Blanchot means by disaster'.[91]

In this interruption called dying in-stead, sovereignty itself is suspended. This, then, is a resistance through death. Politics is always, as Agamben has shown us, a politics of death; but death ultimately kills even the possibilities of necropolitics. Crucially, then, the voice of the human thing is, as Hill writes: 'an interruption of possibility, a deferral or difference that, like a caesura, voiced in the neuter, and irreducible to any opposition between immanence and transcendence, divide[s] the origin from itself, put[s] immediacy at a distance, ruin[s] all prospect of foundation, *and revoke[s] the supremacy of sovereignty as such*.'[92]

In *The Beast and the Sovereign* seminars, Derrida characterizes sovereignty as that which 'causes fear, and fear makes the sovereign' – it is thus terror (with its echoes of the guillotine) that is 'the essential manifestation of sovereignty'; defined as such, fear is 'proper to mankind', and '[l]ife lives in fear' (*BSI*, 40–1). As Julia Kristeva writes, keeping at the forefront a broad view of history: 'a human's greatest fear is to see his life taken, and this fear founds the social pact'.[93] And yet this social pact continually unworks itself. In fact, Derrida continues, the condition of sovereignty 'lasts only as long as law, sovereignty, and the state are able to *protect* fearful subjects against what is causing them fear', and if sovereignty itself constitutes the community of its subjects, they can never be protected from itself (*BSI*, 42). This is what Foucault already understands when writing: 'How could power exercise its highest prerogatives by putting people to death, when its main role was to ensure, sustain, and multiply life, to put this life in order? For such a power, execution was at the same time a limit, a scandal, and a contradiction'.[94]

This is one more way of understanding society as that which is founded in the scandal of the death penalty; what is here being added is that such a society necessarily goes beyond its foundation, undoing what creates it as part of the process of its own contradiction. Hypothetically losing one's head is not the same as literally having it detached; while one can be afraid in life, it is impossible in already living death; without fear, the social pact undoes its foundation. In not being able to be protected from the death penalty that founds the community – indeed, it is the very thing that also annuls it – sovereign subjectivity must necessarily come undone. As Schmitt writes, 'the '*protego ergo obligo* is the *cogito ergo sum* of the state' and, with the death penalty having killed us before we are born, the unravelling of sovereign protection unravels the human *cogito* that belongs to the political subject.[95] As Derrida explains: '"I protect you" means, for the state, I oblige you, you are my subject, I subject you. Being the subject of one's fear and being the subject of the law or the state, being obliged to obey the state as one obeys one's fear, are at bottom the same thing' (*BSI*, 43).

Protection may be 'the essential function of the state', but the state always fails to protect by virtue of its very existence as first and foremost a human society (*BSI*, 46). What emerges in this failure, then, is a lack of fear (and pity, and tragedy) – an indifference belonging to the human of the necropolis. In, like Antigone, not being able to oblige in having always already been executed, we are then in the post-mortal realm of the post-subject that is at once the post-sovereign.

What this means, then, is that the human thing is ultimately the possibility of a beyond the political that is not merely the apolitical. While Agamben believes that sovereignty is what is proper and inalienable to the human being, this book's understanding of death as more sovereign than any sovereignty uncovers, speaking but not heard, acknowledged but not recognized, the human thing.[96]

All this gestures towards the political elsewhere that Butler finds in *Antigone*, and which this project has explored through several other living corpses. This other-than-political does not make of the human thing a new sovereign figure, and this through the negative topography of the neither/nor maintained in relational death. Thinking of an(-)other politics, one recalls Derrida who, speaking of animal society, maintains that one cannot conclude 'that there is *politics* and especially *sovereignty* in communities of non-human living beings. "Social animal" does not necessarily mean "political animal"' (*BSI*, 16).

This 'being without a city', a wholly different condition from the 'being-political of the living being called man', requires us to think otherwise, beyond this '*living being* called man' (*BSI*, 25).[97] It is where the 'who' becomes a 'what', where it is impossible to define one as 'oneself'; in short, it is the end of the *ipsissimus* of the mortal self, the end of the 'sovereignty of the responsible human Me' (*BSI*, 183). What is required in thinking the human thing is thus a 'repoliticization', in Derrida's words, or more accurately a depoliticization that is not Schmittian but thanatopolitical, an end of a politics of the living and living politics itself. In sum, here is the 'ambivalent specter of death that remains inassimilable and incomprehensible within sovereignty's hermetically self-referential [Narcissistic] discourse'.

What remains, then, are remains, 'something even below the [beast]' that is the werewolf-sovereign, not poor in world (*weltarm*) but, like Cincinnatus and the rest of our dead men walking, worldless (*weltlos*).[98] This something is like a stone, for instance, or a corpse: 'the inanimate, the lifeless [. . .], what cannot even die' (*BSII*, 113). If 'the *autos* is indissociable from what happens *in the world*', then exiting the world entails exiting also the *autos*, instead residing with the epilogic thanatography of the neutral, the indifferent (*BSII*, 88). This is being-in-general, the anonymous and unavowable whatever community, beyond the being-mortal that for Heidegger defines the human.

'Whatever singularity has no identity', continues Agamben; 'it is not determinate with respect to a concept, but neither is it simply indeterminate; rather it is determined only through its relation to an *idea*, that is, to the totality of its possibilities'.[99] This quasi-conceptual state is the possibility intimated by the literature of the death penalty: an understanding of death that moves the human away from political life, that is, away from both politics and ontology. The human thing is the ellipsis following 'there is . . .'. It is neither determinable nor indeterminable, neither sovereign nor subject, but rather effortlessly decomposing, naked yet faceless and fundamentally incommunicable in its stygian relation with death, thus opening up what Agamben remains unsure of in *Homo Sacer*, namely: the possibility of a political relation without a ban, where there persists the human without being.

The fragmentary and unavowable community of human things, then, may still be said to be 'coming', for it is never present, but only insofar as one also understands with this that which, as Blanchot writes, 'never comes, except arbitrarily, or has always already come', in the indifferent manner of 'the coming of what does not come, of what would come without an arrival, *outside of Being and as though adrift*'.[100] In other words, this is the being-death-in-abeyance that literature allows us to glimpse and, in so doing, frees us from the tyranny of the self, the subject, the human being.

Conclusion

The death of me

Derrida's textual spectre warns me that unravelling the human is no easy task; that it remains always a continuous process of conceptualization and, indeed, requires considerable heart: 'Courage! Courage, now!', he says, '[y]ou need heart and courage to think, contrary to what many people would be tempted to think. For example, to think the living dead. Whether one is for it or against it, whether one accepts the possibility or the impossibility of it, you need courage to think that' (*BSII*, 147). I would like to think this book of mine has been written with at least some bravery, and that it has not (yet) been the death of me.

'The death of me', as a phrase, has always piqued my interest. It reveals, as an inversion of the philosophically laden syntagm 'my death', how it is always, apparently, something or someone else that is the death of me, and often this is left to the future. 'They will be the death of me', the idiom goes, and this I might say of a neighbour or colleague who is being particularly difficult. I am not dead, not yet, but I will definitely die if they keep on being so difficult. This is all a bit hyperbolic, of course, and perhaps one should try and work things out, but it is indeed an odd phrase. Moreover, I cannot for the life of me work out whether this other reversal – 'I cannot for the life of me' – stands in direct contrast to, or happy agreement with, 'the death of me'.

As a turn of phrase (standing shoulder to shoulder with that other one, the 'dead man walking', so often referred to here), 'the death of me' can be said to encapsulate, to a great degree, what has been argued in this book, namely: that the death penalty holds within its contra-temporal and contra-political turns not only the death of *a* subject but the death of *the* subject, the death of anyone, any human being who could say 'me' and 'my death'. Indeed, this book understands, as does Oliver, how 'by giving death the sovereign state claims a power that calls into question what it means to be human'. Oliver goes on: 'There is much more to be said about this line of reasoning, but that will have to wait for another context'; this book fulfils the necessity of that other context.[1] This does not, of course, make everything clear. As Derrida suggests (here paraphrased by Howells), the death penalty 'is ultimately not an issue susceptible to logical analysis: [a]s a matter of life and death it lies beyond reason, arguably at the heart of what it is to be human'.[2] Although this study has inevitably promoted an inchoate and disjointed formulation of the human enshrined within an anthropocentric universe, this book nevertheless remains a component of a wide-ranging and comprehensive debate around human death within which it retains its own solidity, and its critical lens can be transported to discussions of death and the human more generally beyond the particular focus forwarded here.

One indication of this is how my study very obviously gestures us towards a host of other texts, some literary, some critical. I will not here attempt an exhaustive list but will instead mention some which seem to me most obvious. These range from the commercially popular – such as William Bradford Huie's *The Execution of Private Slovik* (1954), Truman Capote's *In Cold Blood* (1966), John Grisham's *The Chamber* (1994) and Stephen King's *The Green Mile* (1996) – to those rather more obscure – such as Ambrose Bierce's 'An Occurrence at Owl Creek Bridge' (1890), Flann O'Brien's *The Third Policeman* (1967) and Drew Magary's *The Postmortal* (2011). One could also mention numerous other works that are more traditionally consigned to the category of 'literature': Edgar Allen Poe's 'The Pit and the Pendulum' (1842), Henry James's 'The Altar of the Dead' (1895), Herman Melville's *Billy Budd* (1924), Theodore Dreiser's *An American Tragedy* (1925), Robert Musil's *The Man Without Qualities* (1930), Ward Greene's *Death in the Deep South* (1936), Orhan Pamuk's *The White Castle* (1985) and Don DeLillo's *The Body Artist* (2001). And this is not to mention poetry (such as William Wordsworth's series of 'Sonnets on the Punishment of Death', 1837), memoirs (such as François-René de Chateaubriand's *Memoirs from Beyond the Grave*, 1849–50), plays (such as Jean Genet's *Deathwatch*, 1947), films (such as Alejandro G. Iñárritu's *The Revenant*, 2015), paintings (such as Peter Bruegel the Elder's 'The Triumph of Death', *c*. 1562) and all the other media and art forms that interrogate the context and state of the human living death.

Many other literary, legal and historical studies might also have been included here, including Ann Algeo's *The Courtroom as Forum* (1996), Stuart Banner's *The Death Penalty* (2002), Kristin Boudreau's *The Spectacle of Death* (2006) and Mark Camuel's *The Shadow of Death* (2006). Notable interventions, which would have been highly germane here, must also be named, including – this time listed in ascending order of relevance – Austin Sarat, Slavoj Žižek and, especially, Roberto Esposito. Attempting to incorporate this vast discourse would have not only diluted this study but also left no space for the detailed analysis presented here.

But let me now return to this idea of 'my death': I have here contested this syntagm in terms of both its paradoxical subjectivity (the 'I' still somehow whole, untouched by the death it should not even possess) and its endless deflection into an uncertain future. Indeed, Epicurus, Levinas and others like them – those who would forever disassociate self from death – would agree that something can only be the death of me in the future, for I (so long as I am an 'I') am never dead. Heidegger might at first seem diametrically opposed to this, maintaining as he does that life is what it is only because we are marked by death at every moment – hence why the defining characteristic of the human being, for him, is mortality – but there nonetheless remains in Heidegger's thought a strict disassociation between the 'I' and its corpse. The preposition 'towards' betrays a distinct and impermeable (and temporal) separation between being and non-being, and so there is no relation to death *as such* in this supposed ownmost death that is mine-every-time.

On this Derrida offers a counterpoint, noting that, perhaps:

> contrary to what Heidegger says, we did remain beasts [i.e. not mortal humans] who do not have the power to die, to whom death as such never appears, dying remaining, as Blanchot often complains, impossible, alas. No, insists Heidegger, you have to become mortal. But at bottom, is this not pretty much the same thing? Living death beyond life, live to death, living death, etc. This is perhaps the same circle. (*BSII*, 124)

It seems Blanchot is the one to turn to when one tries to imagine a non- or beyond-mortal, when one tries to parse the difference between mortality and finitude, and to understand the condition of the condemned human as the 'what' which is already dead, where self and death collide and yet where there remains absent the immortal being-present of the 'towards' once death is already in the past. It is Blanchot who, in Derrida's words, 'never ceased dwelling in these places that are uninhabitable for thought', whether it be the 'question of the impossible and of the possibility of the impossible, or [. . .] the fictional, even literary space that accepts the living of death, becoming living dead' (*BSII*, 180). And indeed this is why the literary fiction of the death penalty, starting from Blanchot's own, has here been read beyond the more typical discussions around condemnation.

This includes discussion from within psychoanalysis (which maintains at heart a belief in subjectivity) despite its seeming importance in coming to understand ourselves as our own corpses. Freud, as Derrida comments, would suggest 'that the relation to our death is not representable, and that each time we try to represent our own deaths to ourselves, we continue to be there as spectators, observers, voyeurs' (*BSII*, 157).[3] It is my hope that this work has convincingly demonstrated how literary works can evoke or conjure the unexperienced experience of death at the moment of condemnation as more than a mere '*impression*' or psychosomatic '*feeling* of posthumousness', as, for instance, Ebury understands it; it is not merely 'the criminal's *sense* of themselves as a living being [which is] radically reduced',[4] or what Morisi sees as the symbolic death of 'a threatened psyche' trapped within 'premortem carceral existence'.[5] The literary works here studied reveal, at the very moment sovereignty reaches its apotheosis in the death penalty, not psychological destruction but the end of the condemned human's ontological self and its banishment from the onto-political structure.

Antigone, Pablo Ibbieta, Cincinnatus and all the unnameable rest have allowed us to traverse the quasi-conceptual path Blanchot has opened, beyond even Derrida, who – despite thinking through ipseity via hauntology, the *mort-vivant*, the unexperienced experience, the *tout autre*, the deconstruction of the borders of death, and so on – ultimately upholds the dividing wall and deposes the 'I' without properly annulling its gift of death. Blanchot's work allows us to look not only beyond the fundamental definition of the human as mortal but also, intricately woven with this, the dominating sovereignty of its Dasein. Looking through to the other side, looking at the human otherwise, there is indeed here figured a relation to death *as such*.

When one finds oneself a dead man walking, condemned to death by the sovereign power that obliges and subjects because it protects, there is a simultaneous interruption – an in(de)finite, in(de)terminable suspension made most evident through the social event of dying in-stead – of the human as 'ontological subject' (i.e. 'mortal being') as well as 'political subject' (i.e. 'subject being'). Such interruption brings with it a time of limbo, of abeyance, between the onto-political experience of death (banishment) and proper, bodily death. We observe, therefore, a death that is lived, one which characterizes the living corpse as that which survives without surviving, that lives on as a 'laggard shadow' in 'that second, that syncope', in 'the pause, the hiatus, when the heart is like a feather', with an 'extraordinary lightness' or 'abeyance'. This silence is what Heidegger's ontology speaks over.

In the instantaneous meeting of being and non-being, it cannot be said that the living corpse is both 'being' and 'non-being', for that would be the magical Hegelian 'life that endures death and maintains itself in it', or the Heideggerian relation to death *as such* that somehow nonetheless permits us to participate in the presence of the present (his overcoming of metaphysics). If we are not to put death to death – that is, if we are to acknowledge the sovereignty of death beyond any other kind of sovereignty (of the mortal *ipsissimus*, of political being which is headed and beheaded by the sovereign) – then we must see this living corpose, thanatopolitically, as that which is *neither* being *nor* non-being. This is the impossible beyond of ontological thought in which, as Derrida rightly says, Blanchot dwells. Indeed, Blanchot's thought endlessly and in diverse ways circles the question, much heavier than any feather, of what it is 'to be without being'.

This is why I have here examined the Blanchovian Neuter through diverse literary figures who all inhabit the uninhabitable, that is, the topographical yet unmappable spaces of the *chora*, *il y a*, *neutrality* and *whatever being*, each of which keeps as banished the anonymous existence of the neither/nor that populates their placelessness. The word 'populates', crucially, reminds us how the neutral is not the singular (and nor the plural). While the erasure of ontological selfhood necessarily also dissolves the figure of the (ethical) Other – for if Levinas says there is no One without the Other, the facelessness of death reveals there can be no Other without the One – there remains the sociality of the Third that interrupts the dialectical closure of sovereign and condemned, Lord and Bondsman, face to face – and thus reveals a death penalty that spills beyond both its enactment as a judicial punishment and the confines of the self, emerging as the foundation of human society. The limbo seemingly reserved for death row escapes its cells, cue the communal and social necropolis that is politically otherwise and elsewhere, a being-without-polis that is not actively apolitical but which, rather, passively and indifferently, *dwells* and *decomposes*. My study thus provides further elucidation of Bradley's view that 'this state of exception outside of life and death becomes the laboratory in which [...] a new politics is struggling to be born'.[6] Here, then, is the differently politicized human that speaks neither politically nor apolitically through a resistance, the name of which is death.

And yet in death, as evidenced by my decision to now speak in the first person – despite my upholding of the extermination of the 'I' – there remains ... something, and this something speaks on. Here termed the human thing, this is what is '[n]either generic nor individual, neither an image of the divinity nor an animal form' – and so not reducible to the figure of the animal that is also the sovereign, not at the threshold of law and lawlessness but its interruption. This is an assembly of self in death one may characterize but not define, one which must always be left as the example (as whatever) and never the exemplary (as self). As

Derrida argues in *The Beast and the Sovereign* seminars, following what Blanchot wrote around a decade earlier, this is the unidentifiable nature of 'what'.

> 'What,' the 'what': one can call that the thing, the *res,* or the nothing [*rien*] of the thing, a thing that is not someone, neither a subject nor a self, nor a consciousness, nor a human being, nor a *Dasein*, the thing that does not think, does not speak and does nothing, the thing that remains silent [*coite*], if you want to play on this homonym whereby the *quoi* remains *coi* (c.o.i.), i.e. mute and immobile, a tranquil force, and *coite, coite* meaning not *coitus* [*coït*] but coming from *quietus*, which means 'at rest, tranquil, impassive'. (BSI, 199)

It is notable that Derrida here emphasizes 'the becoming-thing of the person' as something 'tranquil' (even if the thing, in truth, is always unbecoming rather than becoming, and, as we have seen, does indeed speak and resist 'in the name of death') (*BSI*, 199). It recalls the notion of equipollence as popularized through Sextus Empiricus's *Outlines of Scepticism*, whereby '[t]he sceptical persuasion' suspends all judgements between oppositions and leads one 'afterwards to tranquillity'.[7] This '[s]uspension of judgement is a standstill of the intellect, owing to which we neither reject nor posit anything', and where '[b]y "opposed accounts" we do not necessarily have in mind affirmation and negation'[8] – and this, indeed, is the realm of the neither/nor, of being without being, where (as Kamuf clarifies) '[t]his "without" between the repetitions does not signal a cancelation; [. . .] but has instead the effect of *suspending* the positing force of language'.[9] This suspension, impassivity or lack of the tragic is the indifference of the community of the human thing, which neither affirms nor negates – but rather tranquilly resists affirming and negating – both human Dasein and what some, like Agamben, would consider its essential and inalienable political mode.[10]

'Such is the last ambiguity', Blanchot writes: 'it vanishes if it awakens; it perishes if it comes to light'; the condition of the fragmentary and unidentifiable human thing 'is to be *buried alive,* and in that it is indeed its own symbol, symbolized by what it symbolizes: death that is life, that is death as soon as it survives'.[11] Blanchot here writes, in 'The Language of Fiction', specifically with Kafka in mind, whose 'heroes are engaged in an intermediate moment between life and death', wandering through 'the strange condition of the dead who do not die' where '[t]he passage from yes to no, from no to yes, is the rule'.[12]

Blanchot does not mention Kafka's 'In the Penal Colony', but it inevitably comes to mind when speaking of fiction and the relational death of condemnation. In the short story, a soldier is 'condemned to death for disobedience and insulting behaviour to a superior', except that, despite being in chains and watched over by another soldier, he does not know he has been condemned.¹³ He '"has had no chance of putting up a defense"' and is to be executed with a complex and ingenuous apparatus the shape of which itself '"corresponds to the human form"' and which is to write the accusing sentence upon the condemned's body with sharp and calligraphic needles.¹⁴ The diplomat who is made to witness the execution is told by the presiding officer that the killing takes around twelve hours, midway through which the condemned's face will reveal, as has always happened, a visible 'enlightenment', 'transfiguration' and 'radiance'.¹⁵ Yet the visitor – whose views are held in high esteem by the colony's commandant – makes it known to the officer that he thinks 'the inhumanity of the execution [is] undeniable', and the latter, in despair at the knowledge that his commander will use this testimony to destroy his beloved machine, frees the condemned and takes his place.¹⁶ He is, in fact, seeking the enlightenment he has seen granted only to the condemned, but the machine, old and dilapidated, breaks down, not writing anything with its needles but only repeatedly jabbing, jabbing, and the officer lies dead.

If there were time, it would be fruitful to read this story through the ontological ramifications of the death penalty as explored in my study: the fact that the sentence of condemnation comes only after the state of condemnation itself; our inability to escape our sentence or actively defend against it; the machinery of the death penalty itself having the form of the human, for it is the most human thing; the death machine being itself condemned to death; the beatitude of the condemned's face, bathed in what Blanchot would describe as 'extraordinary lightness'; the unnamed soldier who accompanies the protagonists as the third, or even the fourth; the twelve-hour execution, when one is very much living death; the dying in-stead, where death is taken and not given and where the one who condemns is also condemned; the inhumanity revealed beyond the human being.¹⁷

What I wish to focus on here, however, is how Kafka figures the act of writing and its ties to death, which above all leads us here to reflect on a certain impossibility of understanding. Kafka's diplomat, being shown a draft or manuscript of the sentence to be corporeally inscribed, can only see an unreadable 'labyrinth of lines crossing and recrossing each other'.¹⁸ Despite the promise of elegant though lethal narration, the machine manages only to jab and kill, not write. In the end, there was not, for anyone involved, any 'promised redemption'.¹⁹

This hearkens back to an almost throwaway remark I made in the last chapter on the impossibility of *poiesis*, of producing either the narrative that autothanatography paradoxically maintains or else the 'I' that lives it. Here, with Kafka's story, comes a reading that presents the unreadable, both in drafted plans and in its execution (in both senses). Kafka's fabular story, then, focuses not on the work of literature but rather the constant unworking of the literary – that which unworks the literary and what the literary itself unworks. What is unworked is the human. The death sentence is illegible, only a murmur or a rustle, as fragmented and unproductive as the multiple disconnected and irregular jabs on the officer's corpse.

Here, then, is what I call the thanatoliterary, a literature that escapes all narrative and provides us only with an epilogue we cannot read: a human neither here nor there, neither with the living nor with the dead, neither being nor non-being. We are thus 'no more than nothing'. It is inevitable that at the heart of the thanatoliterary is death, for that is where all readings end to then begin. Literature thus delivers the non-sentence: the relational death and the condition of the human thing. This of course can have other names too: queer being, for instance, or posthuman being in some of its most literal senses, or else the Unnameable, or Degree Zero. Ultimately, I have here read the literature of the death penalty as that which reveals the human being as itself a fiction.

Notes

Introduction

1 Our knowledge of this ritual in one such culture, that of the ancient Assyrians, is severely limited: the surviving fragments are few relative to the extent of the original writings, their legibility is considerably deteriorated, and one is hindered by the inadequate or general lack of decipherments of the cuneiform tablets. As such, there is no commentary on this ritual that is considered canonical or finalized beyond other interpretations, although Simo Parpola's translations and commentaries are currently considered the most authoritative and Jean Bottéro's work the most frequently cited. Texts that look at specific variations depending on the region or period have not been consulted. See, in particular: Preston Kavanagh and Simo Parpola, *Ezekiel to Jesus: Son of Man to Suffering Servant* (Eugene: Wipf & Stock, 2017), specifically 'The Assyrian Substitute King Ritual' and 'Letters from Assyrian Scholars', 59–103; Jean Bottéro, *Mesopotamia: Writing, Reasoning, and the Gods*, trans. by Zainab Bahrani and Marc Van De Mieroop (London and Chicago: University of Chicago Press, 1992), specifically 'The Substitute King and His Fate', 138–55; M. Rahim Shayegan, *Aspects of History and Epic in Ancient Iran: From Gaumāta to Wahnām* (Washington: Center for Hellenic Studies, 2012), specifically 'The Concepts and Reality of the Substitute King in Mesopotamia and Iran', 35–42; W. G. Lambert, 'A Part of the Ritual for the Substitute King', *Archiv für Orientforschung* 18 (1957–1958): 109–12; John H. Walton, 'The Imagery of the Substitute King Ritual in Isaiah's Fourth Servant Song', *Journal of Biblical Literature* 122, no. 4 (2003): 734–43 (736–8); and Lorenzo Verderame, 'Means of Substitution: The Use of Figurines, Animals, and Human Beings as Substitutes in Assyrian Rituals', *Rivista degli Studi Orientali* 86, Supplemento no. 2 (2013): 300–23 (317–21).

2 Bottéro, *Mesopotamia*, 150. Italics as in original. Henceforth, all quotations will reproduce the italicization of the original unless otherwise stated. Italics added by the author will be acknowledged in the corresponding note.

3 Jacques Derrida would agree that thinkers such as Lacan, Althusser, Foucault, Freud, Marx, Nietzsche and Heidegger 'never [managed] to "liquidate" the subject', and to be added to this list are others such as Hegel, Levinas and Derrida himself. See Jacques Derrida and Jean-Luc Nancy, '"Eating Well", or the Calculation of the

Subject: An Interview with Jacques Derrida', trans. by Peter Connor and Avital Ronnell, in *Who Comes After The Subject?*, ed. by Eduardo Cadava, Peter Connor and Jean-Luc Nancy (New York and London: Routledge, 1991), 97.

4   See Bottéro, *Mesopotamia*, specifically 'Writing and Dialectics, or the Progress of Knowledge', 87–102.

5   Achille Mbembe, 'Necropolitics', trans. by Libby Meintjes, *Public Culture* 15, no. 1 (2003): 27, 11. Mbembe has developed this work further; see Achille Mbembe, *Necropolitics*, trans. by Steven Corcoran (Durham and London: Duke University Press, 2019).

6   Ibid., 13.

7   'Sovereign is he who decides on the exception.' Carl Schmitt, *Political Theology: Four Chapters on the Concept of Sovereignty*, trans. by George Schwab (London and Chicago: University of Chicago Press, 1985), 5. Though it might seem so in the ancient Assyrian context, it is here being argued that is never anachronistic to talk of the state of exception.

8   Bottéro, *Meosopotamia*, 155.

9   Michel Foucault, 'Right of Death and Power over Life', in *The History of Sexuality*, vol. 1, trans. by Robert Hurley (New York: Pantheon Books, 1990), 140.

10 Michel Foucault, *Society Must Be Defended: Lectures at the Collège de France, 1975–1976*, trans. by David Macey, ed. by Mauro Bertani and Alessandro Fontana (London and New York: Allen Lane, The Penguin Press, 2003), 240.

11 For an explanation of *patria potestas*, see Foucault, 'Right of Death and Power over Life', 135.

12 Foucault, *Society Must Be Defended*, 240.

13 Mbembe, 'Necropolitics', 39.

14 Foucault, 'Right of Death and Power over Life', 136–7. 'Positive' here is not to be equated with 'beneficial'; rather, it is used in opposition to the negation of life through death and killing. One can easily administer this line of thought to the handling of the Covid pandemic, though some nation states provide alternative viewpoints.

15 Foucault, *Society Must Be Defended*, 241.

16 Ibid., 246.

17 As Marina Gržinić and Šefik Tatlić concisely summarize: 'Mbembe claims that the concept of biopolitics, due to the war machine and the state of exception being one of the major logics of contemporary capitalist societies, should be replaced with necropolitics.' Marina Gržinić and Šefik Tatlić, *Necropolitics, Racialization, and Global Capitalism: Historicization of Biopolitics and Forensics of Politics, Art, and Life* (Lanham: Lexington Books, 2014), 24.

18 Ibid., 241.

19 Mbembe, 'Necropolitics', 12.

20 Tracy B. Strong, 'Foreword', in Schmitt, *Political Theology*, xxiv.
21 Carl Schmitt, 'The Age of Neutralizations and Depoliticizations', trans. by Matthias Konzen and John P. McCormick, in *The Concept of the Political – Expanded Edition*, trans. by George Schwab (London and Chicago: The University of Chicago Press, 2007), 90, 95.
22 Strong, 'Foreword', xxvii.
23 George Schwab, 'Introduction', in Schmitt, *Political Theology*, xxxviii.
24 Ibid., xlii–xliii.
25 Ibid.
26 Schmitt, *Political Theology*, 13.
27 Achille Mbembe, *On The Postcolony* (Berkely: University of California Press, 2001), 13. The introduction from which this quote is taken was translated by A. M. Berrett.
28 Mbembe, 'Necropolitics', 14. It should here be noted that this is not necessarily or exclusively contradictory of Foucault's ideas, but 'Necropolitics' in effect acts out a thinking through of the sweeping formulations of biopolitics. Mbembe is, therefore, here understood as Timothy Campbell and Adam Sitze's ideal reader. See Timothy Campbell and Adam Sitze, 'Introduction', in *Biopolitics – A Reader*, ed. by Timothy Campell and Adam Sitze (Durham and London: Duke University Press, 2013), 7.
29 Foucault, *Society Must Be Defended*, 248.
30 Mbembe, 'Necropolitics', 15, 16.
31 Ibid., 12. See Carl von Clausewitz, *On War*, ed. by Howard Michael and Peter Paret (Princeton: Princeton University Press, 1984), 87: 'War is the continuation of politics by other means.'
32 Mbembe, 'Necropolitics', 15, 40.
33 Georges Bataille, *The Accursed Share: An Essay on General Economy*, vols2 and 3, trans. by Robert Hurley (New York: Zone Books, 1991), 222.
34 Implicit in this discussion is, of course, the idea of the king's two bodies, the *politic* and the *natural*. See Ernst H. Kantorowicz, *The King's Two Bodies: A Study in Mediaeval Political Theology* (Princeton: Princeton University Press, 1985).
35 Foucault, *Society Must Be Defended*, 248.
36 Stuart J. Murray, 'Thanatopolitics: Reading in Agamben a Rejoinder to Biopolitical Life', *Communication and Critical/Cultural Studies* 5, no. 2 (2008): 205.
37 Ibid., 204.
38 Stuart J. Murray, 'Thanatopolitics: On the Use of Death for Mobilizing Political Life', *Polygraph* 18 (2006): 193.
39 Achille Mbembe, 'On The Postcolony: A Brief Response to Critics', *African Identities* 4, no. 2 (2006): 155, as quoted in Murray, 'Thanatopolitics: On the Use of Death for Mobilizing Political Life', 195.
40 Murray, 'Thanatopolitics: On the Use of Death for Mobilizing Political Life', 208.

41 The only linguistic difference between the two is that the former conjoins 'politics' with a Latinized version of the Greek *nekros*, meaning 'dead body, corpse, dead person', whereas the latter conjoins it with a Latinized version of the Greek *thanatos*, meaning 'death'. Thus, the former emphasizes a particular corporeality, whereas the latter stresses the more generalized state of being dead. See *Chambers Dictionary of Etymology*, ed. by Robert K. Barnhart (Edinburgh: Chambers, 1988), 698, 1130.

42 Murray, 'Thanatopolitics: On the Use of Death for Mobilizing Political Life', 202.

43 Foucault, *Society Must Be Defended*, 240.

44 Murray, 'Thanatopolitics: On the Use of Death for Mobilizing Political Life', 199.

45 Arthur Bradley, *Unbearable Life: A Genealogy of Political Erasure* (New York: Columbia University Press, 2019), 11. Bradley traces Foucault's point on the sovereign gift of life/death back to Rousseau and Hobbes.

46 Ibid., 4.

47 Foucault, *Society Must Be Defended*, 247.

48 Bradley, *Unbearable Life*, 40.

49 See Plato, *The Republic of Plato*, ed. and trans. by Francis MacDonald Cornford (London: Oxford University Press, 1945). See especially 'Part V (Book X, 595A-608B). The Quarrel between Philosophy and Poetry', 321–40.

50 Plato, *The Dialogues of Plato*, vol. 1, 4th edn, ed. and trans. by B. Jowett (Oxford: Clarendon Press, 1953), 435, as quoted in *GD*, 14.

51 Emphasis added.

52 Simon Critchley, 'Preface to the Second Edition', in *Very Little . . . Almost Nothing: Death, Philosophy, Literature*, 2nd edn (Oxon and New York: Routledge, 2004), xvii.

53 Joanna Baillie, 'Introductory Discourse', in *A Series of Plays: In Which It Is Attempted to Delineate the Stronger Passions of the Mind. . .*, 3rd edn (London: T. Cadell, Jun. & W. Davies, 1800), 5.

54 Emphasis added. Importantly, Blanchot forwards this question when contemplating the Terror. For further commentary on this point, see David Wills, *Killing Times: The Temporal Technology of the Death Penalty* (New York: Fordham University Press, 2019), 132–41.

55 As in Levinas's description of the *il y a*, discussed later. See *EE*, 53.

56 Emmanuel Levinas, 'Time and the Other', in *Time and the Other, and Additional Essays*, trans. by Richard A. Cohen (Pittsburgh: Duquesne University Press, 2011), 72. See Richard A. Cohen, *Levinasian Meditations: Ethics, Philosophy, and Religion* (Pittsburgh: Duquesne University Press, 2010), 151.

57 In the interest of properly interrogating the issues at hand, we shall have to put aside these other aspects of the death penalty, despite their propinquity, and discuss them only briefly and intermittently when necessary. There is of course no singular work that fully deals with all these issues; however, works that touch on several of them are referenced here. Derrida's *Death Penalty* seminars, which

will be discussed from the second chapter on, provide ample exploration of most of these aspects and conjoin them with a wealth of bibliographical resources. For a vast interrogation of non-literary public discourse on crime and the death penalty, as well as for an analysis of the impact of particular American novels on their sociopolitical milieu and the concurrent development of psychiatry and criminology, see David Guest, *Sentenced to Death: The American Novel and Capital Punishment* (Jackson: University Press of Mississippi, 1997). For a similarly comprehensive view of the historical development of the American death penalty, as well as how novels and other literary forms influenced the laws and societies around it, see John Cyril Barton, *Literary Executions: Capital Punishment and American Culture, 1820–1925* (Baltimore: John Hopkins University Press, 2014). For deeper insight into the physical and psychological conditions on death row, one may turn to, for instance: *Into the Abyss: A Tale of Death, a Tale of Life*, dir. by Werner Herzog (IFC Films, 2011) as well as this same director's miniseries *On Death Row* (Channel 4, 2012–13), and Michael Johnson, 'Fifteen Years and Death: Double Jeopardy, Multiple Punishments, and Extended Stays on Death Row', *Boston University Public Interest Law Journal* 23, no. 1 (2014): 85–116. For a reading of the medical determination of death in line with this project's own views, one might read *HS*, 160–5.

58 Geoffrey Adelsberg, 'U.S. Racism and Derrida's Theologico-Political Sovereignty', in *Death and Other Penalties: Philosophy in a Time of Mass Incarceration*, ed. by Geoffrey Adelsberg, Lisa Guenther and Scott Zeman (New York: Fordham University Press, 2015), 84, 93.

59 Mbembe overtly recognizes the reality of racism within the context of sovereign othering and enmity; following Hannah Arendt, he underscores the fact that the 'politics of race is ultimately linked to the politics of death' (Mbembe, 'Necropolitics', 17). Foucault may also be read as anticipating the thanatopolitical reading of biopolitics later undertaken by Mbembe and Agamben (as the former to a degree acknowledges) through his concept of 'modern racism' – essentially, 'the break between what must live and what must die', a form of state eugenics under the umbrella of social Darwinism that is epitomized by Nazi Germany (Foucault, *Society Must Be Defended*, 254). According to Foucault, racism allows biopolitics to function in letting the other must die so as to allow the state to live – and live better – thereby extending the reach of biopower into death, apart from life. Thus, 'racism alone can justify the murderous function of the State' (256). See Bradley, *Unbearable Life*, 34–5. See also Kim Su Rasmussen, 'Foucault's Genealogy of Racism', *Theory, Culture & Society* 28, no. 5 (2011): 34–51.

60 Stephanie M. Straub, 'Introduction. From Capital Punishment to Abolitionism: Deconstructing the Death Penalty', in *Deconstructing the Death Penalty: Derrida's Seminars and the New Abolitionism*, ed. by Kelly Oliver and Stephanie M. Straub

(New York: Fordham University Press, 2018), 8. On this issue of the death penalty and race, see also Sarah Tyson, 'The Heart of the Other?', and Lisa Guenther, 'An Abolitionism Worthy of the Name: From the Death Penalty to the Prison Industrial Context', both in *Deconstructing the Death Penalty*. Additionally, see: (i) Angela Y. Davis, *Abolition Democracy: Beyond Empire, Prisons, and Torture* (New York: Seven Stories Press, 2005); (ii) Adelsberg, Guenther and Zeman, eds., *Death and Other Penalties*, especially 'Part I: Legacies of Slavery', 13–74; (iii) Katherine Ebury, *Modern Literature and the Death Penalty, 1890–1950* (London: Palgrave Macmillan, 2021), 197–222; and (iv) Wills, *Killing Times*, 150–67.

61 Victor Hugo, 'Preface', in *LD*, 4.
62 Ève Morisi, *Capital Letters: Hugo, Baudelaire, Camus, and the Death Penalty* (Evanston: Northwestern University Press, 2020), 27.
63 Peggy Kamuf, *Literature and the Remains of the Death Penalty* (New York: Fordham University Press, 2019), 125.
64 Straub, 'Introduction', 4. 'Beginning with Literature', the first chapter of Kamuf's book as referenced in the following endnote, is also published as the first chapter in Oliver and Straub, eds., *Deconstructing the Death Penalty*, 13–31.
65 Kamuf, *Literature and the Remains of the Death Penalty*, 25. Writing in particular of *The Executioner's Song*, Kamuf makes the deconstructionist point that this power of fictional writing is there even in supposedly non-fictional accounts of the death penalty (97).
66 Ibid., 28.
67 Morisi, *Capital Letters*, 54.
68 Ebury, *Modern Literature and the Death Penalty*, 14.
69 Ève Morisi, 'Introduction: Capital Literature', in *Death Sentences: Literature and State Killing*, ed. by Birte Christ and Ève Morisi (Cambridge: Legenda, 2019), 4.
70 Bradley, *Unbearable Life*, 1–2.
71 *The Tragedy of Hamlet, Prince of Denmark*, ed. by Burton Raffel (New Haven and London: Yale University Press, 2003), I.1.3.

Chapter 1

1 This same episode is also recounted, albeit much more briefly and ambiguously, in Blanchot's much earlier *La Folie du Jour*: 'I was made to stand against the wall like many others. Why? For no reason. The guns did not go off. I said to myself, God, what are you doing? [. . .] The world hesitated, then regained its equilibrium'. Maurice Blanchot, *The Madness of the Day*, trans. by Lydia Davis (Barrytown: Station Hill Press, 1981), 6.

2. Epicurus, 'Letter to Monoceus', as quoted in Giovanni Reale, *A History of Ancient Philosophy III: Systems of the Hellenistic Age*, ed. and trans. by John R. Catan (Albany: SUNY Press, 1985), 173.
3. Michael Dillon and Paul Fletcher, 'Real Time: The Instant of My Death', *Journal for Cultural Research* 12, no. 4 (2008): 397.
4. Ibid.
5. Their joint publication in the *Meridian: Crossing Aesthetics* series evidences this close relation. For further information on the publication of *The Instant of My Death*, see also note 8 in this chapter.
6. Ginette Michaud, 'Literature in Secret: Crossing Derrida and Blanchot', trans. by Pamela Lipson, Patrick Poirier and Roger Starling, *Angelaki* 7, no. 2 (2002): 76, 69.
7. For further details of Blanchot and Derrida's first meeting, see Benoît Peeters, 'A Period of Withdrawal: 1968', in *Derrida: A Biography*, trans. by Andrew Brown (Cambridge and Maiden: Polity Press, 2013), 186–206. Derrida comments most directly on his friendship with Blanchot upon the latter's death: see *BSII*, 175–6.
8. Following problems between Blanchot and publishers Fata Morgana, presumably because of its laconic length, Derrida quotes *The Instant of My Death* 'in extenso' so as to 'free Blanchot from the burden of his contractual restraints'; thus, Derrida 'discreetly "passes" Blanchot's text to Galilée, sheltering him within the text of *Demeure*'. Michaud, 'Literature in Secret', 70.
9. Michaud, 'Literature in Secret', 71.
10. "Supplementary" here consciously recalls Derrida's double-edged concept as that which is both 'a plenitude enriching another plenitude', that is, that which 'cumulates and accumulates presence' while being itself 'quite ex[-]orbitant in every sense of the word', as well as that which 'intervenes or insinuates itself', that is, that which is 'alien', 'acting through the hands of others'. Jacques Derrida, *Of Grammatology*, trans. by Gayatri Chakravorti Spivak (Baltimore and London: John Hopkins University Press, 1997), 144–5, 163, 147. For the development of this concept more generally, see 'Part II: Nature, Culture, Writing', in *Of Grammatology*, 95–316.
11. On 22 December 1849, Dostoevsky was one of the subjects of a mock execution by firing squad, also deferred only at the last moment as a political move on the part of Tsar Nicholas I. For further details, see Nancy Ruttenburg, '"Why is this man alive?": The Unconsummated Conversion', in *Dostoevsky's Democracy* (Princeton: Princeton University Press), 31–41.
12. Blanchot himself writes about the impossible non-experience of when 'one' experiences the disaster which makes that same 'one' disappear. See Maurice Blanchot, *The Writing of the Disaster*, trans. by Ann Smock (Lincoln and London: University of Nebraska Press, 1992), 110.

13 Susan Bainbrigge, 'Introduction', *Forum for Modern Language Studies* 41, no. 4 (2005): 359, 363–4.
14 Emphasis added.
15 Ebury, *Modern Literature and the Death Penalty*, 71.
16 This statement shall be examined more thoroughly in the second chapter in light of the distinction, made by Derrida around six years after *Demeure*, between 'condemned to die' and 'condemned to death'. While it is true that death is inevitable for all individuals, the case of the death sentence is markedly singular.
17 One is immediately reminded of that stanza from 'The Tollund Man': 'The scattered, ambushed | Flesh of labourers, | Stockinged corpses | Laid out in the farmyards', and of note is that the namesake of the poem was himself a victim of execution, hanged by a braided leather rope. Seamus Heaney, 'The Tollund Man', in *Opened Ground – Poems 1966–1996* (London: Faber & Faber, 1998), 64–5 (65).
18 Rei Terada, 'Review', *SubStance* 30, no. 3 (2001): 132. It should here be noted that Terada is of the opinion that 'some of the explication [in *Demeure*] lacks energy, at least in comparison with Derrida's literary reading in the sixties and seventies', a comment that is not really substantiated and is unlikely given *Demeure*'s exhaustive relation to the narrative (134).
19 Jungah Kim, 'Ethical Complexities in Reading and Writing Autobiography: Thinking the Humanity of Others in the Instant of My Death', *Life Writing* 9, no. 1 (2012): 106.
20 Christopher Fynsk, 'Compassion for Suffering Humanity: *The Instant of My Death*', in *Last Steps – Maurice Blanchot's Exilic Writing* (New York: Fordham University Press, 2013), 110.
21 Ibid., 117.
22 Ibid., 111.
23 Cf. Bainbrigge, 'Introduction', 361: 'alterity in autobiography recurs as a key theme, with death and the other often featuring as the "unknowns"'. As such, the whole idea of 'autothanatography' might need re-examination, as shall be done in the last chapter.
24 'If it were done when 'tis done, then 'twere well | It were done quickly. If th' *assassination* | Could trammel up the consequence, and catch | With his surcease success'. *Macbeth*, ed. by Burton Raffel (New Haven and London: Yale University Press, 2005), I.7.1-4. Emphasis added.
25 'Haile brave friend; | Say to the king, the knowledge of the Broyle, | As thou didst leave it'. *Macbeth*, I.2.23-25. Of course, counter-balancing this, one cannot forget that it is nonetheless in Duncan's name that the war is fought in the first place, or the fact that the character is based on the less-than-virtuous, and certainly not innocent, historical figure of King Duncan in Raphael Holinshed's *Chronicles of England, Scotland, and Ireland*.

26 While Macbeth shall be referred to later on, one must be mindful, however, of 'placing Shakespeare in the space of Blanchot' when 'Blanchot himself seems to resist doing this', seeing as how there is a marked lack of engagement between Shakespeare and Blanchot, where, in the latter's oeuvre, Shakespeare only 'appears a handful of times as a name' and, even then, his characters are given priority over their author. See Mario Aquilina, '"Everything and Nothing": Shakespeare in Blanchot', *Word and Text* 5, no. 1–2 (2015): 95.
27 Kamuf, *Literature and the Remains of the Death Penalty*, 41–2.
28 The problems of the French Revolution, so close to this discussion, will be brought into the discussion in the third chapter.
29 Fynsk does acknowledge that, in the narrative, there is evidenced 'the collapse of any conceptual and social walls between [the protagonist] and "suffering humanity"'. Fynsk, 'Compassion for Suffering Humanity', 111.
30 Does not the '"Bois des buyères"' – 'Heath Woods' (my translation) – point almost irreverently at the heath upon which the witches appear to Macbeth? 'Upon this blasted Heath you stop our way'. *Macbeth*, I.3.177.
31 *The Compact Edition of the Oxford English Dictionary*, vol. 1 (Oxford: Clarendon Press, 1971), 5. Emphasis added. It is of note that Rottenberg translates '*en instance*' as abeyance, bringing to light the idea of vacancy or suspension implicit in Blanchot's phrase.
32 Queen Gertrude tells Hamlet that he 'know'st 'tis common; all that lives must die, | Passing through nature to eternity', to which he replies: 'Ay, madam, it is common'. *Hamlet*, I.2.72-4.
33 See, for instance, Kavanagh and Parpola, *Ezekiel to Jesus*, 64, and Verderame, 'Means of Substitution', 316. Bottéro writes of only one particular king who 'was called *the farmer*', and this 'perhaps in opposition to *the shepherd*, which was a common royal epithet in ancient Mesopotamia'. Bottéro, *Mesopotamia*, 149.
34 Walton, 'The Imagery of the Substitute King Ritual', 737. With some exceptions, the substitute was generally 'a prisoner of war, a prisoner, a criminal condemned to death, a political enemy of the king, a gardener or a simpleton' – in short, 'a person whose life did not matter much or who would have deserved death anyway'. Kavanagh and Parpola, *Ezekiel to Jesus*, 64.
35 Bottéro, *Mesopotamia*, 147.
36 Aside from what Derrida writes in 'Living On', survival is here also read in the same manner Derrida reads it decades later in *BSII*, 130–2.
37 Jacques Derrida, 'Living On', trans. by James Hulbert, in Harold Bloom, Paul de Man, et al., *Deconstruction and Criticism* (New York: The Seabury Press, 1979), 108.
38 Ibid., 135.
39 While this discussion limits itself quite restrictively, much more can be derived should one bring in the cultural and literary resonances of the 'revenant' in all its

manifestations, extending even to the zombie, ghost and vampire figurations, in both oriental and occidental cultures. One could also easily read theological or religious interpretations into this continuation of life after death and its not-quite-synonym of 'afterlife'. For more on the supernatural elements of the revenant, see Ebury, *Modern Literature and the Death Penalty*, 64–70.

40 Dillon and Fletcher, 'Real Time', 395.
41 The word shares its etymology with 'rupture', from the Latin '*rupta* [which] came to mean (1) a defeat, flying mass of broken troops; (2) a fragment of an army, a troop; (3) a way broken or cut through a forest' – all three meanings are incorporated into Blanchot's narrative. Walter W. Skeat, *The Concise Etymological Dictionary of the English Language* (London: Clarendon Press, 1887), 409–10.
42 Dillon and Fletcher, 'Real Time', 400.
43 Ibid., 401.
44 In his notes to *Aporias*, Dutoit writes that *arrivant* 'can mean "arrival", "newcomer", or "arriving"' (*AP*, 86).
45 Emphasis added.
46 Emmanuel Levinas, *Otherwise Than Being, or Beyond Essence*, trans. by Alphonso Lingis (Pittsburgh: Duquesne University Press, 2011), 191, n. 2, as quoted in Jacques Derrida, *Adieu to Emmanuel Levinas*, trans. by Pascale-Anne Brault and Michael Naas (Stanford: Stanford University Press, 1999), 30.
47 Derrida, *Adieu*, 29, 31.
48 In a long, academic and correspondence-based friendship which lasted until their death, Blanchot was to Levinas 'always the friend, the unique and brotherly interlocutor'. Michaël Levinas and Sarah Hammerschlag, 'The Final Meeting between Emmanuel Levinas and Maurice Blanchot', *Critical Inquiry* 36, no. 4 (2010): 650. See also Emmanuel Levinas, 'On Maurice Blanchot', in *Proper Names*, trans. by Michael B. Smith (Stanford: Stanford University Press, 1996), 127–70.
49 Cf. Derrida, speaking of the multiple passions: '"Passion" implies finitude [. . .] but also a certain passivity in the heteronomic relation to the law and to the other' (*D*, 26).

Chapter 2

1 Paul Muldoon's *Horse Latitudes*, for instance, was written '"as the US embarked on its foray into Iraq"', meditating '"a series of battles [. . .] in which horses or mules played a major role"'. James Fenton, 'A Poke in the Eye with a Poem', *The Guardian*, 21 October 2006, para. 2, accessed 2 July 2022, https://www.theguardian.com/books/2006/oct/21/featuresreviews.guardianreview6. See Paul Muldoon, *Horse Latitudes* (London: Faber & Faber Ltd., 2006).

2   *Macbeth*, II.4.18.
3   Friedrich Nietzsche, 'The Birth of Tragedy', in *The Birth of Tragedy and Other Writings*, ed. by Raymond Guess and Ronald Speirs, trans. by Ronald Speirs (Cambridge: Cambridge University Press, 2007), 23. The original quote is taken from a fragment of Aristotle's *Eudemos*. A horse was, after all, the omen that saw Nietzsche to his grave.
4   Mark A. Marinella, 'On the Hippocratic Facies', *Journal of Clinical Oncology* 26, no. 21 (2008): 3638–40.
5   From '*hippos*' and '*kratiá*'. See *Chambers*, 483, 230.
6   Cary Wolfe, 'Introduction', in *Zoontologies: The Question of the Animal*, ed. by Cary Wolfe (Minneapolis and London: Minnesota University Press, 2003), xi. For more on the blurring of the human/animal divide in view of the death penalty, see (i) Nicole Anderson, 'A Proper Death: Penalties, Animals, and the Law', in *Deconstructing the Death Penalty*, 159–74, and (ii) Ebury, *Modern Literature and the Death Penalty*, 117–39.
7   Indeed, if one can even encapsulate the human as a 'political animal', the implications of which shall be progressively troubled across this and the upcoming chapters, especially through Agamben. Aristotle, *The Politics*, trans. by T. A. Sinclair (London and New York: Penguin Books, 1992), 60. Cf. *HS*, 2–3, where Agamben explicitly comments on this particular Aristotelian phrase, as well as *BSI*, 315–34 and 343–9, where Derrida comments on both Aristotle's phrase as well as Agamben's and Heidegger's interpretations of it.
8   For more on animal substitution (though horses in particular are not mentioned, likely because of their esteemed position in the historical context to which they belonged), see Verderame, 'Means of Substitution', 313–17.
9   As defined under 'acorn' in Francis Grose, *1811 Dictionary of the Vulgar Tongue: A Dictionary of Buckish Slang, University Wit, and Pickpocket Eloquence*, 1811, http://www.gutenberg.org/cache/epub/5402/pg5402-images.html. However, the phrase has been in use at least since John Ray's *A Collection of English Proverbs*, published in 1678, and has since also been adapted, with the same meaning, into such phrases as 'the wooden horse' and 'the timber mare'. For more details, see Pascal Tréguer, '"A Horse That Was Foaled Of An Acorn": Meaning and Origin', in *Word Histories*, 5 October 2016, https://wordhistories.net/2016/10/05/horse-foaled-of-an-acorn/.
10 Immanuel Kant, *Anthropology from a Pragmatic Point of View*, ed. and trans. by Robert B. Lauden (Cambridge: Cambridge University Press, 2006), 15.
11 Elsewhere, in surprising terms, Kant writes that man is 'completely above the animal *society*'. Immanuel Kant, 'Conjectures on the Beginning of Human History', in *An Answer to the Question: What is Enlightenment?*, trans. by H. B. Nisbet (London and New York: Penguin Books, 2009), 94. Emphasis added.

This and the above quotation, conjoined with several instances of seeming self-contradiction in what Kant writes about the animal, leads to several problems on the issue of animals' exclusion from the Categorical Imperative as well as their moral treatment. See, for instance, J. Skidmore, 'Duties to Animals: The Failure of Kant's Moral Theory', *Journal of Value Inquiry* 35, no. 4 (2001): 541–59. See also the discussion between Alexander Broadie, Elizabeth M. Pybus and Tom Regan: Broadie and Pybus, 'Kant's Treatment of Animals', *Philosophy* 41, no. 190 (1974): 375–83, and Regan, 'Broadie and Pybus on Kant', *Philosophy* 51, no. 198 (1976): 471–2 (and their rejoinder to Regan in 1978, 'Kant's Maltreatment of Animals', with the same journal). For a reworded reassertion of the above distinction Kant draws between man and animal, see Immanuel Kant, *Groundwork of the Metaphysics of Morals*, ed. and trans. by Mary Gregor (Cambridge: Cambridge University Press, 2006), 37.

12 Although Kant never dwells too long on the clarification of this distinction, it is in one instance made lucid when he writes of how these aspects of man need to be 'contradistinguished' as explained earlier. See Immanuel Kant, *The Metaphysic of Ethics*, trans. by J. W. Semple (Edinburgh: T. & T. Clark, 1836), 204.

13 Immanuel Kant, *Lectures on Ethics*, ed. by Peter Heath and J. B. Schneewind, trans. by Peter Heath (Cambridge: Cambridge University Press, 1997), 147. Emphasis added. Of course, although other commentators have not really addressed this, this seems to directly contradict both the analogies Kant sees between man and animal as well as the indirect duties Kant tries to outline using this same example of the dog and the horse: 'Even gratitude for the long service of an old horse or dog (just as if they were members of the household) belongs *indirectly* to man's duties *with regard to* these animals; considered as a direct duty, however, it is always only a duty of man *to* himself'. Immanuel Kant, *The Metaphysics of Morals*, trans. by Mary Gregor (Cambridge: Cambridge University Press, 1991), 238.

14 Kant, *Lectures on Ethics*, 127.

15 Kant, *The Metaphysics of Morals*, 144. This is why Derrida says, with not much conviction: 'Execution is sui-cide. For the autonomy of juridical reason there is only auto-execution' (*DPII*, 67).

16 Ibid., 143, 237.

17 Arthur Schopenhauer, *The World as Will and Idea*, vol. 3, trans. by R. B. Haldane and J. Kemp (London: Routledge and Kegan Paul, 1957), 413. Schopenhauer's notion of 'bestiality' comes very close and shall be briefly returned to later. In terms of the relativistic devaluation of a select few to some status below 'the rational/political human', an affinity can be identified with Peter Singer, who claims that not all human beings can be considered persons, as well as neoliberalism's focus on the so-called inhumanity of the enemy. See, for instance, Peter Singer, *Practical Ethics* (Cambridge: Cambridge University Press, 2011).

18 Here one sees, too, 'the Cartesian mind-body dualism that haunts Kant's philosophy'. Cohen, *Levinasian Meditations*, 23.
19 Attila Ataner, 'Kant on Capital Punishment and Suicide', *Kant Studien* 97, no. 4 (2006): 472, 470.
20 This point is reiterated several times, and the Kantian logic interrogated more deeply, in *DPII*, 37–43, 84–102.
21 See *Chambers*, 142.
22 There are other closely related conversations of equal importance but which must be reserved for elsewhere. See, for instance, Michel Foucault, *Discipline and Punish: The Birth of the Prison*, trans. by Alan Sheridan (New York: Vintage Books, 1995).
23 Epictetus, 'On "Indifference"', in *Discourses and Selected Writings*, ed. and trans. by Robert Dobbin (London: Penguin Books, 2008), 91.
24 Emphasis added.
25 See Ippolit's letter in *TI*, in particular 350–7.
26 Janet Price and Ruth Gould, 'Experience and Performance whilst Living with Disability and Dying: Disability Art as a Pathway to Flourishing', in *On the Feminist Philosophy of Gillian Howie: Materialism and Mortality*, ed. by Victoria Browne and Daniel Whistler (London and New York: Bloomsbury Academic, 2016), 268. For a deeper look at the philosophical relation of terminal illness with the idea of 'my death', see the entire volume from which the above quotation was taken. It is important to note here, with Derrida, that this 'limit between *condemning to death* and *condemning to die* is not always airtight', and neither is the distinction 'between *letting die* and *making die*' (*DPII*, 198). One clear example of this is the *fatwa*, especially in its differing treatment as *part of the law* and as *apart from the law*; specifically, one can mention Ayatollah Khomeini's 1989 *fatwa* ordering the death of Salman Rushdie for his *Satanic Verses* as putting such distinctions into question. See *DPII*, 197.
27 Cf. *HS*, 32: 'the sovereign is the point of indistinction between violence and law, the threshold on which violence passes over into law and law passes over into violence'.
28 Harrold Tarrant, 'Justice and Duty (II): Socrates in Prison – Introduction to *Crito*', in Plato, *The Last Days of Socrates: Euthyphro, Apology, Crito, Phaedo*, trans. by Hugh Tredennick and Harrold Tarrant (London: Penguin Books, 1993), 73.
29 Emphasis added.
30 Walter Benjamin, 'Critique of Violence', in *Reflections: Essays, Aphorisms, Autobiographical Writings*, trans. by Edmund Jephcott, ed. by Peter Demetz (New York: Schocken Books, 1986), 286.
31 Kant, *The Metaphysics of Morals*, 168. Derrida quotes this repeatedly in his seminars on the penalty.

32 Derrida also makes this point in the chapter 'Death Penalties', in Jacques Derrida and Elisabeth Roudinesco, *For What Tomorrow . . . A Dialogue*, trans. by Jeff Fort (Stanford: Stanford University Press, 2004), 139–65.
33 Adeslberg, 'U.S. Racism and Derrida's Theologico-Political Sovereignty', 84–5.
34 Ibid., 89. Adelsberg thus calls not for 'opposition to all sovereign decision over life and death' but rather for 'abstinence from the death penalty as punishment', wherein one 'is limited to questioning the death penalty as practice rather than death penalty as sovereign capacity to decide' (87, 89).
35 Christina Howells, 'The Death Penalty and Its Exceptions', in *Deconstructing the Death Penalty*, 88–9. Kamuf takes this one step further: 'If one has a concept of death, it is because the death penalty is inscribed within it' (*Literature and the Remains of the Death Penalty*, 120).
36 Should one like to keep law at the forefront of these concerns, then one could perhaps bring in the very relevant *jus accrescendi* (right of survivorship) and *jus tertii* (the law of the third as applicable in disputes over possession). See *A Dictionary of Law*, 8th edn, ed. by Jonathan Law (Oxford: Oxford University Press, 2015), 234–5.
37 Barton, *Literary Executions*, 253.
38 Kamuf, *Literature and the Remains of the Death Penalty*, 88.
39 As cited from the precursory prose version of the poem. John Donne, 'Meditation 17', in *Devotions Upon Emergent Occasions Together with Death's Duell*, ed. by John Sparrow (Cambridge: Cambridge University Press, 1923), 98.
40 Timothy Clark, *Martin Heidegger* (London and New York: Routledge, 2011), 12, 15.
41 From 'Der Ackermann aus Böhmen'. See 'Author's Notes', in *BT*, 494. When relevant, Heidegger's original German terms will be provided in text in square brackets. This is in acknowledgement of most translators of Heidegger's work who recognize the difficulty, or indeed impossibility, of an 'accurate' translation of his neologistic and at times even colloquial use of the German language. Original page numbers, chapters and sections will not be provided in text, as the edition of *Being and Time* used here offers rigorous clarity in and of itself. See John Macquarrie and Edward Robinson, 'Translators' Preface', in *BT*, xxiii–xxvi. Most of the quotations in this chapter are taken from the introductory and first chapters of 'Division Two: Dasein and Temporality', 45–53, 274–311.
42 Martin Heidegger, *Gesamtausgabe: Reden und andere Zeugnisse eines Lebenswegs*, vol. 19 (Frankfurt am Main: Klostermann, 2000), 605, as quoted in George Pattison, *Heidegger on Death: A Critical Theological Essay* (Surry: Ashgate Publishing Ltd., 2013), 147.
43 Pattison, *Heidegger on Death*, 130, 7. Cf. Jacques Derrida, 'Faith and Knowledge: The Two Sources of "Religion" at the Limits of Reason Alone', trans. by Samuel

Weber, in *Acts of Religion*, ed. by Gil Anidjar (New York and London: Routledge, 2002), 51, 94–8.
44 Emphasis added.
45 Cf. Derrida: 'the identity of the oneself is *given* by death' (*GD*, 45).
46 This same sentiment is uttered, word for word, by Van in Vladimir Nabokov, *Ada or Ardor: A Family Chronicle* (New York: McGraw-Hill, 1969), 164. Heidegger himself repeats this throughout his works. Perhaps closest to this formulation, in a 1935 lecture course, he says: 'Insofar as humans *are*, they stand in the no-exit of death'. Martin Heidegger, *Introduction to Metaphysics*, trans. by Gregory Fried and Richard Polt (New Haven and London: Yale University Press, 2000), 169. The translators note how Heidegger recommended these lectures, in the preface to the seventh edition of *Being and Time* (1953), to those seeking further elucidations of its ideas.
47 Ovid, 'The Story of Narcissus', in *Metamorphoses*, trans. by Sir Samuel Garth, John Dryden, et al., stanza 5, accessed 2 July 2022, http://classics.mit.edu/Ovid/metam.3.third.html. 'Book 3' was translated by Joseph Addison in 1727.
48 Ibid., stanza 2.
49 Ibid., stanza 3.
50 Ibid., stanza 6.
51 Ibid., stanza 5.
52 Ibid., stanza 5.
53 Ovid, 'Narcissus', in *Metamorphoses*, ed. and trans. by Charles Martin (New York and London: Norton, 2009), 77–80, lns. 607–8.
54 Ovid, 'The Story of Narcissus', stanza 5. On this spatiality of possession and selfhood, the original Latin is very revealing: 'o utinam a nostro secedere corpore possem', where Narcissus speaks of himself in the plural: 'our' body.
55 Ibid., stanza 7.
56 Ovid, 'Narcissus', lns. 649–50.
57 From the Greek Στύξ. *Oxford English Dictionary*, ed. by Catherine Soanes and Angus Stevenson (Oxford: Oxford University Press, 2006), 1757.
58 Ovid, 'The Story of Narcissus', stanza 3.
59 In the fourth chapter, this view shall be further reinforced through Levinas (mainly), who, as Colin Davis explains, believes that 'sociality in Heidegger is found in the subject alone' (Colin Davis, *Levinas: An Introduction* (Cambridge: Polity Press, 1996), 30). It is where, in Levinas's words, Being seems 'an imprisonment' leading to 'the need to leave oneself behind, that is, *to break the most radical, the most irremissible bond, the fact that the I is itself*' (Emmanuel Levinas, *De l'évasion* (Montpellier: Fata Morgana, 1982), 73, as quoted in and translated by Davis, *Levinas*, 18). Levinas's intersubjectivity may be appositely described as the purposeful antithesis of Heideggerian Narcissism: in the language

of Ecclesiastes, 'the opposite of vanity, [. . .] of the vanity of vanities' (Emmanuel Levinas, 'Dying For . . .', in Emmanuel Levinas, *Entre Nous*, trans. by Michael B. Smith and Barbara Harshav (New York: Columbia University Press, 1998), 216). This kind of critique of self-enclosed or self-referential Being is made frequently, even if not on this particular basis of death. One of the earliest of Heidegger's critics, Martin Buber, attacks the solitude of Dasein from several fronts, stating (in very relevant terms) how 'Heidegger's "existence" is monological' and that '[i]t is not my existence which calls to me, but the being which is not I' (Martin Buber, 'What is Man', in *Between Man and Man*, trans. by Ronald Gregor-Smith (London and New York: Routledge, 2004), 199, 197).

60 Derrida comments on 'the strange and stupefying and shocking fact that never, but never, it turns out, has any philosophical discourse as such, in the system of its properly philosophical argument, opposed the principle, I repeat, the principle, of the death penalty' (*DPII*, 2). Derrida also makes this identical point in *What For Tomorrow . . . A Dialogue*, 146.

61 See Blanchot, *The Madness of the Day*, and Maurice Blanchot, *Death Sentence*, trans. by Lydia Davis (Barrytown: Station Hill, 1978). One could also here add Malraux, mentioned by name in *ID*. See, in particular, André Malraux, *Lazarus*, trans. by Terence Kilmartin (New York: Grove Press, 1978). The original title of the latter of Blanchot's works, *L'Arrêt de Mort* – which can also be translated to the 'stopping', 'suspension', 'rupture' or 'interruption' of death – makes sense of why Blanchot looks at terminal illness rather than the death penalty, refusing to draw the conceptual line between 'condemned to die' and 'condemned to death'.

62 Cf. Gil Anidjar, 'Introduction – "Once More, Once More": Derrida, The Arab, The Jew', in Derrida, *Acts of Religion*, 2: 'Derrida has been seen as performing *acts of religion*, as enacting a return to his own "religious" origins, though within the constraints of a necessarily complicated reappropriation'. The miracle, as a central concept of deconstruction, and its ties with the exception (as central to Schmitt's *political theology*) will be mentioned once more in Chapter 4.

63 This is made clear even in Derrida's disagreement with Levinas's critique of Heidegger's prioritization of the death of the self over that of the other (see *AP*, 38–9). See also Derrida's non-problematization of the impossibility of dying in-stead (*AP*, 25–6).

64 See *GD*, 41–5.

65 The translation of Levinas is here Derrida's own. The emphasis on 'be' in the quotation from *GD* is added here.

66 Stefano Cochetti, 'The Lethal Narcissus: Heidegger on Sacrifice/Sacrifice on Heidegger', *Contagion: Journal of Violence, Mimesis, and Culture* 4 (1997): 93–4.

67 Ibid., 93, 96.

68 Cochetti, 'The Lethal Narcissus', 91–2. Cf. Derrida on victims of war in relation to Heidegger's idea of death (*GD*, 86–7).

69 Alison Stone, 'Natality and Mortality: Rethinking Death with Cavarero', *Continental Philosophy Review* 43, no. 3 (2010): 357, 354.
70 Ibid., 358, 361–2.
71 Ibid., 363.
72 Ibid., 364. The fear of one's death is, then, a fear of the end of a relation to the other-in-me.
73 Alison Stone, 'The Relationality of Death', in *On the Feminist Philosophy of Gillian Howie*, 166. It is worth noting here that Gillian Howie, who is the focus of the collection, finds this idea to be an asymmetrical one: while the death of others occurs in my life, my death does not, and cannot, take place in mine; essentially, this is a Heideggerian rejoinder. It is important to note that Stone's argument nonetheless bears some similarities to what Heidegger himself said of mourning, previously quoted (see *BT*, 282).
74 Stone, 'Natality and Mortality', 355, 370.
75 As he points out: 'In *Being and Time* there is little acknowledgement of the "lived-body" (Leib) that prereflectively negotiates its way through the world', and this to the degree of flaw. Kevin A. Aho, *Heidegger's Neglect of the Body* (Albany: SUNY Press, 2009), 2.
76 Stone, 'Natality and Mortality', 369.
77 Cf. 'I posthume as I breathe'. Jacques Derrida, 'Circumfession', trans. by Geoffrey Bennington, in Jacques Derrida and Geoffrey Bennington, *Circumfession/Derridabase* (Chicago and London: The University of Chicago Press, 1999), 26.
78 Stone, 'Natality and Mortality', 363–4.
79 Stone concludes, however, that 'nothing of [the other] can survive', and that we 'exist less the more we are bereaved'. Ibid., 366–7.
80 Donne, 'Meditation 17', 99, as quoted in Pattison, *Heidegger on Death*, 111. This same quotation is also used, for identical purposes, in Stone's 'The Relationality of Death', 167.
81 Pattison, *Heidegger on Death*, 108. Pattison previously writes, in the second chapter, of the links between Heidegger and Kant, Fichte, Hegel, and Kierkegaard, especially on the basis of the 'I'.
82 Ibid., 113.
83 Ibid.
84 Ibid., 116.
85 Ibid.
86 Ibid., 104, 145. This, of course, is tied in by Pattison with the thoughts of Kierkegaard and Levinas. Among many other poems, one strongly echoed here is one by Thomas Campbell, where we read that '[t]o live in the hearts of those we leave behind | Is not to die'. Thomas Campbell, 'Hallowed Ground', in *The Complete Poetical Works of Thomas Campbell*, ed. by J. Logie Robertson (London: Oxford University Press, 1907), lines 35–6.

87 Cf. *BT*, 282–3.
88 Jacques Derrida, 'Foreword: *Fors*: The Anglish Words of Nicolas Abraham and Maria Torok', trans. by Barbara Johnson, in Nicolas Abraham and Maria Torok, *The Wolf Man's Magic Word: A Cryptonomy*, trans. by Nicholas Rand (Minneapolis: University of Minnesota Press, 1986), xvi. Although Torok maintains a strict topographical division between 'incorporation' and 'introjection', Derrida does make it a point to state that 'the purity of such a disassociation remains in fact only a theoretical ideal' (xviii). It is only between self and other that '[t]he dividing wall is *real*' (xix). Derrida would later also say: 'Nothing is stronger than love, save death' (*BSI*, 210).
89 Derrida, 'Foreword: *Fors*', xvii.
90 Jacques Derrida, *Memoires for Paul de Man*, revised edn, trans. by Cecile Lindsay, Jonathan Culler, Eduardo Cadava and Peggy Kamuf (New York: Columbia University Press, 1989), 35. Cf. *BSII*, 121, 126–7, 169.
91 Derrida, 'Foreword: *Fors*', xvii, xlv, xxii.
92 Derrida, in his notes to 'Foreword: *Fors*', 119.
93 Stone, 'Natality and Mortality', 362.
94 This would possibly be an apt place to venture into antinatalist philosophy, which returns us chiefly but not solely to Schopenhauer, whose preference for non-Being is most evident in *The World as Will and Representation*. See also, for instance, E. M. Cioran, *The Trouble with Being Born*, trans. by Richard Howard (New York: Arcade Publishing, 2012), and, for a wider conception of this strand of philosophy, see the excellent work of David Benatar, *Better Never To Have Been: The Harm of Coming into Existence* (Oxford and New York: Oxford University Press, 2006).
95 Judith Butler, *Precarious Life: The Powers of Mourning and Violence* (London and New York: Verso, 2004), 22.
96 Ibid., 23.
97 Derrida, 'Foreword: *Fors*', xviii.
98 This term appears very rarely, although even then in very close proximity to this work's concerns: (i) in the context of theology, as in the as of yet untranslated 1937 work by Wilhelm Traugott Hahn, 'Das Mitsterben und Mitauferstehen mit Christus bei Paulus: Ein Beitrag zum Problem der Gleichzeitigkeit des Christen mit Christus' ['Dying and Resurrecting with Christ in [St] Paul: A Contribution to the Problem of *Simultaneity* for the Christian with Christ'] (my translation and emphasis); (ii) the term also resurges as the title of a 2003 documentary film produced by Heike Bittner (which appears to have been unpopular) following people who care for children with terminal illness. For (i) Hahn, see: https://ia600502.us.archive.org/0/items/MN41529ucmf_0/MN41529ucmf_0.pdf; for (ii) Bittner, see: http://www.cinema.de/film/mitsterben,1320904.html.

99 Leo Tolstoy, 'The Death of Ivan Ilyich', in *The Death of Ivan Ilyich and Other Stories*, trans. by Alymer Maude and J. D. Duff (New York: Signet Classic, 2003), 129. Ultimately, Tolstoy too can be read as thinking through the idea of the relational death, as strongly evidenced by the final scenes of another of his short stories. See also Leo Tolstoy, 'Master and Man', in *The Death of Ivan Ilyich*, especially 274–87. Tolstoy was 'a fervent opponent of the death penalty, and who wrote against the death penalty' (*DPII*, 247).

100 Pattison, *Heidegger on Death*, 68. For more and even biographical detail around Heidegger's (non-)relation to Dostoevsky, see Pattison, *Heidegger on Death*, 65–79.

101 Emphasis added except for the last instance.

102 By this term is meant something entirely different to Levinas's similar rephrasing of Heidegger's words into 'the impossibility of possibility'; Levinas, as shall be discussed later on, understands death as transcending all possible human experience. See Levinas, 'Time and the Other', 70, footnote.

103 See Mikhail Bakhtin, *Problems of Dostoevsky's Poetics*, ed. and trans. by Caryl Emerson (Minneapolis and London: Minnesota University Press, 1999). Barton's *Literary Executions* consciously employs Bakhtinian theory as a way of interrogating its own texts, adopting 'a Bakhtinian approach to the novel, short fiction, and popular discourse concerning capital punishment that strives to show the polyphony in what is frequently considered the monologic authority of (the) law' (8).

104 Pattison, *Heidegger on Death*, 77.

105 1 Cor. 15.54-55.

Chapter 3

1 Martin Heidegger, *The Fundamental Concepts of Metaphysics: World, Finitude, Solitude*, trans. by William McNeil and Nicholas Walker (Bloomington and Indianapolis. Indiana University Press, 1995), 93. It must immediately be noted that Heidegger distinguishes between three kinds of boredom. For an insightful reading of these three types, see Eran Dorfman, 'Everyday Life between Boredom and Fatigue', in *Boredom Studies Reader: Frameworks and Perspectives*, ed. by Michael E. Gardiner and Julian Jason Haladyn (London and New York: Routledge, 2017), especially 185–9, and Derrida's comments on Heidegger's boredom in *BSII*, 70–2. For a contextualization of Heidegger's mood of boredom more generally across philosophy and the arts, see Lars Svendson, *A Philosophy of Boredom*, trans. by John Irons (London: Reaktion Books, 2008), especially 'The Phenomenology of Boredom', 107–32.

2 Heidegger, *Fundamental Concepts*, 93.
3 Maurice Blanchot, *Awaiting Oblivion*, trans. by John Gregg (Lincoln: University of Nebraska Press, 1997), 27.
4 William McNeil and Nicholas Walker, 'Translators' Foreword', in *Fundamental Concepts*, xix–xx.
5 Heidegger, *Fundamental Concepts*, 94.
6 Ibid., 87.
7 Ibid., 82.
8 Ibid., 100.
9 Ibid., 152. Emphasis added.
10 Dorfman makes a good argument for the breaking of this particular dichotomy against the context of Heideggerian boredom (180–3).
11 See *Chambers*, 1062. It would be beneficial, here and throughout this study, to keep in mind Agamben's understanding of 'stasis' and its relation to the *oikos* and the *polis*. See Giorgio Agamben, *Stasis: Civil War as a Political Paradigm*, trans. by Nicholas Heron (Stanford: Stanford University Press, 2015).
12 Heidegger, *Fundamental Concepts*, 103.
13 Ibid., 105.
14 Although this is claimed in a completely different context, a certain complementarity to this present discussion may still be read, not least in terms of the *hetero-* prefix of 'heterotopia': 'a train is an extraordinary bundle of relations because it is something through which one goes'. Michel Foucault, 'Of Other Spaces: Utopias and Heterotopias', trans. by Jay Miskoviec, *Architecture/Mouvement/Continuité* 5 (1984): 3.
15 Wills, *Killing Time*, 99–100. A discussion of Hegel follows both in this book and in *Killing Time* – however, in the latter, the focus is on blood, whereas here the focus shall be on the death penalty's interruption of historical progress.
16 Heidegger, *Fundamental Concepts*, 80.
17 Kelly Oliver, 'Making Death a Penalty: Or, Making "Good" Death a "Good" Penalty', in *Death and Other Penalties*, 102.
18 Ebury, *Modern Literature and the Death Penalty*, 73.
19 Julian Jason Haladyn and Michael E. Gardiner, 'Momentous Splendour: An Introduction to Boredom Studies', in *Boredom Studies*, 9.
20 Heidegger, *Fundamental Concepts*, 103.
21 This idea of being buried alive also implicates, of course, the idea of surviving, of living one's death, and this is at length analysed by Derrida, although with slightly differing emphasis, in terms of Daniel Defoe's *Robinson Crusoe*. See especially *BSII*, 127–39.
22 Cf. 'biopolitics is at least as old as the sovereign exception' (*HS*, 6).
23 Critchley writes that '[t]he key term in Lacan's extraordinary reading of *Antigone* is ἄτη [*até*], which he renders as transgression'. Simon Critchley, 'Das

Ding: Lacan and Levinas', *Research in Phenomenology* 28 (1998): 77. With its multifarious resonances in different oeuvres and discourses, varied even in the interpretations of the thinkers discussed here and later, transgression is here understood as that which demands the political decision on the state of exception through the death penalty (and not, for instance, as crimes to be punished by incarceration) and which in turn leads to the transgression of autonomous, solitary subjectivity. The close relation of incarceration and condemnation, however, is not unremarkable.

24 Jacques Lacan, *The Ethics of Psychoanalysis, 1959-1960*, ed. by Jacques-Allain Miller, trans. by Dennis Porter (New York: W.W. Norton & Company, 1992), 269. Critics are often quick to assume that Antigone committed suicide without Haemon's assistance, a fact that remains unascertainable.
25 Paul Allen Miller, 'Lacan's Antigone: The Sublime Object and the Ethics of Interpretation', *Phoenix* 61, no. 1–2 (2007): 1.
26 Lacan, *The Ethics of Psychoanalysis*, 248.
27 Ibid., 247, 254.
28 Ibid., 258, 267.
29 Ibid., 270, 280. Cf. Miller, 'Lacan's Antigone', 2: 'Beauty for Lacan represents the perfect moment between life and death'.
30 Lacan, *The Ethics of Psychoanalysis*, 280.
31 Judith Butler, *Antigone's Claim: Kinship Between Life and Death* (New York: Columbia University Press, 2000), 44, 23. Although such quotes make it seem pertinent to further discuss Butler's ideas in relation to *Antigone*, her central themes are only tangential here: the relationship between kinship and state, language, gender and resistance. Butler views Antigone's life as 'a living death' (23) more in relation to the issues of kinship, incest and the unliveable life rather than in terms of the death penalty, which remains surprisingly undiscussed in Butler's monograph despite being the central mechanism within the drama.
32 Lacan, *The Ethics of Psychoanalysis*, 263.
33 G. W. F. Hegel, *Aesthetics: Lectures on Fine Art*, vol. 1, trans. by T. M. Knox (Oxford: Oxford University Press, 1975), 464.
34 Patricia Jagentowicz Mills, 'Hegel's Antigone', in *The Phenomenology of Spirit Reader*, ed. by Jon Stewart (Albany: State University of New York Press, 1998), 243. It is on the lines of this quote that Hegel sees a transcendence of death (along with other readers of Hegel and *Antigone*, such as Lacan and Butler). Through burial, mourning and ethical family relations (even, or especially, with those dead), humanity continues to move towards the Spirit.
35 Cf. 'That is the position of heroes in world history generally; through them a new world dawns. [. . .] [T]he heroes appear, therefore, as violent, transgressing laws. Individually, they are vanquished; but this principle persists, if in a different form, and buries the present': as translated by Mark William Roche in *Tragedy*

and Comedy: A Systematic Study and Critique of Hegel (Albany: State University of New York Press, 1998), 53, from G. W. F. Hegel, *Vorlesungen über die Geschichte der Philosophie I*, volume 18 in the Suhrkamp Taschenbuch Wissenschaft (Berlin: Suhrkamp Verlag, 1986), 515.

36 The *PS* sections under discussion here are 'IV. The Truth of Self-Certainty, Introduction', and 'A. Independence and Dependence of Self-Consciousness: Lordship and Bondage', 104–18.

37 Kojève will here be significantly foregrounded for two reasons. The first is that he dedicates much more time to the significations of death in the Lord–Bondsman dialectic than Hegel himself does, which is of most relevance here. For some, like Agata Bielik-Robson, this is a distortive emphasis that amounts to a 'thanatic' or 'cryptotheological' reading to be remedied by interpretations such as that of Franz Rosenzweig (see Agata Bielik-Robson, 'The Thanatic Strain. Kojève and Rosenzweig as Two Readers of Hegel', *Journal for Cultural Research* 19, no. 3 (2015): 274–90). However, and this is the second reason, the main thinkers here engaged with (mainly those belonging to twentieth century French philosophy) very often, through reference, manner of interpretation and ideas, make it clear that it was Kojève, and not Hegel, who played a shaping and even determinative role in their writings. For more on Kojève's influence – apart from Bielik-Robson (specifically 278–81) – see also, for instance: Christoph Kletzer, 'Alexandre Kojève's Hegelianism and the Formation of Europe', in *Cambridge Yearbook of European Legal Studies, Vol. 8, 2005–2006*, ed. by John Bell and Claire Kilpatrick (Oxford: Hart Publishing, 2006), 133–51. Given that Kojève's death-centric interpretation has influenced the thinkers engaged with here, it is with his interpretation one must engage in order to understand the questions at hand. It is, however, important to note that other differences between Kojève and Hegel are not to be understated, particularly Kojève's valorization of the figure of the master.

38 Emphasis added.

39 Butler, *Precarious Life*, 36.

40 On "ill-fittingness", cf.: 'What tragedy depicts is one *dikē* in conflict with another, a law that is not fixed, but rather shifting and changing into its opposite'. Jean-Pierre Vernant, 'The Historical Moment of Tragedy in Greece', in Jean-Pierre Vernant and Pierre Nidal-Naquet, *Myth and Tragedy in Ancient Greece* (Cambridge: Zone Books, 1990), 26.

41 Here Kantorowicz is speaking of Shakespeare's *Richard II*. He goes on: 'The king that "never dies" here has been replaced by the king that always dies and suffers death more cruelly than other mortals. Gone is the oneness of the body natural with the immortal body politic, "this double Body, to which no Body is equal" [. . .]. Gone also is the fiction of royal prerogatives of any kind, and all that

remains is the feeble human nature of a king'. Kantorowicz, *The King's Two Bodies*, 30.

42 Adelsberg, 'U.S. Racism and Derrida's Theological-Political Sovereignty', 84.
43 Implicated in this point is the idea of "the great criminal", a figure Benjamin sketched in 'Critique of Violence' and which Derrida discusses (see especially *DPII*, 45–7): 'the one condemned to death', Derrida states, is 'an absolute, almost sovereign power' (*DPII*, 46). The concept of (political, rather than legislative) pardon is also both related and fecund.
44 Jean Hyppolite, *Genesis and Structure of Hegel's 'Phenomenology of Spirit'*, trans. S. Cherniak and J. Heckman (Evanston: Northwestern University Press, 1974), 172.
45 Bradley, *Unbearable Life*, 44.
46 A fuller examination of this statement shall be proffered nearer the end of this chapter and in the next.
47 Butler, *Antigone's Claim*, 2. Cf. *An Introduction to Metaphysics*, 152, where Heidegger defines the *polis* as 'the foundation and scene of man's being-there [. . .] wherein and as which historical being-there is'.
48 Bradley, *Unbearable Life*, 18–19. Bradley is here citing Jean-Luc Nancy, *The Truth of Democracy*, trans. Michael Naas and Pascale-Anne Brault (New York: Fordham University Press, 2010), 31.
49 Jean Paulhan, *The Flowers of Tarbes, or, Terror in Literature*, trans. by Michael Syrotinski (Urbana and Chicago: University of Illinois Press, 2006), 33.
50 Stathis Gourgouris, *Does Literature Think? Literature as Theory for an Antimythical Era* (Stanford: Stanford University Press, 2003), 133. Antigone thus truly occupies an 'immanent position in the task of thought' and 'sustains itself as philosophy's open wound' as long as 'she remains the community's question mark' (128–9, 132).
51 Richard Braun, *Antigone* (New York and Oxford: Oxford University Press, 1973), 7.
52 From *antagōnizesthai*. *Chambers*, 38.
53 On this point, see Alain Badiou, 'Hegel's Master and Slave', trans. by Frank Ruda, *Crisis and Critique*, no. 1 (2017), who is 'not persuaded that [*PS*] really deals with slavery' in historical terms (37).
54 Bradley, *Unbearable Life*, 120 (see also 134–7). Bradley's fifth chapter, from where this quote is taken, deals directly with the politics of the 'already dead' and the revolutionary resistance that this space offers. This shall be taken up in this book's fifth chapter.
55 Rebecca Comay, *Mourning Sickness: Hegel and the French Revolution* (Stanford: Stanford University Press, 2011), 72–4. Emphasis added. A further difference is that Comay holds with Foucault's notion that biopolitics emerges from the Revolution, where 'sovereign power relinquished its need to display itself everywhere' (51).

56 Cf. *BSI*, 138: 'The sovereign is the one who is at the head, the chief, the king, the capital, the first, the *arkhē* of commencement or commandment, the prince, but also the one whose head can spin, who can lose his head, in madness or decapitation. And lose, along with his head, meaning'.
57 Comay, *Mourning Sickness*, 73, 76, 90.
58 Warren J. Lane and Ann M. Lane, 'The Politics of *Antigone*', in *Greek Tragedy and Political Theory*, ed. by J. Peter Euben (Berkeley: University of California Press, 1986), 163. The authors link Antigone's fate to the state of woman in Ancient Greece: she 'symbolizes the ultimate oppressive situation of women at Athens, and her actual fate is emblematic of the effect of such a situation: death in life' (182).
59 Moreover, see Elissa Marder, 'Figures of Interest: The Widow, the Telephone, and the Time of Death', in *Deconstructing the Death Penalty*, 175–85, for a relevant discussion of the feminization of the guillotine and the feminine in the death sentence more generally.
60 Lane and Lane, 'The Politics of *Antigone*', 171.
61 Antigone can revolt from the space of the Greek polis (as opposed to from the French state) because, as Comay notes, 'untimeliness itself is an ineluctable condition of historical experience'. As such, '[t]here is no right time or "ripe" time for revolution' (and thus even the idea that revolution can come only as the fruit of labour is troubled); it is 'a matter of perpetual discontinuity and disjunction', and 'real terror predates the Terror'. Comay, *Mourning Sickness*, 7, 49, 40. This puts under erasure any distinction between antiquity and modernity.
62 Bradley, *Unbearable Life*, 136.
63 Luce Irigaray, *Speculum of the Other Woman*, trans. by Gillian C. Hill (Ithaca: Cornell University Press, 1985), 219. For her feminist reading of *Antigone*, see 216–20.
64 As quoted in Comay, Hegel in 1806 'salutes Napoleon as the "world soul on horseback"'. In Blanchot, the colour grey appears to serve a symbolic function, and could connote the collapsed borders of life and death, since the colour 'is what you get when you mix white and black', where 'gray announces an impossible mourning for a revolution that did not occur as such' (Comay, *Mourning Sickness*, 138, 142–4). Of course, Kojève builds further on the paramount symbolic and revelatory importance of Napoleon to Hegel; see Alexandre Kojève, 'Hegel, Marx and Christianity', trans. by Hilail Gildin, *Interpretation* 1, no. 1 (1970): 21–42.
65 Lacan, *The Ethics of Psychoanalysis*, 263.
66 Jagentowicz Mills, 'Hegel's *Antigone*', 254.
67 Due to constrictions of space, and the fact that *The Third Man* does not incorporate the problematics of the death penalty, this novella will not be discussed. However, pertinent ideas – such as how the mystery pivots on whether Harry's death was *instantaneous*, how Harry "returns" from the dead, or the search for the figure of the third man – are more than complementary with this book's concerns. See

Graham Greene, 'The Third Man', in *The Third Man and The Fallen Idol* (London: Vintage, 2001), 13–120. Although *TM* was first published later (1985) than 'The Third Man', it was drafted during the 1940s: see Graham Greene, 'Introduction', in *TM*, 3–5. Of our present novel, Greene writes: 'I prefer it in many ways to *The Third Man*' ('Introduction', 4). Despite this, not much at all has been written about *TM* (with more attention devoted, instead, to *The Third Man*), much less about the ideas under discussion here. However, it would be beneficial to see, in particular, Stephen K. Land, *The Human Imperative: A Study of the Novels of Graham Greene* (New York: AMS Press, 2008).

68 Cf. farmer Roche's remark that Charlot is 'a bit like Chavel himself. It's the voice: the face of course is quite different' (*TM*, 97).

69 Richard Maxwell's 'Introduction' and appendices (ix–xxxiii, 391–447) to *TC* serve as an excellent overview of Dickens's personal relation to and literary influences around the Revolution, as well as its treatment in the novel. Maxwell traces Carton's substitution for Darnay, here discussed, as a plot twist derived from five main sources: (i) Dickens's previous work on Wilkie Collins's *The Frozen Deep* (1856; originally a stage production starring Collins and Dickens themselves); (ii) Watt Phillips's *The Dead Heart* (1857); (iii) a historical incident recounted in Thomas Carlyle's *French Revolution* (1837); (iv) Edward Bulwer-Lytton's *Zanoni* (1842); and, closest to the present discussion, (v) Alexandre Dumas's *Chevalier de la Maison-Rouge* (1845). See Maxwell, 'Introduction', xxv, and appendices, 431–40. There is obviously a wealth of other critical resources around this novel which the reader may refer to.

70 Andrew Sanders, *The Victorian Historical Novel* (London: MacMillan, 1978), 86, 92.

71 See *TC*, 231–3 for Foulon's execution (an actual historical figure), who pretended he was dead and died properly only on his third hanging. See *TC*, 288–9 for the description of the Carmagnole, where people danced 'a ferocious time that was like a gnashing of teeth in unison. [. . .]. No fight could have been half so terrible as this dance'. Furthermore, the fact that Dr Manette refers to his imprisonment as his 'living grave' raises the question of whether lifetime incarceration can be equated to a condemnation to death (*TC*, 344).

72 Emphasis added.

73 Emphasis added.

74 Maxwell, 'Introduction', ix, xii.

75 Georg Lukács, *The Historical Novel*, trans. by Hannah and Stanley Mitchell (Boston: Beacon Press, 1963), 243–4.

76 Libby Purves, 'Foreword', in *LD*, viii. Writing of *Les Misérables*, but in terms applicable also to *The Last Day of a Condemned Man* under discussion here, Maxwell writes that 'Hugo may have learned a little from Dickens, or at least been encouraged by his example' of writing *TC* ('Introduction', xxix).

77 Morisi, *Capital Letters*, 211–12.
78 The 1832 'Preface' (in *LD*, 3–24) makes Hugo's position on the death penalty starkly clear. In *DPI*, Derrida engages with this Preface, Hugo's public addresses, and his *Écrits sur la peine de mort*, but mentions the novella only in passing. For further context on *Last Day*, especially in terms of its influence on later death penalty narratives and its ties with the author's own abolitionist struggle, see Morisi, *Capital Letters*, 15–19. The two chapters that follow Morisi's preface to the first section engage Hugo's work through a close and astute reading of several of its aspects, including the poetic and linguistic elements employed by Hugo in the name of immediate affect.
79 This is, of course, one of Benjamin's main points in 'Critique of Violence'.
80 Emphasis added.
81 Emmanuel Levinas, *Totality and Infinity*, trans. by Alphonso Lingis (Pittsburgh: Duquesne University Press, 2012), 44.
82 Clothes were indeed highly important in the cultures surrounding the ritual, which 'were carefully crafted to relay messages about the identity of the sovereign'. For more on this, see Omar N'Shea, 'Dressed to Dazzle, Dressed to Kill: Staging Ashurbanipal in the Royal Hunt Reliefs from Nineveh', in *Fashioned Selves: Dress and Identity in Antiquity*, ed. by Megan Cifarelli (Oxford: Oxbow, 2019), 175–84.
83 Jean-Paul Sartre, *Being and Nothingness*, trans. by Hazel E. Barnes (Oxon: Routledge Classics, 2005), 565. It is important to keep in mind that Sartre sees the coat as insubstantial, only 'an outer shell' (415), whereas the literary texts above indicate something deeper than an extraneous and disposable layer.
84 Catherine Malabou, *The Future of Hegel: Plasticity, Temporality and Dialectic*, trans. by Lisabeth During (Oxon and New York: Routledge, 2005), 115.
85 Louis-Sébastien Mercier, *Tableau de Paris*, vol. 3, 295; as quoted by Maxwell, 297. It is unclear whether Maxwell offers his own translation. The original reads: 'Ce n'est pas mourir qui est terrible, c'est mourir le dernier'. See https://archive.org/stream/tableaudeparisv00mercgoog#page/n298/mode/2up. My translation.
86 E. M. Forster, *A Room With A View* (London: Penguin Books, 1990), 122. Henry David Thoreau offers similar thoughts in *Walden: A Fully Annotated Edition*, ed. by Jeffrey S. Cramer (New Haven and London: Yale University Press, 2004), 20–1.
87 Comay, *Mourning Sickness*, 82–4.
88 Heidegger, *Fundamental Concepts*, 125.
89 Malabou, *The Future of Hegel*, 3.
90 What should have been 'the dawn of a human freedom that recognizes no authority but itself', with its 'distinctive mark of Absolute Freedom' being 'the capacity to *begin anew*', fails in requiring its own destruction. David Ciavatta, 'The Event of Absolute Freedom: Hegel and the French Revolution and Its Calendar', *Philosophy and Social Criticism* 40, no. 6 (2014): 585, 590.

91 Georges Danton is assumed to have made the point that 'to guillotine' cannot be conjugated in the past – as paraphrased by Peter Brooks, 'Death in the First Person', *South Atlantic Quarterly* 107, no. 3 (2008): 534.
92 Malabou, *The Future of Hegel*, 20, 176.
93 Ibid., 191.
94 Ibid., 6.
95 Ibid., 188. On this latter moment, and here is once more the constant spectre of theology, the movements of the accidental Third, through Malabou's understanding of revolution and revelation, may even be likened to the unique and negational incarnation of God, 'the figure of pure event' and pure accident which happens in a 'moment', coming from an infinite time ahead of subjectivity (117).
96 Ibid., 103, 122.
97 Ibid., 122. Emphasis added.
98 Ibid., 34. See also 146.
99 Ibid., 5, 12.
100 Ibid., 13.
101 Ibid., 33.
102 Ibid., 31.
103 Ibid., 36, 38.
104 Ibid., 163.
105 Ibid., 81.
106 Ibid., 14. Cf. *PS*, 105.
107 Levinas, *Totality and Infinity*, 57.
108 Gourgouris, *Does Literature Think*, 146, 141.
109 Derrida repeatedly equates the two in his preface to Malabou's work: see Jacques Derrida, 'A Time for Farewells: Heidegger (read by) Hegel (read by) Malabou', trans. by Joseph D. Cohen, in Malabou, *The Future of Hegel*, vii–xlvii (especially x–xi, xxvi–xxvii). He asks of the event of alterity that arrives without being (able to be) seen: 'Is it in any way comprehensible for a subject or even reducible to any subjectivity? Does it still belong in a history of the "becoming-subject"?' Derrida answers this with: 'Perhaps' (xxxiii–xxxiv). Here, this is answered with 'perhaps not'.
110 Gourgouris, *Does Literature Think*, 153, 151.

Chapter 4

1 Cohen, *Levinasian Meditations*, 250. It is to be noted here that the 'face' is first phenomenological, and it is only later that the face of the Other is shown to bear the trace of God.
2 'Western philosophy has most often been an ontology: a reduction of the other to the same'. Levinas, *Totality and Infinity*, 43.

3 Levinas, 'Dying For . . .', 213.
4 Ibid., 184.
5 See Emmanuel Levinas, *Ethics and Infinity: Conversations with Philippe Nemo*, trans. by Richard A. Cohen (Pittsburgh: Duquesne University Press, 1985), 89.
6 Levinas, *Totality and Infinity*, 80.
7 Richard A. Cohen, 'Foreword', in Levinas, *Otherwise Than Being*, xi. For more on the concept of the face in Levinas, see especially: *EE*, 97–100; *Totality and Infinity*, 79–81, 187–247; Emmanuel Levinas, 'Diachrony and Representation', in Levinas, *Time and the Other, and Additional Essays*, 105–8; and *Ethics and Infinity*, 85–92. For further commentary, see, for instance: Davis, *Levinas*, 45, 131–6, and Cohen, *Levinasian Meditations*, 236–54.
8 Levinas, 'Time and the Other', 74. This is of course in direct opposition to the melding of solitude and finitude in Heidegger's *Fundamental Concepts*.
9 Levinas, 'Diachrony and Representation', 112, 99. Emphasis added. In full, diachrony is '[t]he signification of a[n immemorial] past that has not been my present [. . .], and the signification of a [pure] future that commands me in mortality or in the face of the Other' (118). On this, despite some notable differences, Levinas works with Henri Bergson's notion of duration. See, for instance, Cohen, *Levinasian Meditations*, 44–56, and Emmanuel Levinas, *God, Death, and Time*, ed. by Jacques Rolland, trans. by Bettina Bergo (Stanford: Stanford University Press, 2000), 50–6.
10 Levinas, 'Diachrony and Representation', 114.
11 Emphasis added.
12 Cohen, *Levinasian Meditations*, 28. Here, then, emerges one of the principal differences between Levinasian and Blanchovian thought.
13 Levinas, 'Time and the Other', 77–8.
14 This is a concept that Levinas grapples with throughout his entire oeuvre, and one of the strongest links Levinas makes bridging alterity and ethics. See especially Emmanuel Levinas, *Difficult Freedom: Essays on Judaism*, trans. by Seán Hand (Baltimore: John Hopkins University Press, 1990). This is often in opposition to Sartre's concept of freedom, and the descriptor he uses is telling: 'Man is *condemned* to be free'. Jean-Paul Sartre, *Existentialism Is a Humanism* (London: Methuen, 1960), 34. Emphasis added.
15 See Maria Torok, 'The Illness of Mourning and the Fantasy of the Exquisite Corpse', in Nicolas Abraham and Maria Torok, *The Shell and the Kernel: Renewals of Psychoanalysis*, vol. 1, ed. and trans. by Nicholas T. Rand (Chicago and London: University of Chicago Press, 1994), 107–24.
16 The verb denotes the act of encryption and decryption which 'one can never do alone'. Derrida, 'Foreword: *Fors*', xxxvi.
17 First published as the eponymous story of a collection, entitled *Le Mur* in 1939.

18 And yet Derrida, once more in Heidegger's camp despite his continual troubling of Heideggarian boundaries of death, says: 'it is certain that we are "not capable" of our own corpse, we will never see it and feel it' (*BSII*, 161).
19 Levinas, *Otherwise Than Being*, 119.
20 Ibid., 112.
21 Ibid., 117. This, Levinas would also say, is the metaphysical desire *for* the other and *for* justice: 'Desire is desire for the absolutely other', a 'desire without satisfaction' where 'power, by essence murderous of the other, becomes [. . .] the consideration of the other, or justice'. Levinas, *Totality and Infinity*, 34, 47.
22 Cohen, *Levinasian Meditations*, 8.
23 Davis, *Levinas*, 70.
24 Levinas, *Otherwise Than Being*, 12.
25 John Wild, 'Introduction', in Levinas, *Totality and Infinity*, 16.
26 Levinas, *Totality and Infinity*, 35.
27 Emmanuel Levinas, 'Toward the Other', in *Nine Talmudic Readings*, trans. by Annette Aronowicz (Bloomington: Indiana University Press, 1990), 16.
28 Levinas, *Totality and Infinity*, 213.
29 Davis, *Levinas*, 82.
30 Levinas, *Otherwise Than Being*, 159–61.
31 Levinas, 'Time and the Other', 94.
32 Davis, *Levinas*, 83–4.
33 Levinas, *Otherwise Than Being*, 11.
34 Cohen, *Levinasian Meditations*, 284. Cf. Levinas, *Totality and Infinity*, 21–2.
35 See Cohen, *Levinasian Meditations*, 50.
36 Davis, *Levinas*, 99.
37 And this without even going into a critique of whether this 'utopia' is at all utopian, taking it instead at face value. '[T]he non-violence that Levinas seems to promote', as Butler writes, 'does not come from a peaceful place, but rather from a constant tension between the fear of undergoing violence and the fear of inflicting violence'. Butler, *Precarious Life*, 137.
38 See, for instance, David R. Carrier and Michael H. Morgan, 'Protective Buttressing of the Hominin Face', *Biological Reviews* 90 (2015): 330–46. This continues the long debate, as Carrier told the BBC in an interview, '"of whether our past was violent or peaceful"', and, in its focus on the human face, can be seen as a scientific transposition of the juxtaposition between the violent and the 'pacific' highlighted here (though the role of gender is, in the scientific discussion, more pertinent than it is here). See Jonathan Webb, 'Male Faces "buttressed" against Punches by Evolution', in *BBC News*, 9 June 2014, para. 18, accessed 2 July 2022, http://www.bbc.co.uk/news/science-environment-27720617.

39 In the original texts, both Levinas and Sartre deploy the verb *écraser*. '[J]e me sentis *écrasé* sous un poids énorme', Ibbieta says. As quoted earlier, Levinas asks: 'Se elle [la mort] ouvre une issue à la solitude, ne va-t-elle pas simplement *écraser* cette solitude, *écraser* la subjectivité même?'. Emphasis added.
40 Simon Critchley, *The Ethics of Deconstruction: Derrida and Levinas* (Oxford: Blackwell, 1992), 8. This is why there is not here staged a clash between Heideggerian ontology and Levinasian ethics, and why, in the manner of decomposition and unbecoming, Levinas's trajectory is here followed in reverse, from later to early Levinas, to his ontological (rather than ethical) conceptions of a before-becoming-subject.
41 Levinas, 'Diachrony and Representation', 100.
42 See, for instance, Josh Bowers, 'Mandatory Life and Death of Equitable Discretion', in Charles J. Ogletree and Austin Sarat, *Life without Parole: America's New Death Penalty?* (New York: New York University Press, 2012), 25-65.
43 Dylan Thomas, 'Do Not Go Gentle into That Good Night', in *Collected Poems 1934-1952* (London: J.M. Dent & Sons, 1957), 148.
44 Derrida would elsewhere call this 'singular event' or interruption *messianic*, in 'Faith and Knowledge', 56. Here once more is not only the theologico-political aspect of sovereignty but the theological aspect of deconstruction.
45 Luke 16.26. One can indeed draw extensive commentary between this Lazarus and the Lazarus who rose from the dead, especially since the former is '[t]he only character to be given a name in Jesus's parables'. See W. R. F. Browning, *A Dictionary of the Bible*, 2nd edn (Oxford: Oxford University Press, 2009).
46 Albeit the *il y a* is the obvious source of Blanchot's Neuter, which will be discussed in the next chapter.
47 Cohen, *Levinasian Meditations*, 70.
48 Levinas, *Totality and Infinity*, 232. See also Cohen, *Levinasian Meditations*, 71–2: 'Death is not only a future that always comes but never arrives; its transcendence is like nothing so much as [. . .] the approach of another human being'.
49 Cohen, *Levinasian Meditations*, 69.
50 Levinas, *Totality and Infinity*, 36.
51 Ibid., 51.
52 *Hamlet*, III.1.56.
53 Levinas, 'Time and the Other', 72.
54 Ibid., 73. In this same section – which is principally a critique of Heidegger – Levinas also reads Macbeth's death. *Macbeth* has only briefly been discussed in the first chapter, and further discussion on these lines, had there been space enough here, would certainly be fruitful – for is there not, in the later prophecies, also a kind of death sentence, where Macbeth is already dead? And what is one to make of his 'borrow'd robes' in relation to both alterity and sovereignty? *Macbeth*, I.3.109.

55 Emmanuel Levinas, 'Bad Conscience and the Inexorable', in *Face to Face with Levinas*, ed. by Richard Cohen (Albany: SUNY Press, 1986), 40.
56 Levinas, 'Time and the Other', 48–51. The question of suicide and absurdity, like the beinglessness before birth, is indeed very close to this discussion.
57 The absurd laughter at the end of 'The Wall' is not entirely dissimilar from the collective laughter after the execution in 'The Hanging'. See George Orwell, 'A Hanging', in *Why I Write* (London: Penguin, 2004), 95–101.
58 Speaking of the devil, similarly enriching discussion could be had around Sartre's *Nausea* and *No Exit* especially, with the latter's titular theme, setting, three characters, and infamous 'Hell is other people' pointing us once more to the demonic other and the relational death. Of course, one could write volumes on how the tenets of *Being and Nothingness* relate to the ones here, and Sartre's idea that 'man is *condemned* to be free', as he writes in *Existentialism Is a Humanism*, may be understood very differently here (34).
59 Alexander J. Argyros, 'The Sense of an Ending: Sartre's "The Wall"', *Modern Language Studies* 18, no. 3 (1988): 46.
60 Maurice Cranston, *Jean-Paul Sartre* (New York: Grove Press, 1962), 24–5, as quoted in ibid.
61 Ibid., 47–8.
62 Kevin W. Sweeney, 'Lying to the Murderer: Sartre's Use of Kant in "The Wall"', *Mosaic* 18, no. 2 (1985): 6. Sweeney's discussion of the debate between Kant and Benjamin Constant, of lying to a murderer who seeks your friend, is interesting in light of the present discussion, as a dynamic between *three*.
63 He goes on: 'What the hearty laugh screens from us [. . .] [is] the identity between being and non-being, between the living and the death-stricken being'. Georges Bataille, preface to 'Madame Edwarda', in *The Bataille Reader*, ed. by Fred Botting and Scott Wilson (Oxford and Malden: Blackwell Publishers Ltd., 1997), 224–5.
64 See Maurice Blanchot, *The Space of Literature*, trans. by Ann Smock (Lincoln and London: University of Nebraska Press, 1982), 96.
65 Levinas, *Otherwise Than Being*, 182. My emphasis.
66 Emmanuel Levinas, 'Preface', in *Time and the Other*, 33.
67 Levinas primarily mentions art as that which frees from inwardness (see *EE*, 45–51).
68 Levinas, 'Time and the Other', 46.
69 See Plato, 'Timaeus', in *Gorgias and Timaeus*, ed. by Tom Crawford, trans. by B. Jowett (Mineola: Dover Publications, 2003), 188–249 (especially 213–14).
70 Brandon Wocke, 'Derrida at Villette: (An)aesthetic of Space', in *University of Toronto Quarterly* 83, no. 3 (2014): 741. Emphasis added. Wocke's essay deals with the fascinating transcripts, essays and sketches recording Derrida's collaboration with Peter Eisenman and Bernard Tschumi, who were to create a 'garden' for *Parc*

de la Villette, drawing inspiration from the idea of the *chora*, but which ultimately failed to be created because of budgetary reasons. See Jacques Derrida and Peter Eisenman, *Chora L Works*, ed. by Jeffrey Kipnis and Leeser Thomas (New York: Monacelli Press, 1997).

71 Yvonne Sherwood and John D. Caputo, 'Otobiographies, Or How a Torn and Disembodied Ear Hears a Promise of Death [A Prearranged Meeting between Yvonne Sherwood and John D. Caputo and the Book of Amos and Jacques Derrida]', in *Derrida and Religion: Other Testaments*, ed. by Yvonne Sherwood and Kevin Hart (New York and Oxon: Routledge, 2005), 213, 233.

72 In Samuel Beckett's words, this would be an '[u]nmoreable unlessable unworseable evermost almost void'. Samuel Beckett, 'Worstward Ho', in *Company / Ill Seen Ill Said / Worstward Ho / Stirrings Still*, ed. by Dirk Van Hulle (London: Faber and Faber, 2009), 101. For more on Beckett's entire oeuvre and how it relates to the present discussion, see Critchley's *Very Little, Almost Nothing*.

73 Derrida, 'Faith and Knowledge', 55, 57–9. The original text quoted here is all italicized. This passage can be read as both extension and distillation of what Derrida writes three years earlier in *Khôra* (1993): see Jacques Derrida, 'Khôra', trans. by Ian McLeod, in *On The Name*, ed. by Thomas Dutoit (Stanford: Stanford University Press, 1995), 89–127. The two other essays in *On The Name*, along with Dutoit's introduction (which also includes a translation of the unbound insert that served as an introduction to the original three publications that are here published together), also feature what would here be very relevant commentary on the name.

74 *As You Like It*, ed. by Barbara A. Mowat and Paul Werstine (New York and London: Washington Square, 2004), II.7.148. Blanchot writes elsewhere: 'Mortal, immortal: does this reversal have any meaning?'. The answer here is yes. Blanchot, *The Writing of the Disaster*, 119.

75 Sherwood and Caputo, *Derrida and Religion*, 237, 216.

76 Maurice Blanchot, *The Gaze of Orpheus*, ed. by P. Adams Sitney, trans. by Lydia Davis (New York: Station Hill, 1981), 55.

77 'Old English (685-6) *thing* meeting, assembly; later, entity, being, matter (before 899); also, act, deed, event (about 1000); cognate with Old Frisian and Old Saxon *thing* assembly, action, matter [. . .]. Old High German *ding* assembly, lawsuit, thing (modern German *Ding* matter, affair, thing), Old Icelandic *thing* assembly, meeting, parliament, council (Norwegian *ting* assembly, being, creature, thing). Swedish *ting* court session [. . .]. Gothic has the cognate *theis* time, appointed time [. . .] suggesting that the original Germanic sense of *thing* may have been "day of assembly", ultimately from a base meaning "stretch or extent of time" (from Indo-European **tenk-* draw out, or draw together [. . .] and related to the source of Old English *thennan* stretch out [. . .]). Similar semantic developments are found in the

Romance languages, in which Latin *causa*, legal case, has given rise to French *chose*, Italian and Spanish *cosa*, all meaning "thing". *Chambers*, 1134.

78 Julian Young, *Schopenhauer* (London and New York: Routledge, 2005), 169–70.
79 *Othello*, ed. by Burton Raffel (New Haven and London: Yale University Press, 2005), II.3.247-48.
80 On this, one might look, for instance, to *The Vegetarian*, where the protagonist Yeong-hye passes 'into a border area between different states of being' in 'trying to shuck off the human'. Han Kang, *The Vegetarian*, trans. by Deborah Smith (London: Portobello Books, 2015), 70–1, 85.
81 Lacan, *The Ethics of Psychoanalysis*, 46, 56. Lacan also brings up the German *die Sache*, to be distinguished in psychoanalysis from *das Ding* despite sharing etymological connotations (43–4). For a very relevant discussion relating Lacan's *Das Ding* both to Freud's *Nebenmensch* and to Levinas's ethics, see Critchley, 'Das Ding: Lacan and Levinas'.
82 Badiou, 'Hegel's Master and Slave', 44.
83 Lacan, *The Ethics of Psychoanalysis*, 43. While definite links could be drawn between "assembly" as discussed here, in its multifarious resonances, and Gilles Deleuze and Felix Guattari's theory of assemblage – as multiplicities that are 'neither a part nor a whole' – such work must be left for elsewhere. Thomas Nail, 'What is an Assemblage?', *SubStance* 46, no. 1 (2017): 23.
84 For Levinas on clothes and nudity, see especially *EE*, 31. Of course sex and death have a long history and a unique relation, one grounded in the disappearance of self and identity, the '*petite mort*' (although this relation is often clumsily intermeshed with the concept of love). Looking at this relation critically, one can mention – apart from de Sade, an important figure for Blanchot – several works of Bataille's and the many works, such as those by Leo Bersani, interrogating the links between identity, sex and death through AIDS. For a more general overview of the interrelation, see, for instance: Beverly Clack, *Sex and Death: A Reappraisal of Human Mortality* (Cambridge and Malden: Polity Press, 2002).
85 While this cannot be discussed at length, one thinks not only of the idea of the double and the twin face from *Twelfth Night*'s Sebastian and Viola stretching back to, for instance, the myth of Romulus and Remus, but also, in light of the present interest in death, the doppelgänger, that antithetical twin stranger that often ominously prophesizes the end. E. T. A. Hoffman's *The Devil's Elixirs* is another fecund tale where the protagonist's doppelgänger is condemned to death instead.
86 Of the few illustrations in the Penguin edition, one of these depicts this doubling as 'The Likeness'. See *TC*, 78.
87 Emphasis added. The one who took Chavel's death is named Janvier, perhaps a conscious echo of Janus, the two-faced god of duality in one.
88 Morisi, *Capital Letters*, 46.

89 Svetlana Kozlova, 'The Utopia of Truth and the Gnoseology of the Severed Head in *Invitation to a Beheading*', trans. by Vladimir Talmy, *Russian Studies in Literature* 37, no. 3 (2001): 7. One must also keep in mind how '[f]or every possible allegorical reading of the novel there are portions of material that fail to fit', though this is true for all literary works discussed here. Leona Toker, *Nabokov: The Mystery of Literary Structures* (Ithaca and London: Cornell University Press, 2016), 127.

90 The epigraph is written by Delalande: 'an invented, apparently Gnostic sage', as Dale Peterson explains. See Dale Peterson, 'Nabokov's *Invitation*: Literature as Execution', in *Nabokov's Invitation to a Beheading: A Critical Companion*, ed. by Julian W. Connolly (Evanston: Northwestern University Press, 1997), 88. My translation.

91 James I. Porter, 'The Death Masque of Socrates: Nabokov's *Invitation to a Beheading*', *International Journal of Classical Tradition* 17, no. 3 (2010): 389 (abstract).

92 Ibid., 400. Though thinking on different lines, Porter's argument that Cincinnatus 'has become trapped in Plato's cave' maps extremely well unto the current discussion of the *il y a* without exit (see especially 396–9). This entire discussion can be related to Nabokov's own world view, evidenced most clearly by his comments on Nikolai Gogol (see 392) and how he says of *IB* that 'the worldling will deem it a trick' (Nabokov, 'Foreword', in *IB*, ix).

93 *As You Like It*, II.7.146.

94 Davis, *Levinas*, 84. Emphasis added.

95 Victor Hugo, *The Man Who Laughs* (Auckland: Floating Press, 2011), 74. Following the original subtitle, this book has also been translated as *By Order of the King*. Morisi's translation of this passage is arguably more powerful (*Capital Letters*, 3, second epigraph).

96 Hugo, *The Man Who Laughs*, 74.

97 Derrida, 'Foreword: *Fors*', xviii–xix.

Chapter 5

1 The fictional example earlier has followed the execution procedure in the state of Arizona. For more information, see 'Arizona Department of Corrections: Department Order 710 – Execution Procedures', accessed 2 July 2022, https://deathpenaltyinfo.org/files/pdf/ExecutionProtocols/ArizonaProtocol_06.17.17.pdf. For more information on the Lazarus phenomenon, see, for instance: Vaibhav Sahni, 'The Lazarus Phenomenon', *Journal of the Royal Society of Medicine* 7, no. 8 (2016): 1–6; and Douglas Stranges, Alan Lucerna, James Espinosa, et al., 'A Lazarus Effect: A Case Report of Bupropion Overdose Mimicking Brain Death', *World Journal of Emergency Medicine* 9, no. 1 (2018): 67–9. No proof-based cases of the

Lazarus phenomenon have been documented in relation to the death penalty; however, seeing as how most cases of the phenomenon do include lethal chemical doses, brainstem death and the declaration of 'clinically dead', this example lies within the realm of the extremely unlikely but nonetheless possible. For more on the (paradoxes and cruelty) of the usage of the lethal injection, especially in the contemporary United States, see Oliver, 'Making Death a Penalty: Or, Making "Good" Death a "Good" Penalty', 95–105. The legal and social confusion in the wake of a corpse's resurrection is also exuberantly explored through Ethel Rosenberg's survival in Robert Coover's *The Public Burning* (New York: Grove Press, 1977).

2 One similar, historical case is that of Benjamin Schreiber, who was sentenced for life at Iowa State Penitentiary and was taken to hospital because of illness. There, he died and was resuscitated (against his will). He argued that he had served his lifelong sentence. The court's outcome refused to entertain the notion 'because "life" is not defined by the state's code'. See Nicholas Bogel-Burroughs, 'A Prisoner Who Briefly Died Argues That He's Served His Life Sentence', *The New York Times*, 8 November 2019, accessed 2 July 2022, https://www.nytimes.com/2019/11/08/us/prisoner-dies-life-sentence.html.

3 Adriana Cavarero, *Relating Narratives: Storytelling and Selfhood*, trans. by Paul A. Kottman (Oxon: Routledge, 2000), xiv.

4 Jacques Derrida, *The Ear of the Other: Otobiography, Transference, Translation*, trans. by Peggy Kamuf, ed. by Christie V. McDonald (New York: Schocken Books, 1985), 51.

5 Blanchot, *Space of Literature*, 171.

6 Ivan Callus, 'Comparatism and (Auto)thanatography: Death and Mourning in Blanchot, Derrida, and Tim Parks', *Comparative Critical Studies* 1, no. 3 (2004): 339.

7 Ibid., 340. See also, especially, 352–6.

8 Jean-Luc Nancy, 'Introduction', in *Who Comes After the Subject*, 5.

9 Peter Brooks, *Reading for the Plot: Design and Intention in Narrative* (Cambridge, MA: Harvard University Press, 1992), 22. Brooks is here forwarding Walter Benjamin's thought.

10 Mark C. Taylor, 'Ghost Stories', in Mark C. Taylor and Christian Dietrich Lammerts, *Grave Matters* (London: Reaktion Books Ltd., 2002), 35.

11 Bede Rundle, *Grammar in Philosophy* (Oxford: Clarendon Press, 1979), 46, as quoted in Ann Banfield, 'The Name of the Subject: The "Il"?', *Yale French Studies* 93 (1998): 139. Emphasis added.

12 See Levinas, 'On Maurice Blanchot'.

13 Blanchot, *Space of Literature*, 96. The possessive pronoun 'his' is here emphasized. For more on Blanchot's possible proximity to Heidegger, see, for instance, Pascal Massie, 'The Secret and the Neuter: On Heidegger and Blanchot', *Research in Phenomenology* 37 (2007): 32–55.

14 Blanchot, *Space of Literature*, 96.
15 Ibid., 95.
16 Maurice Blanchot, 'The Myth of Mallarmé', in Maurice Blanchot, *The Work of Fire*, trans. by Charlotte Mandell (Stanford: Stanford University Press, 1995), 41.
17 Rustam Singh, 'Not This, Not That: Maurice Blanchot and Poststructuralism', *Comparative and Continental Philosophy* 8, no. 1 (2016): 73. Singh's central argument that Blanchot goes beyond poststructuralism is here strongly supported.
18 Blanchot, 'The Myth of Mallarmé', 39.
19 Garth Gillan and Levinas in Garth Gillan and Emmanuel Levinas, 'About Blanchot: An Interview', *SubStance* 5, no. 14 (1976): 55. Cf. Maurice Blanchot, *Thomas the Obscure*, trans. by Robert Lamberton (Barrytown: Station Hill Press, 1988), 99. In Lamberton's translation, the quote referenced in the interview is 'I think, therefore I am not'.
20 Blanchot, *Space of Literature*, 55. Emphasis added.
21 Walter Brogan, 'Broken Words: Maurice Blanchot and the Impossibility of Writing', *Comparative and Continental Philosophy* 1, no. 2 (2015): 182, 191.
22 A proper commentary on 'The Hollow Men' could take the entirety of this chapter, or more, especially in consideration of their living of death, their 'quiet and meaningless' voices (and the other voices at an infinite distance), the lack of faces and eyes, their being-in-'deliberate[-]disguises', their anonymity and place of placelessness and so on; in short, their whole paradoxical 'being'. Another aspect of the Hollow Men shall be mentioned in passing in the following section. T. S. Eliot, 'The Hollow Men', in *T. S. Eliot: Collected Poems, 1909 – 1962* (London: Faber and Faber, 2002), 79, 81, 80.
23 Singh, 'Not This, Not That', 75.
24 The tension between the Neuter and the aporetic deserves attention, with Derrida description of the latter as either/or (see *BSII*, 35) being in tension with the former's neither/nor.
25 Maurice Blanchot, *The Step Not Beyond*, trans. by Lycette Nelson (Albany: University of New York Press, 1992), 19. The fact that Blanchot compares this space to a 'garden' and 'desert' makes clearer the links between this space and the Derridean *chora*.
26 Blanchot, *Space of Literature*, 133.
27 Arleen Ionescu, William Large and Laura Marin, 'Introduction: Blanchot's Spaces', *Word and Text* 5, no. 1–2 (2015): 6. Here the authors are quoting Gerald L. Bruns, *Maurice Blanchot: The Refusal of Philosophy* (Baltimore and London: John Hopkins University Press, 1997), 82.
28 Blanchot, *The Writing of the Disaster*, 65.
29 Garth and Levinas, 'About Blanchot: An Interview', 55.
30 Critchley, *Very Little . . . Almost Nothing*, 203.

31 Ibid., 206–7.
32 Singh, 'Not This, Not That', 80.
33 Stone, 'The Relationality of Death', 165.
34 Gary Saul Morson, *Narrative and Freedom: The Shadows of Time* (New Haven and London: Yale University Press, 1994), 197.
35 Garth and Levinas, 'About Blanchot: An Interview', 55.
36 Blanchot, *The Writing of the Disaster*, 101.
37 Blanchot, *Space of Literature*, 48. It is worth mentioning that W. H. Auden's infamous 'poetry makes nothing happen' works on similar lines, and the fact that this is an elegy is not inconsequential. See W. H. Auden, 'In Memory of W.B. Yeats', in *The Norton Anthology of Poetry*, ed. by Margaret Ferguson, Mary Jo Salter and Jon Stallworthy, 5th edn (New York and London: W.W. Norton & Co, 2005), 1473.
38 Morson, *Narrative and Freedom*, 191.
39 Blanchot, *The Step Not Beyond*, 85.
40 Blanchot, *Space of Literature*, 122–3.
41 Ibid., 128.
42 Ibid., 149.
43 Foucault, *Society Must Be Defended*, 240.
44 Blanchot, *Space of Literature*, 147. Emphasis added.
45 Maurice Blanchot, 'The Athenaeum', in Maurice Blanchot, *The Infinite Conversation*, trans. by Susan Hanson (Minneapolis and London: Minnesota University Press, 2003), 353.
46 Blanchot, *The Step Not Beyond*, 1.
47 Blanchot, 'The Athenaeum', 353. With this particular quotation, Deborah Esch and Ian Balfour's translation might be more insightful, if not more accurate, in translating the latter phrase as 'shattering it', thus further clarifying Blanchot's notion of the fragment. See Maurice Blanchot, 'The Athenaeum', trans. by Deborah Esch and Ian Balfour, in *Studies in Romanticism* 22, no. 2 (1983): 165.
48 Singh, 'Not This, Not That', 76.
49 Blanchot, 'The Athenaeum', trans. by Hanson, 357.
50 Callus, 'Comparatism and (Auto)Thanatography', 340.
51 Maurice Blanchot, 'Who?', trans. by Eduardo Cadava, in *Who Comes After the Subject?*, 58. Emphasis added. Cf. Derrida, who says that '[e]ven if *Dasein* is not the subject [. . .] [i]t is from the standpoint of *Dasein* that Heidegger defines the humanity of man' (Derrida and Nancy, '"Eating Well": An Interview', 104–5). This thinking of the death of the 'what', therefore, runs directly counter to the thinking of the *Jemeingkeit*.
52 Blanchot, *The Madness of the Day*, 9.
53 Blanchot, *Space of Literature*, 96.
54 Brogan, 'Broken Words', 182.

55 Bataille, *The Accursed Share*, 256.
56 Blanchot, *The Writing of the Disaster*, 131.
57 Bataille, *The Accursed Share*, 204.
58 Georges Bataille, 'Hegel, Death and Sacrifice', trans. by Jonathan Strauss, *Yale French Studies* 78 (1990): 19.
59 Bataille has only been infrequently referred to throughout this book. Apart from, by and large, the constrictions of space and time, this is also because Bataille's lexicon, which requires extensive clarification, would most likely have distracted us from the argument that is being proffered here. It would certainly not have been fruitless to discuss some of his overarching concepts: the inner experience and its economy (one close to that of the unexperienced experience); his readings of Hegel, which suggest that while Hegel momentously grasped the crucial negation at the heart of man and language, death is ultimately historicized and thus consumed by dialectical synthesis; his conceptualization of the *Acéphale* – and here the *beheaded* is particularly important – and his intellectual friendship with and proximity to Blanchot; or his ideas on community, poetry, negativity, and of course sovereignty. His thought is centrally important here if understood as a thinker 'who wishes to shatter the composed rationality of the isolated individual', and who finds 'subjectivity [. . .] torn apart' at 'the limit of knowledge' (Fred Botting and Scott Wilson, 'Introduction: From Experience to Economy', in *The Bataille Reader*, 1–2). This is not to say there would not have been divergences between Bataille and what is presented here, specifically on the central concept of sacrifice, among other things. Apart from the works by Bataille quoted in this book, see also Benjamin Noys, *Georges Bataille – A Critical Introduction* (London: Pluto Press, 2000).
60 Emphasis added. Agamben makes the interesting point that 'Homeric Greek does not even know a term to designate the living body. The term *sōma*, which appears in later epochs as a good equivalent to our term "life," originally meant only "corpse"' (*HS*, 66). This lack of individual life will continue to inform Agamben's work, who, in the sequel to *HS*, describes this reduction to anonymity, in terms of the USA Patriot Act, as the production of 'a legally unnameable and unclassifiable being'. Giorgio Agamben, *State of Exception*, trans. Kevin Attell (Chicago and London: University of Chicago Press, 2005), 3.
61 Emphasis added.
62 Howells, 'The Death Penalty and Its Exceptions', 96.
63 Agamben explains this point also through the *patria potestas*. See *HS*, 89–90. He states this most clearly in one of his concluding statements, inverting Freud: '"Where there is a People, there will be bare life"' (*HS*, 179).
64 Emphasis added.
65 Emphasis added.

66 Derrida's slightly later musings on the *loup* and its relation to sovereignty in *The Beast and the Sovereign* (especially the first volume) can be made to correspond, at least to some extent, to Agamben's meditations on the figure of the werewolf, where 'sovereign and beast seem to have in common their being-outside-the-law', with 'the beast being the sovereign, the sovereign being the beast' (*BSI*, 17, 32). Derrida makes direct, contentious, and only very fleeting references to Agamben in these seminars (see *BSI*, 92).

67 Foucault, interviewed by Pierre Dumayet on television after his publication of *Les mots et les choses*. See 'Michel Foucault à propos du livre "Les mots et les choses"', online video recording, *Institut National de l'Audiovisuel*, 15 June 1966, accessed 2 July 2022, https://www.ina.fr/video/i05059752/michel-foucault-a-propos-du-livre-les-mots-et-les--video.html. Indeed, it is against the invention of the apotheosis of Man as being-towards-death that this book, with Blanchot, situates itself.

68 Giorgio Agamben, *The Coming Community*, trans. Michael Hardt (Minneapolis: Minnesota University Press, 2009), 5. On Bartleby, see 35–7.

69 Agamben, *Coming Community*, 17, 10–11.

70 Ibid., 18–19.

71 Ibid., 48.

72 Emphasis added.

73 Eliot, 'The Hollow Men', 79, 81. An extended discussion could here be had on the human thing and what Derrida says of the 'undecidable figure of the marionette as life *and* death, life-death' (*BSI*, 256). The marionette is a 'living "being" that perhaps "is" not – a *living without being*', that which is the 'inhuman *what*', and not a *who*, '[n]either animal nor human', where there is a 'being-at-home-with-the-other', who is neither guest nor host, in the multiple and impossible polis, a 'multipli-city' (*BSI*, 219, 222, 205, 201). Indeed, the human thing of the present discussion is an elaboration, interrogation, and deepening of Derrida's marionette which Derrida ultimately leaves vague (and this not only because of the vagueness necessitated by such a figure of the neither/nor).

74 Agamben, *Coming Community*, 64–5.

75 Maurice Blanchot, *The Unavowable Community*, trans. by Pierre Joris (Barrytown: Station Hill Press, 1998), 12.

76 See *HS*, 48, 59, 153.

77 Derrida and Nancy, '"Eating Well": An Interview', 99–100.

78 Agamben, *Coming Community*, 29.

79 Leslie Hill, '"Not In Our Name": Blanchot, Politics, the Neuter', *Paragraph* 30, no. 3 (2007): 142.

80 Taylor, 'Ghost Stories', 22.

81 Agamben, *Coming Community*, 10.

82 Ibid., 29.
83 Ibid., 67. See also 23–5.
84 While there is no *Stimmung*, as such, attributed to the *chora*, that of the *il y a* is specifically horror, and not indifference. One must keep in mind that the *il y a* as understood here is impassable, and thus there can be no horror from a Being that never arrives.
85 Here are clear resonances with some forms of contemporary resistance, for instance: (i) the Zapatista movement, the members of which participate in a '[r]esistant subjectivity [that] is in a sense already dead, a posthumous subjectivity', who describe themselves as 'the nameless, the always dead' and whose death is an indifferent and 'useless death' (Howard Caygill, *On Resistance: A Philosophy of Defiance* (London and New York: Bloomsbury, 2013), 98, 127, 112); (ii) the Turkish death fasters and self-immolators, whose forms of necroresistance directly (and thanatopolitically) respond to, and take power away from, 'the sovereign power of life and death', thinking instead of an 'alternative [to] sovereignty' (Banu Bargu, *Starve and Immolate: The Politics of Human Weapons* (New York: Columbia University Press, 2014), 27, 2). It should be noted that the specific idea of wilful self-destruction highlighted in the latter example is not what is being explored here; rather, this is the transgression first identified through *Antigone*; that is, the transgression that is the refusal to participate in *presence* or the *made-to-be* and instead remain within the *neither/nor*. For more on the concept of passive resistance as 'resistance beyond the closure of being', see Shokoufeh Sakhi, 'Prison and the Subject of Resistance: A Levinasian Inquiry', in *Death and Other Penalties*, 250–65 (quote taken from 258).
86 Cf. Bataille, 'Hegel, Death and Sacrifice', 20: 'In tragedy, at least, it is a question of our identifying of some character who dies, and of believing that we die, although we are alive'.
87 See Pierre Joris, 'Translator's Preface', in *The Unavowable Community*, xxii–xxv. See also *The Unavowable Community*, 10–11, 24–6. Blanchot quotes a crucial sentence from Bataille: 'If the community is revealed by the death of the other person, it is because death itself is the true community of mortal beings: their impossible communion' (10–11).
88 Hill, 'Not In Our Name', 154.
89 Giorgio Agamben, *Language and Death: The Place of Negativity*, trans. by Karen E. Pinknus and Michael Hardt (Minneapolis and Oxford: Minneapolis University Press, 1991), 46. The original Hegelian quote under discussion here is taken from the 'Preface' to the *Phenomenology*, 19. Derrida (see *BSII*, 152–4) ignores this point when reading this same passage from Hegel, despite the acknowledgement that enduring death within life – a life that is somehow maintained – would be a power over death, a putting to *work* of death, or at the very least the transformation of

death from impossibility to concept (on this, Blanchot writes very clearly: see *The Writing of the Disaster*, 68).

90 Critchley, *Very Little . . . Almost Nothing*, 61.
91 Brogan, 'Broken Words', 192.
92 Hill, 'Not In Our Name', 151–2. Emphasis added. Here she is discussing Pindar's fragment 'Das Höchste' and Hölderlin's, Schmitt's, and Blanchot's translations and discussions of it.
93 Julia Kristeva, 'On the Inviolability of Human Life', trans. by Lisa Walsh, in *Death and Other Penalties*, 132.
94 Foucault, 'Right of Death and Power over Life', 138.
95 Carl Schmitt, 'The Concept of the Political', trans. by George Schwab, in *The Concept of the Political – Expanded Edition*, 52. Here Schmitt is quoting Thomas Hobbes, and the thoughts of Agamben and Derrida as quoted in this chapter also bear multiple and overt references to Hobbes; the centrality of his thought on sovereignty, obligation and punishment cannot be understated. See Thomas Hobbes, *Leviathan*, ed. by J. C. A. Gaskin (Oxford, New York: Oxford University Press, 2008). See also Arthur Bradley, 'Jus Puniendi: La questione della pena in Foucault, Agamben ed Esposito', in *Teologie e Politica: Genealogia e Actualita*, ed. by Elettra Stimilli (Roma: Quodlibet, 2019), 105–26.
96 Indeed, Derrida, in these same lectures, also makes evident that he does not believe sovereignty to be the 'proper' of mankind, and that sovereignty can be successfully deconstructed: 'Sovereignty is a *posited law*, a thesis or prosthesis, and not a natural given' (*BSI*, 77). On this, see also *BSI*, 57, 75, 138.
97 Foucault too stresses how the sovereign rules 'over men insofar as they are living beings' (*Society Must Be Defended*, 247).
98 Here Derrida's discussion of Heidegger's three definitions (*weltlos* for the thing, *weltarm* for the animal, and *weltbildend* for the human being) is being kept in view, which he discusses throughout *BSII*.
99 Agamben, *Coming Community*, 67.
100 Blanchot, 'Who?', 59. Emphasis added.

Conclusion

1 Oliver, 'Making Death a Penalty: Or, Making "Good" Death a "Good" Penalty', 102.
2 Howells, 'The Death Penalty and Its Exceptions', 91.
3 Derrida here refers to a particular work of Freud's. See Sigmund Freud, 'Our Attitude towards Death', in *The Standard Edition of the Complete Psychological Works of Sigmund Freud, Vol. XIV (1914-1916)*, ed. and trans. by James Strachey, Anna Freud, Alix Strachey and Alan Tyson (London: Vintage, 2001), 289–300.

4 Ebury, *Modern Literature and the Death Penalty*, 62, 74, 73. Emphasis added.
5 Morisi, *Capital Letters*, 28, 57.
6 Bradley, *Unbearable Life*, 20.
7 Sextus Empiricus, *Outlines of Scepticism*, ed. by Julia Annas and Jonathan Barnes (Cambridge and New York: Cambridge University Press, 2007), 4.
8 Ibid., 5.
9 Kamuf, *Literature and the Remains of the Death Penalty*, 29. Emphasis added.
10 In this context of neither affirmation nor negation, one might appreciate the linguistic fact that 'impassivity' can often be synonymous with 'passivity' despite the prefix.
11 Maurice Blanchot, 'The Language of Fiction', in *The Work of Fire*, 84.
12 Ibid., 81–3.
13 Franz Kafka, 'In the Penal Colony', trans. by Willa and Edwin Muir, in *The Complete Short Stories of Franz Kafka*, ed. by Nahum N. Glatzer (London: Vintage, 2005), 140.
14 Ibid., 145–6.
15 Ibid., 150, 154.
16 Ibid., 151.
17 In *Killing Times*, Wills also turns to Kafka at the conclusion of his book (see 206–14). 'In the Penal Colony' is read in line with Wills's concept of prosthetic time (in part, an unnatural and technological certainty of mortal time imposed by the death sentence, wherein *punishment* is *duration*) akin to the concept of limbo/*Langweile* as discussed here. Wills, however, does not acknowledge that the death penalty machine breaks down in the manner Kafka here makes explicit, interrupting its own enclosures of mortal time through an interruption of sovereignty itself, returning the living dead to finitude (but not to mortal time). Wills also presents a deeply insightful reading of two other works of Kafka's, namely *The Trial* and 'Metamorphosis'. The reading of the latter is especially apropos, as Wills focuses on the thingness of the transformed Gregor Samsa: 'his metamorphosis is first a reduction to an unnameable liminal creature unworthy even of sacrifice, and ultimately, as the charwoman makes clear, he is merely a "thing" that she is proud to have disposed of' (213).
18 Kafka, 'In the Penal Colony', 148.
19 Ibid., 166.

Bibliography

Abu-Jamal, Mumia. *Live from Death Row*. New York: Perennial, 2002.
Adelsberg, Geoffrey. 'U.S. Racism and Derrida's Theologico-Political Sovereignty'. In *Death and Other Penalties: Philosophy in a Time of Mass Incarceration*, edited by Geoffrey Adelsberg, Lisa Guenther, and Scott Zeman, 83–94. New York: Fordham University Press, 2015.
Adelsberg, Geoffrey, Lisa Guenther and Scott Zeman, eds. *Death and Other Penalties: Philosophy in a Time of Mass Incarceration*. New York: Fordham University Press, 2015.
Agamben, Giorgio. *Homo Sacer: Sovereign Power and Bare Life*. Translated by Daniel Heller-Roazen. Stanford: Stanford University Press, 2007.
Agamben, Giorgio. *Language and Death: The Place of Negativity*. Translated by Karen E. Pinknus and Michael Hardt. Minneapolis and Oxford: Minneapolis University Press, 1991.
Agamben, Giorgio. *Stasis: Civil War as a Political Paradigm*. Translated by Nicholas Heron. Stanford: Stanford University Press, 2015.
Agamben, Giorgio. *State of Exception*. Translated by Kevin Attell. Chicago and London: University of Chicago Press, 2005.
Agamben, Giorgio. *The Coming Community*. Translated by Michael Hardt. Minneapolis: Minnesota University Press, 2009.
Aho, Kevin A. *Heidegger's Neglect of the Body*. Albany: SUNY Press, 2009.
Anderson, Nicole. 'A Proper Death: Penalties, Animals, and the Law'. In *Deconstructing the Death Penalty: Derrida's Seminars and the New Abolitionism*, edited by Kelly Oliver and Stephanie M. Straub, 159–74. New York: Fordham University Press, 2018.
Anidjar, Gil. 'Introduction – "Once More, Once More": Derrida, The Arab, The Jew'. In Jacques Derrida, *Acts of Religion*, edited by Gil Anidjar, 1–39. New York and London: Routledge, 2002.
Aquilina, Mario. '"Everything and Nothing": Shakespeare in Blanchot'. *Word and Text* 5, no. 1–2 (2015): 87–97.
Argyros, Alexander J. 'The Sense of an Ending: Sartre's "The Wall"'. *Modern Language Studies* 18, no. 3 (1988): 46–52.
Aristotle. *The Politics*. Translated by T. A. Sinclair. London and New York: Penguin Books, 1992.
'Arizona Department of Corrections: Department Order 710: Execution Procedures', https://files.deathpenaltyinfo.org/legacy/files/pdf/ExecutionProtocols/ArizonaProtocol_06.17.17.pdf.

Ataner, Attila. 'Kant on Capital Punishment and Suicide'. *Kant Studien* 97, no. 4 (2006): 452–82.

Auden, W. H. 'In Memory of W.B. Yeats'. In *The Norton Anthology of Poetry*, edited by Margaret Ferguson, Mary Jo Salter, and Jon Stallworthy, 5th edn, 1470–2. New York and London: W.W. Norton & Co, 2005.

Badiou, Alain. 'Hegel's Master and Slave'. Translated by Frank Ruda. *Crisis and Critique* 4, no. 1 (2017): 35–47.

Baillie, Joanna. 'Introductory Discourse'. In *A Series of Plays: In which it is Attempted to Delineate the Stronger Passions of the Mind . . .*, 3rd edn, 1–71. London: T. Cadell, Jun. & W. Davies, 1800.

Bainbrigge, Susan. 'Introduction'. *Forum for Modern Language Studies* 41, no. 4 (2005): 359–64.

Bakhtin, Mikhail. *Problems of Dostoevsky's Poetics*. Edited and translated by Caryl Emerson. Minneapolis and London: Minnesota University Press, 1999.

Banfield, Ann. 'The Name of the Subject: The "Il"?' *Yale French Studies* 93 (1998): 133–74.

Bargu, Banu. *Starve and Immolate: The Politics of Human Weapons*. New York: Columbia University Press, 2014.

Barnhart, Robert K., ed. *Chambers Dictionary of Etymology*. Edinburgh: Chambers, 1988.

Barton, John Cyril. *Literary Executions: Capital Punishment and American Culture, 1820–1925*. Baltimore: John Hopkins University Press, 2014.

Bataille, Georges. 'Hegel, Death and Sacrifice'. Translated by Jonathan Strauss. *Yale French Studies* 78 (1990): 9–28.

Bataille, Georges. 'Madame Edwarda'. In *The Bataille Reader*, edited by Fred Botting and Scott Wilson, 223–36. Oxford and Malden: Blackwell Publishers Ltd., 1997.

Bataille, Georges. *The Accursed Share: An Essay on General Economy*, vols 2 and 3. Translated by Robert Hurley. New York: Zone Books, 1991.

Beckett, Samuel. 'Worstward Ho'. In *Company / Ill Seen Ill Said / Worstward Ho / Stirrings Still*, edited by Dirk Van Hulle, 79–104. London: Faber and Faber, 2009.

Benatar, David. *Better Never To Have Been: The Harm of Coming into Existence*. Oxford and New York: Oxford University Press, 2006.

Benjamin, Walter. 'Critique of Violence'. In *Reflections: Essays, Aphorisms, Autobiographical Writings*, translated by Edmund Jephcott and edited by Peter Demetz, 277–300. New York: Schocken Books, 1986.

Bielik-Robson, Agata. 'The Thanatic Strain. Kojève and Rosenzweig as Two Readers of Hegel.' *Journal for Cultural Research* 19, no. 3 (2015): 274–90.

Bittner, Heike, dir. *MitSterben?* Götz Walter Filmproduktion, 2003.

Blanchot, Maurice. *Awaiting Oblivion*. Translated by John Gregg. Lincoln: University of Nebraska Press, 1997.

Blanchot, Maurice. *Death Sentence*. Translated by Lydia Davis. Barrytown: Station Hill, 1978.

Blanchot, Maurice. 'Literature and the Right to Death'. Translated by Lydia Davis. In *The Work of Fire*, translated by Charlotte Mandell, 300–44. Stanford: Stanford University Press, 1995.

Blanchot, Maurice. 'The Athenaeum'. Translated by Deborah Esch and Ian Balfour. *Studies in Romanticism* 22, no. 2 (1983): 163–72.

Blanchot, Maurice. 'The Athenaeum'. In Maurice Blanchot, *The Infinite Conversation*, translated by Susan Hanson, 351–9. Minneapolis and London: Minnesota University Press, 2003.

Blanchot, Maurice. *The Gaze of Orpheus*. Edited by P. Adams Sitney and translated by Lydia Davis. New York: Station Hill, 1981.

Blanchot, Maurice. *The Instant of My Death*. Translated by Elizabeth Rottenberg. Stanford: Stanford University Press, 2000.

Blanchot, Maurice. 'The Language of Fiction'. In Maurice Blanchot, *The Work of Fire*, translated by Charlotte Mandell, 74–84. Stanford: Stanford University Press, 1995.

Blanchot, Maurice. *The Madness of the Day*. Translated by Lydia Davis. Barrytown: Station Hill Press, 1981.

Blanchot, Maurice. 'The Myth of Mallarmé'. In Maurice Blanchot, *The Work of Fire*, translated by Charlotte Mandell, 27–42. Stanford: Stanford University Press, 1995.

Blanchot, Maurice. *The Space of Literature*. Translated by Ann Smock. Lincoln and London: University of Nebraska Press, 1982.

Blanchot, Maurice. *The Step Not Beyond*. Translated by Lycette Nelson. Albany: University of New York Press, 1992.

Blanchot, Maurice. *The Unavowable Community*. Translated by Pierre Joris. Barrytown: Station Hill Press, 1998.

Blanchot, Maurice. *The Writing of the Disaster*. Translated by Ann Smock. Lincoln and London: University of Nebraska Press, 1992.

Blanchot, Maurice. *Thomas the Obscure*. Translated by Robert Lamberton. Barrytown: Station Hill Press, 1988.

Blanchot, Maurice. 'Who?' Translated by Eduardo Cadava. In *Who Comes After The Subject?*, edited by Eduardo Cadava, Peter Connor, and Jean-Luc Nancy, 58–60. New York and London: Routledge, 1991.

Bogel-Burroughs, Nicholas. 'A Prisoner Who Briefly Died Argues That He's Served His Life Sentence'. *The New York Times*, 8 November 2019, accessed 2 July 2022, https://www.nytimes.com/2019/11/08/us/prisoner-dies-life-sentence.html.

Bottéro, Jean. *Mesopotamia: Writing, Reasoning, and the Gods*. Translated by Zainab Bahrani and Marc Van De Mieroop. London and Chicago: University of Chicago Press, 1992.

Botting, Fred and Scott Wilson. 'Introduction: From Experience to Economy'. In *The Bataille Reader*, edited by Fred Botting and Scott Wilson, 1–34. Oxford and Malden: Blackwell Publishers Ltd., 1997.

Bowers, Josh. 'Mandatory Life and Death of Equitable Discretion'. In Charles J. Ogletree and Austin Sarat, *Life without Parole: America's New Death Penalty?*, 25–65. New York: New York University Press, 2012.

Bradley, Arthur. 'Jus Puniendi: La questione della pena in Foucault, Agamben ed Esposito'. In *Teologie e Politica: Genealogia e Actualita*, edited by Elettra Stimilli, 105–26. Roma: Quodlibet, 2019.

Bradley, Arthur. *Unbearable Life: A Genealogy of Political Erasure*. New York: Columbia University Press, 2019.

Braun, Richard. *Antigone*. New York and Oxford: Oxford University Press, 1973.

Broadie, Alexander and Elizabeth M. Pybus. 'Kant's Treatment of Animals'. *Philosophy* 41, no. 190 (1974): 375–83.

Brogan, Walter. 'Broken Words: Maurice Blanchot and the Impossibility of Writing'. *Comparative and Continental Philosophy* 1, no. 2 (2015): 181–92.

Brooks, Peter. 'Death in the First Person'. *South Atlantic Quarterly* 107, no. 3 (2008): 531–46.

Brooks, Peter. *Reading for the Plot: Design and Intention in Narrative*. Cambridge, MA: Harvard University Press, 1992.

Browning, W. R. F. *A Dictionary of the Bible*, 2nd edn. Oxford: Oxford University Press, 2009.

Bruns, Gerald L. *Maurice Blanchot: The Refusal of Philosophy*. Baltimore and London: John Hopkins University Press, 1997.

Buber, Martin. 'What Is Man'. In *Between Man and Man*, translated by Ronald Gregor-Smith, 140–244. London and New York: Routledge, 2004.

Butler, Judith. *Antigone's Claim: Kinship Between Life and Death*. New York: Columbia University Press, 2000.

Butler, Judith. *Precarious Life: The Powers of Mourning and Violence*. London and New York: Verso, 2004.

Callus, Ivan. 'Comparatism and (Auto)thanatography: Death and Mourning in Blanchot, Derrida, and Tim Parks'. *Comparative Critical Studies* 1, no. 3 (2004): 337–58.

Campbell, Thomas. 'Hallowed Ground'. In *The Complete Poetical Works of Thomas Campbell*, edited by J. Logie Robertson, 248–51. London: Oxford University Press, 1907.

Campbell, Timothy and Adam Sitze. 'Introduction'. In *Biopolitics – A Reader*, edited by Timothy Campell and Adam Sitze, 1–40. Durham and London: Duke University Press, 2013.

Carrier, David R. and Michael H. Morgan. 'Protective Buttressing of the Hominin Face'. *Biological Reviews* 90 (2015): 330–46.

Cavarero, Adriana. *Relating Narratives: Storytelling and Selfhood*. Translated by Paul A. Kottman. Oxon: Routledge, 2000.

Caygill, Howard. *On Resistance: A Philosophy of Defiance*. London and New York: Bloomsbury, 2013.

Christ, Birte and Ève Morisi, eds. *Death Sentences: Literature and State Killing*. Cambridge: Legenda, 2019.

Ciavatta, David. 'The Event of Absolute Freedom: Hegel and the French Revolution and Its Calendar'. *Philosophy and Social Criticism* 40, no. 6 (2014): 577–605.

Cioran, E. M. *The Trouble with Being Born*. Translated by Richard Howard. New York: Arcade Publishing, 2012.

Clack, Beverly. *Sex and Death: A Reappraisal of Human Mortality*. Cambridge and Malden: Polity Press, 2002.

Clark, Timothy. *Martin Heidegger*. London and New York: Routledge, 2011.

Cochetti, Stefano. 'The Lethal Narcissus: Heidegger on Sacrifice/Sacrifice on Heidegger'. *Contagion: Journal of Violence, Mimesis, and Culture* 4 (1997): 87–100.

Cohen, Richard A. 'Foreword'. In Emmanuel Levinas, *Otherwise Than Being, or Beyond Essence*, translated by Alphonso Lingis, xi–xvi. Pittsburgh: Duquesne University Press, 2011.

Cohen, Richard A. *Levinasian Meditations: Ethics, Philosophy, and Religion*. Pittsburgh: Duquesne University Press, 2010.

Comay, Rebecca. *Mourning Sickness: Hegel and the French Revolution*. Stanford: Stanford University Press, 2011.

Cranston, Maurice. *Jean-Paul Sartre*. New York: Grove Press, 1962.

Critchley, Simon. 'Das Ding: Lacan and Levinas'. *Research in Phenomenology* 28 (1998): 72–90.

Critchley, Simon. 'Preface to the Second Edition'. In *Very Little ... Almost Nothing: Death, Philosophy, Literature*, 2nd edn, xv–xxviii. Oxon and New York: Routledge, 2004.

Critchley, Simon. *The Ethics of Deconstruction: Derrida and Levinas*. Oxford: Blackwell, 1992.

Critchley, Simon. *Very Little ... Almost Nothing: Death, Philosophy, Literature*, 2nd edn. Oxon and New York: Routledge, 2004.

Davis, Angela Y. *Abolition Democracy: Beyond Empire, Prisons, and Torture*. New York: Seven Stories Press, 2005.

Davis, Colin. *Levinas: An Introduction*. Cambridge: Polity Press, 1996.

de Beauvoir, Simone. *A Very Easy Death*. New York: Random House, 1999.

de Beauvoir, Simone. *All Men Are Mortal*. Croydon: Virago Press, 2004.

Derrida, Jacques. 'A Time for Farewells: Heidegger (read by) Hegel (read by) Malabou'. Translated by Joseph D. Cohen. In Catherine Malabou, *The Future of Hegel: Plasticity, Temporality and Dialectic*, translated by Lisabeth During, vii–xlvii. Oxon and New York: Routledge, 2005.

Derrida, Jacques. *Adieu to Emmanuel Levinas*. Translated by Pascale-Anne Brault and Michael Naas. Stanford: Stanford University Press, 1999.

Derrida, Jacques. *Aporias*. Translated by Thomas Dutoit. Stanford: Stanford University Press, 1993.

Derrida, Jacques. 'Circumfession'. Translated by Geoffrey Bennington. In Jacques Derrida and Geoffrey Bennington, *Circumfession/Derridabase*, 3–315. Chicago and London: The University of Chicago Press, 1999.

Derrida, Jacques. *Demeure: Fiction and Testimony*. Translated by Elizabeth Rottenberg. Stanford: Stanford University Press, 2000.

Derrida, Jacques. 'Faith and Knowledge: The Two Sources of "Religion" at the Limits of Reason Alone'. Translated by Samuel Weber. In *Acts of Religion*, edited by Gil Anidjar, 40–101. New York and London: Routledge, 2002.
Derrida, Jacques. 'Foreword: *Fors*: The Anglish Words of Nicolas Abraham and Maria Torok'. Translated by Barbara Johnson. In Nicolas Abraham and Maria Torok, *The Wolf Man's Magic Word: A Cryptonomy*, translated by Nicholas Rand, xi–xlvii. Minneapolis: University of Minnesota Press, 1986.
Derrida, Jacques. 'Khôra'. Translated by Ian McLeod. In *On The Name*, edited by Thomas Dutoit, 89–127. Stanford: Stanford University Press, 1995.
Derrida, Jacques. 'Living On'. Translated by James Hulbert. In Harold Bloom, Paul de Man, et al., *Deconstruction and Criticism*, 75–176. New York: The Seabury Press, 1979.
Derrida, Jacques. *Memoires for Paul de Man*, revised edn. Translated by Cecile Lindsay, Jonathan Culler, Eduardo Cadava and Peggy Kamuf. New York: Columbia University Press, 1989.
Derrida, Jacques. *Of Grammatology*. Translated by Gayatri Chakravorti Spivak. Baltimore and London: John Hopkins University Press, 1997.
Derrida, Jacques. *The Beast and the Sovereign*, vol. 1. Edited by Michel Lisse, Marie-Louise Mallet, and Ginette Michaud and translated by Geoffrey Bennington. Chicago and London: University of Chicago Press, 2009.
Derrida, Jacques. *The Beast and the Sovereign*, vol. 2. Edited by Michel Lisse, Marie-Louise Mallet, and Ginette Michaud and translated by Geoffrey Bennington. Chicago and London: University of Chicago Press, 2011.
Derrida, Jacques. *The Death Penalty*, vol. 1. Edited by Geoffrey Bennington, Marc Crépon, and Thomas Dutoit, and translated by Peggy Kamuf. Chicago and London: Chicago University Press, 2014.
Derrida, Jacques. *The Death Penalty*, vol. 2. Edited by Geoffrey Bennington and Peggy Kamuf and translated by Elizabeth Rottenburg. Chicago and London: The University of Chicago Press, 2017.
Derrida, Jacques. *The Ear of the Other: Otobiography, Transference, Translation*. Edited by Christie V. McDonald and translated by Peggy Kamuf. New York: Schocken Books, 1985.
Derrida, Jacques. *The Gift of Death*. Translated by David Wills. Chicago and London: The University of Chicago Press, 1995.
Derrida, Jacques and Peter Eisenman. *Chora L Works*. Edited by Jeffrey Kipnis and Leeser Thomas. New York: Monacelli Press, 1997.
Derrida, Jacques and Jean-Luc Nancy. '"Eating Well," or the Calculation of the Subject: An Interview with Jacques Derrida'. Translated by Peter Connor and Avital Ronnell. In *Who Comes After The Subject?*, edited by Eduardo Cadava, Peter Connor and Jean-Luc Nancy, 96–119. New York and London: Routledge, 1991.
Derrida, Jacques and Elisabeth Roudinesco. *For What Tomorrow . . . A Dialogue*. Translated by Jeff Fort. Stanford: Stanford University Press, 2004.
Dickens, Charles. *A Tale of Two Cities*. London: Penguin Books, 2003.

Dillon, Michael and Paul Fletcher. 'Real Time: The Instant of My Death'. *Journal for Cultural Research* 12, no. 4 (2008): 389–402.

Donne, John. 'Meditation 17'. In *Devotions Upon Emergent Occasions Together with Death's Duell*, edited by John Sparrow, 96–102. Cambridge: Cambridge University Press, 1923.

Dorfman, Eran. 'Everyday Life between Boredom and Fatigue'. In *Boredom Studies Reader: Frameworks and Perspectives*, edited by Michael E. Gardiner and Julian Jason Haladyn, 180–92. London and New York: Routledge, 2017.

Dostoevsky, Fyodor. *The Idiot*. Translated by Constance Garnett. Hertfordshire: Wordsworth Classics, 2010.

Ebury, Katherine. *Modern Literature and the Death Penalty, 1890–1950*. London: Palgrave Macmillan, 2021.

Eliot, T. S. 'The Hollow Men'. In *T. S. Eliot: Collected Poems, 1909–1962*, 79–82. London: Faber and Faber, 2002.

Empiricus, Sextus. *Outlines of Scepticism*. Edited by Julia Annas and Jonathan Barnes. Cambridge and New York: Cambridge University Press, 2007.

Epictetus. 'On "Indifference"'. In *Discourses and Selected Writings*, edited and translated by Robert Dobbin, 89–91. London: Penguin Books, 2008.

Fenton, James. 'A Poke in the Eye with a Poem'. In *The Guardian*, 21 October 2006, https://www.theguardian.com/books/2006/oct/21/featuresreviews.guardianreview6.

Forster, E. M. *A Room With A View*. London: Penguin Books, 1990.

Foucault, Michel. *Discipline and Punish: The Birth of the Prison*. Translated by Alan Sheridan. New York: Vintage Books, 1995.

Foucault, Michel. 'Of Other Spaces: Utopias and Heterotopias'. Translated by Jay Miskoviec. *Architecture/Mouvement/Continuité* 5 (1984): 1–9.

Foucault, Michel. 'Right of Death and Power over Life'. In *The History of Sexuality*, vol. 1, translated by Robert Hurley, 135–59. New York: Pantheon Books, 1990.

Foucault, Michel. *Society Must Be Defended: Lectures at the Collège de France, 1975–1976*. Edited by Mauro Bertani and Alessandro Fontana and translated by David Macey. London and New York: Allen Lane, The Penguin Press, 2003.

Foucault, Michel and Pierre Dumayet. 'Michel Foucault à propos du livre "Les mots et les choses"'. online video recording, *Institut National de l'Audiovisuel*, 15 June 1966, accessed 2 July 2022, https://www.ina.fr/video/i05059752/michel-foucault-a-propos-du-livre-les-mots-et-les--video.html.

Freud, Sigmund. 'Our Attitude towards Death'. In *The Standard Edition of the Complete Psychological Works of Sigmund Freud, Vol. XIV (1914-1916)*, edited and translated by James Strachey, Anna Freud, Alix Strachey, and Alan Tyson, 289–300. London: Vintage, 2001.

Fynsk, Christopher. 'Compassion for Suffering Humanity: *The Instant of My Death*'. In *Last Steps – Maurice Blanchot's Exilic Writing*, 109–21. New York: Fordham University Press, 2013.

Gillan, Garth and Emmanuel Levinas. 'About Blanchot: An Interview'. *SubStance* 5, no. 14 (1976): 54–7.

Gourgouris, Stathis. *Does Literature Think? Literature as Theory for an Antimythical Era*. Stanford: Stanford University Press, 2003.

Greene, Graham. *The Tenth Man*. New York: Washington Square Press, 1998.

Greene, Graham. 'The Third Man'. In *The Third Man and The Fallen Idol*, 13–120. London: Vintage, 2001.

Grose, Francis. *1811 Dictionary of the Vulgar Tongue: A Dictionary of Buckish Slang, University Wit, and Pickpocket Eloquence*, 1811, accessed 2 July 2022, http://www.gutenberg.org/cache/epub/5402/pg5402-images.html.

Gržinić, Marina and Šefik Tatlić. *Necropolitics, Racialization, and Global Capitalism: Historicization of Biopolitics and Forensics of Politics, Art, and Life*. Lanham: Lexington Books, 2014.

Guenther, Lisa. 'An Abolitionism Worthy of the Name: From the Death Penalty to the Prison Industrial Context'. In *Deconstructing the Death Penalty: Derrida's Seminars and the New Abolitionism*, edited by Kelly Oliver and Stephanie M. Straub, 239–57. New York: Fordham University Press, 2018.

Guest, David. *Sentenced to Death: The American Novel and Capital Punishment*. Jackson: University Press of Mississippi, 1997.

Hahn, Wilhelm Traugott. 'Das Mitsterben und Mitauferstehen mit Christus bei Paulus: Ein Beitrag zum Problem der Gleichzeitigkeit des Christen mit Christus', 1937, https://ia600502.us.archive.org/0/items/MN41529ucmf_0/MN41529ucmf_0.pdf.

Haladyn, Julian Jason and Michael E. Gardiner. 'Momentous Splendour: An Introduction to Boredom Studies'. In *Boredom Studies Reader: Frameworks and Perspectives*, edited by Michael E. Gardiner and Julian Jason Haladyn, 3–17. London and New York: Routledge, 2017.

Heaney, Seamus. 'The Tollund Man'. In *Opened Ground – Poems 1966-1996*, 64–5. London: Faber & Faber, 1998.

Hegel, Georg Wilhelm Friedrich. *Aesthetics: Lectures on Fine Art*, vol. 1. Translated by T. M. Knox. Oxford: Oxford University Press, 1975.

Hegel, Georg Wilhelm Friedrich. *Phenomenology of Spirit*. Translated by A. V. Miller. Oxford: Oxford University Press, 2004.

Hegel, Georg Wilhelm Friedrich. *Vorlesungen über die Geschichte der Philosophie I*, volume 18 in der Suhrkamp Taschenbuch Wissenschaft. Berlin: Suhrkamp Verlag, 1986.

Heidegger, Martin. 'Author's Notes'. In *Being and Time*, translated by John Macquarrie and Edward Robinson, 489–501. New York and London: Harper and Row, 2008.

Heidegger, Martin. *Being and Time*. Translated by John Macquarrie and Edward Robinson. New York and London: Harper and Row, 2008.

Heidegger, Martin. *Gesamtausgabe: Reden und andere Zeugnisse eines Lebenswegs*, vol. 19. Frankfurt am Main: Klostermann, 2000.

Heidegger, Martin. *Introduction to Metaphysics*. Translated by Gregory Fried and Richard Polt. New Haven and London: Yale University Press, 2000.

Heidegger, Martin. *The Fundamental Concepts of Metaphysics: World, Finitude, Solitude*. Translated by William McNeil and Nicholas Walker. Bloomington and Indianapolis: Indiana University Press, 1995.

Herzog, Werner, dir. *Into the Abyss: A Tale of Death, a Tale of Life*. IFC Films, 2011.

Herzog, Werner, dir. *On Death Row*. Aired 2012-2013 on Channel 4.

Hill, Leslie. '"Not In Our Name": Blanchot, Politics, the Neuter'. *Paragraph* 30, no. 3 (2007): 141-59.

Hobbes, Thomas. *Leviathan*. Edited by J. C. A. Gaskin. Oxford and New York: Oxford University Press, 2008.

Hoffman, E. T. A. *The Devil's Elixirs*. Translated by Ian Sumter. Surrey: Grosvenor House, 2007.

Holinshed, Raphael. *Holinshed's Chronicles: The Historie of England Bookes 1-IV*. Oxford: Benediction Classics, 2012.

Howells, Christina. 'The Death Penalty and Its Exceptions'. In *Deconstructing the Death Penalty: Derrida's Seminars and the New Abolitionism*, edited by Kelly Oliver and Stephanie M. Straub, 87-98. New York: Fordham University Press, 2018.

Hugo, Victor. 'Preface'. In *The Last Day of a Condemned Man*, translated by Geoff Woollen, 3-24. London: Hesperus Press Limited, 2002.

Hugo, Victor. *The Last Day of a Condemned Man*. Translated by Geoff Woollen. London: Hesperus Press Limited, 2002.

Hugo, Victor. *The Man Who Laughs*. Auckland: Floating Press, 2011.

Hyppolite, Jean. *Genesis and Structure of Hegel's 'Phenomenology of Spirit'*. Translated by S. Cherniak and J. Heckman. Evanston: Northwestern University Press, 1974.

Ionescu, Arleen, William Large, and Laura Marin. 'Introduction: Blanchot's Spaces'. *Word and Text* 5, no. 1-2 (2015): 5-16.

Irigaray, Luce. *Speculum of the Other Woman*. Translated by Gillian C. Hill. Ithaca: Cornell University Press, 1985.

Jagentowicz Mills, Patricia. 'Hegel's *Antigone*'. In *The Phenomenology of Spirit Reader*, edited by Jon Stewart, 243-71. Albany: State University of New York Press, 1998.

Johnson, Michael. 'Fifteen Years and Death: Double Jeopardy, Multiple Punishments, and Extended Stays on Death Row'. *Boston University Public Interest Law Journal* 23, no. 1 (2014): 85-116.

Joris, Pierre. 'Translator's Preface'. In Maurice Blanchot, *The Unavowable Community*, transated by Pierre Joris, xi-xxv. Barrytown: Station Hill Press, 1998.

Kafka, Franz. 'In the Penal Colony'. Translated by Willa and Edwin Muir. In *The Complete Short Stories of Franz Kafka*, edited by Nahum N. Glatzer, 140-67. London: Vintage, 2005.

Kamuf, Peggy. *Literature and the Remains of the Death Penalty*. New York: Fordham University Press, 2019.

Kang, Han. *The Vegetarian*. Translated by Deborah Smith. London: Portobello Books, 2015.
Kant, Immanuel. *Anthropology from a Pragmatic Point of View*. Edited and translated by Robert B. Lauden. Cambridge: Cambridge University Press, 2006.
Kant, Immanuel. 'Conjectures on the Beginning of Human History'. In *An Answer to the Question: What is Enlightenment?*, translated by H. B. Nisbet, 87–105. London and New York: Penguin Books, 2009.
Kant, Immanuel. *Groundwork of the Metaphysics of Morals*. Edited and translated by Mary Gregor. Cambridge: Cambridge University Press, 2006.
Kant, Immanuel. *Lectures on Ethics*. Edited by Peter Heath and J. B. Schneewind and translated by Peter Heath. Cambridge: Cambridge University Press, 1997.
Kant, Immanuel. *The Metaphysic of Ethics*. Translated by J. W. Semple. Edinburgh: T. & T. Clark, 1836.
Kant, Immanuel. *The Metaphysics of Morals*. Translated by Mary Gregor. Cambridge: Cambridge University Press, 1991.
Kantorowicz, Ernst H. *The King's Two Bodies: A Study in Mediaeval Political Theology*. Princeton: Princeton University Press, 1985.
Kavanagh, Preston and Simo Parpola. *Ezekiel to Jesus: Son of Man to Suffering Servant*. Eugene: Wipf & Stock, 2017.
Kim, Jungah. 'Ethical Complexities in Reading and Writing Autobiography: Thinking the Humanity of Others in the Instant of My Death'. *Life Writing* 9, no. 1 (2012): 97–110.
Kletzer, Christoph. 'Alexandre Kojève's Hegelianism and the Formation of Europe'. In *Cambridge Yearbook of European Legal Studies, Vol. 8, 2005-2006*, edited by John Bell and Claire Kilpatrick, 133–51. Oxford: Hart Publishing, 2006.
Kojève, Alexandre. 'Hegel, Marx and Christianity'. Translated by Hilail Gildin. *Interpretation* 1, no. 1 (1970): 21–42.
Kojève, Alexandre. *Introduction to the Reading of Hegel: Lectures on the Phenomenology of Spirit*. Edited by Allan Bloom and translated by James H. Nichols, Jr. Ithaca and London: Cornell University Press, 1980.
Kozlova, Svetlana. 'The Utopia of Truth and the Gnoseology of the Severed Head in *Invitation to a Beheading*'. Translated by Vladimir Talmy. *Russian Studies in Literature* 37, no. 3 (2001): 6–17.
Kristeva, Julia. 'On the Inviolability of Human Life'. Translated by Lisa Walsh. In *Death and Other Penalties: Philosophy in a Time of Mass Incarceration*, edited by Geoffrey Adelsberg, Lisa Guenther, and Scott Zeman, 130–7. New York: Fordham University Press, 2015.
Lacan, Jacques. *The Ethics of Psychoanalysis, 1959–1960*. Edited by Jacques-Allain Miller and translated by Dennis Porter. New York: W.W. Norton & Company, 1992.
Lambert, W. G. 'A Part of the Ritual for the Substitute King'. *Archiv für Orientforschung* 18, (1957–1958): 109–12.
Land, Stephen K. *The Human Imperative: A Study of the Novels of Graham Greene*. New York: AMS Press, 2008.

Lane, Warren J. and Ann M. Lane. 'The Politics of *Antigone*'. In *Greek Tragedy and Political Theory*, edited by J. Peter Euben, 162–82. Berkeley: University of California Press, 1986.

Law, Jonathan, ed. *A Dictionary of Law*, 8th edn. Oxford: Oxford University Press, 2015.

Levinas, Emmanuel. 'Bad Conscience and the Inexorable'. In *Face to Face with Levinas*, edited by Richard Cohen, 35–40. Albany: SUNY Press, 1986.

Levinas, Emmanuel. *De l'évasion*. Montpellier: Fata Morgana, 1982.

Levinas, Emmanuel. 'Diachrony and Representation'. In Emmanuel Levinas, *Time and the Other, and Additional Essays*, translated by Richard A. Cohen, 97–120. Pittsburgh: Duquesne University Press, 2011.

Levinas, Emmanuel. *Difficult Freedom: Essays on Judaism*. Translated by Seán Hand. Baltimore: John Hopkins University Press, 1990.

Levinas, Emmanuel. 'Dying For . . .'. In Emmanuel Levinas, *Entre Nous*, translated by Michael B. Smith and Barbara Harshav, 207–18. New York: Columbia University Press, 1998.

Levinas, Emmanuel. *Ethics and Infinity: Conversations with Philippe Nemo*. Translated by Richard A. Cohen. Pittsburgh: Duquesne University Press, 1985.

Levinas, Emmanuel. *Existence and Existents*. Translated by Alphonso Lingis. Pittsburgh: Duquesne University Press, 2014.

Levinas, Emmanuel. *God, Death, and Time*. Edited by Jacques Rolland and translated by Bettina Bergo. Stanford: Stanford University Press, 2000.

Levinas, Emmanuel. 'On Maurice Blanchot'. In *Proper Names*, translated by Michael B. Smith, 127–70. Stanford: Stanford University Press, 1996.

Levinas, Emmanuel. *Otherwise Than Being, or Beyond Essence*. Translated by Alphonso Lingis. Pittsburgh: Duquesne University Press, 2011.

Levinas, Emmanuel. 'Preface'. In *Time and the Other, and Additional Essays*, translated by Richard A. Cohen, 29–37. Pittsburgh: Duquesne University Press, 2011.

Levinas, Emmanuel. 'Time and the Other'. In *Time and the Other, and Additional Essays*, translated by Richard A. Cohen, 39–94. Pittsburgh: Duquesne University Press, 2011.

Levinas, Emmanuel. *Totality and Infinity*. Translated by Alphonso Lingis. Pittsburgh: Duquesne University Press, 2012.

Levinas, Emmanuel. 'Toward the Other'. In *Nine Talmudic Readings*, translated by Annette Aronowicz, 12–29. Bloomington: Indiana University Press, 1990.

Levinas, Michaël and Sarah Hammerschlag. 'The Final Meeting between Emmanuel Levinas and Maurice Blanchot'. *Critical Inquiry* 36, no. 4 (2010): 649–51.

Lukács, Georg. *The Historical Novel*. Translated by Hannah and Stanley Mitchell. Boston: Beacon Press, 1963.

Macquarrie, John and Edward Robinson. 'Translator's Preface'. In *Being and Time*, translated by John Macquarrie and Edward Robinson, xiii–xvi. New York and London: Harper and Row, 2008.

Mailer, Norman. *The Executioner's Song*. New York and Boston: Grand Central Publishing, 2012.

Malabou, Catherine. *The Future of Hegel: Plasticity, Temporality and Dialectic*. Translated by Lisabeth During. Oxon and New York: Routledge, 2005.

Malraux, André. *Lazarus*. Translated by Terence Kilmartin. New York: Grove Press, 1978.

Marder, Elissa. 'Figures of Interest: The Widow, the Telephone, and the Time of Death'. In *Deconstructing the Death Penalty: Derrida's Seminars and the New Abolitionism*, edited by Kelly Oliver and Stephanie M. Straub, 175–85. New York: Fordham University Press, 2018.

Marinella, Mark A. 'On the Hippocratic Facies'. *Journal of Clinical Oncology* 26, no. 21 (2008): 3638–40.

Massie, Pascal. 'The Secret and the Neuter: On Heidegger and Blanchot'. *Research in Phenomenology* 37 (2007): 32–55.

Maxwell, Richard. 'Appendix I-IV'. In Charles Dickens, *A Tale of Two Cities*, 391–447. London: Penguin Books, 2003.

Maxwell, Richard. 'Introduction'. In Charles Dickens, *A Tale of Two Cities*, ix–xxxiii. London: Penguin Books, 2003.

Mbembe, Achille. 'Necropolitics'. Translated by Libby Meintjes. *Public Culture* 15, no. 1 (2003): 11–40.

Mbembe, Achille. *Necropolitics*. Translated by Steven Corcoran. Durham and London: Duke University Press, 2019.

Mbembe, Achille. *On The Postcolony*. Translated by A. M. Berrett, Janet Roitman, Murray Last and Steven Rendall. Berkely: University of California Press, 2001.

Mbembe, Achille. 'On The Postcolony: A Brief Response to Critics'. *African Identities* 4, no. 2 (2006): 143–78.

McNeil, William and Nicholas Walker. 'Translators' Foreword'. In Martin Heidegger, *The Fundamental Concepts of Metaphysics: World, Finitude, Solitude*, translated by William McNeil and Nicholas Walker, xix–xxi. Bloomington and Indianapolis: Indiana University Press, 1995.

Melville, Herman. 'Bartleby, the Scrivener: A Story of Wall Street'. In *Melville's Short Novels*, edited by Dan McCann, 3–34. New York: Norton, 2002.

Mercier, Louis-Sébastien, *Tableau de Paris*, vol. 3. Neuchâtel, 1781–1788, accessed July 2, 2022, https://archive.org/stream/tableaudeparisv00mercgoog#page/n298/mode/2up.

Michaud, Ginette. 'Literature in Secret: Crossing Derrida and Blanchot'. Translated by Pamela Lipson, Patrick Poirier and Roger Starling. *Angelaki* 7, no. 2 (2002): 69–90.

Miller, Paul Allen. 'Lacan's Antigone: The Sublime Object and the Ethics of Interpretation'. *Phoenix* 61, no. 1–2 (2007): 1–14.

Moore, Billy Neal. *I Shall Not Die: Seventy-two Hours on Death Watch*. Bloomington: AuthorHouse, 2005.

Morisi, Ève. *Capital Letters: Hugo, Baudelaire, Camus, and the Death Penalty*. Evanston: Northwestern University Press, 2020.

Morisi, Ève. 'Introduction: Capital Literature'. In *Death Sentences: Literature and State Killing*, edited by Birte Christ and Ève Morisi, 1–10. Cambridge: Legenda, 2019.

Morson, Gary Saul. *Narrative and Freedom: The Shadows of Time*. New Haven and London: Yale University Press, 1994.

Muldoon, Paul. *Horse Latitudes*. London: Faber & Faber Ltd., 2006.

Murray, Stuart J. 'Thanatopolitics: On the Use of Death for Mobilizing Political Life'. *Polygraph* 18 (2006): 191–215.

Murray, Stuart J. 'Thanatopolitics: Reading in Agamben a Rejoinder o Biopolitical Life'. *Communication and Critical/Cultural Studies* 5, no. 2 (2008): 203–7.

N'Shea, Omar. 'Dressed to Dazzle, Dressed to Kill: Staging Ashurbanipal in the Royal Hunt Reliefs from Nineveh'. In *Fashioned Selves: Dress and Identity in Antiquity*, edited by Megan Cifarelli, 175–84. Oxford: Oxbow, 2019.

Nabokov, Vladimir. *Ada or Ardor: A Family Chronicle*. New York: McGraw-Hill, 1969.

Nabokov, Vladimir. *Invitation to a Beheading*. Translated by Dmitri Nabokov and Vladimir Nabokov. London: Penguin Classics, 2016.

Nail, Thomas. 'What is an Assemblage?' *SubStance* 46, no. 1 (2017): 21–37.

Nancy, Jean-Luc. 'Introduction'. In *Who Comes After The Subject?*, edited by Eduardo Cadava, Peter Connor, and Jean-Luc Nancy, 1–8. New York and London: Routledge, 1991.

Nancy, Jean-Luc. *The Truth of Democracy*. Translated by Michael Naas and Pascale-Anne Brault. New York: Fordham University Press, 2010.

Nietzsche, Friedrich. 'The Birth of Tragedy'. In *The Birth of Tragedy and Other Writings*, edited by Raymond Guess and Ronald Speirs and translated by Ronald Speirs, 1–116. Cambridge: Cambridge University Press, 2007.

Noys, Benjamin. *Georges Bataille – A Critical Introduction*. London: Pluto Press, 2000.

Oliver, Kelly. 'Making Death a Penalty: Or, Making "Good" Death a "Good" Penalty'. In *Death and Other Penalties: Philosophy in a Time of Mass Incarceration*, edited by Geoffrey Adelsberg, Lisa Guenther, and Scott Zeman, 95–105. New York: Fordham University Press, 2015.

Oliver, Kelly and Stephanie M. Straub, eds. *Deconstructing the Death Penalty: Derrida's Seminars and the New Abolitionism*. New York: Fordham University Press, 2018.

Orwell, George. 'A Hanging'. In *Why I Write*, 95–101. London: Penguin, 2004..

Ovid. 'Narcissus'. In *Metamorphoses*, translated and edited by Charles Martin, 77–80. New York and London: Norton, 2009.

Ovid. 'The Story of Narcissus'. In *Metamorphoses*, translated by Sir Samuel Garth, John Dryden et al., 1727. Accessed 2 July 2022, http://classics.mit.edu/Ovid/metam.3.third.html.

Pattison, George. *Heidegger on Death: A Critical Theological Essay*. Surry: Ashgate Publishing Ltd., 2013.

Paulhan, Jean. *The Flowers of Tarbes, or, Terror in Literature*. Translated by Michael Syrotinski. Urbana and Chicago: University of Illinois Press, 2006.

Peeters, Benoît. 'A Period of Withdrawal: 1968'. In *Derrida: A Biography*, translated by Andrew Brown, 186–206. Cambridge and Maiden: Polity Press, 2013.
Peterson, Dale. 'Nabokov's *Invitation*: Literature as Execution'. In *Nabokov's Invitation to a Beheading: A Critical Companion*, edited by Julian W. Connolly, 66–92. Evanston: Northwestern University Press, 1997.
Plato. *The Dialogues of Plato*, vol. 1, 4th edn, edited and translated by B. Jowett. Oxford: Clarendon Press, 1953.
Plato. *The Republic of Plato*, edited and translated by Francis MacDonald Cornford. London: Oxford University Press, 1945.
Plato. 'Timaeus'. In *Gorgias and Timaeus*, edited by Tom Crawford and translated by B. Jowett, 188–249. Mineola: Dover Publications, 2003.
Porter, James I. 'The Death Masque of Socrates: Nabokov's *Invitation to a Beheading*'. *International Journal of Classical Tradition* 17, no. 3 (2010): 389–422.
Prejean, Sister Helen. *Dead Man Walking: The Eyewitness Account of the Death Penalty That Sparked a National Debate*. New York: Vintage Books, 1994.
Price, Janet and Ruth Gould. 'Experience and Performance whilst Living with Disability and Dying: Disability Art as a Pathway to Flourishing'. In *On the Feminist Philosophy of Gillian Howie: Materialism and Mortality*, edited by Victoria Browne and Daniel Whistler, 267–83. London and New York: Bloomsbury Academic, 2016.
Purves, Libby. 'Foreword'. In Victor Hugo, *The Last Day of a Condemned Man*, translated by Geoff Woollen, vi–xiv. London: Hesperus Press Limited, 2002.
Reale, Giovanni. *A History of Ancient Philosophy III: Systems of the Hellenistic Age*. Edited and translated by John R. Catan. Albany: SUNY Press, 1985.
Regan, Tom. 'Broadie and Pybus on Kant'. *Philosophy* 51, no. 198 (1976): 471–2.
Roche, Mark William. *Tragedy and Comedy: A Systematic Study and Critique of Hegel*. Albany: State University of New York Press, 1998.
Rossi, Richard M. *Waiting to Die: Life on Death Row*. Harrisonburg: Vision, 2004.
Rundle, Bede. *Grammar in Philosophy*. Oxford: Clarendon Press, 1979.
Ruttenburg, Nancy. '"Why is this man alive?": The Unconsummated Conversion'. In *Dostoevsky's Democracy*, 31–41. Princeton: Princeton University Press, 2010.
Sahni, Vaibhav. 'The Lazarus Phenomenon'. *Journal of the Royal Society of Medicine* 7, no. 8 (2016): 1–6.
Sakhi, Shokoufeh. 'Prison and the Subject of Resistance: A Levinasian Inquiry'. In *Death and Other Penalties: Philosophy in a Time of Mass Incarceration*, edited by Geoffrey Adelsberg, Lisa Guenther, and Scott Zeman, 150–65. New York: Fordham University Press, 2015.
Sanders, Andrew. *The Victorian Historical Novel*. London: MacMillan, 1978.
Sartre, Jean-Paul. *Being and Nothingness*. Translated by Hazel E. Barnes. Oxon: Routledge Classics, 2005.
Sartre, Jean-Paul. *Existentialism is a Humanism*. London: Methuen, 1960.
Sartre, Jean-Paul. *Nausea*. Translated by Lloyd Alexander. New York: New Directions, 2013.

Sartre, Jean-Paul. 'No Exit'. In *No Exit and Three Other Plays*, 1–46. New York: Vintage International, 1989.

Sartre, Jean-Paul. 'The Wall'. In *Intimacy*, translated by Lloyd Alexander, 49–74. London: Panther Books, 1968.

Schmitt, Carl. *Political Theology: Four Chapters on the Concept of Sovereignty*. Translated by George Schwab. London and Chicago: University of Chicago Press, 1985.

Schmitt, Carl. 'The Age of Neutralizations and Depoliticizations'. Translated by Matthias Konzen and John P. McCormick. In *The Concept of the Political – Expanded Edition*, translated by George Schwab, 80–96. London and Chicago: University of Chicago Press, 2007.

Schmitt, Carl. 'The Concept of the Political'. Translated by George Schwab. In *The Concept of the Political – Expanded Edition*, translated by George Schwab, 19–79. London and Chicago: University of Chicago Press, 2007.

Schopenhauer, Arthur. *The World as Will and Idea*, vol. 3. Translated by R. B. Haldane and J. Kemp. London: Routledge and Kegan Paul, 1957.

Schwab, George. 'Introduction'. In Carl Schmitt, *Political Theology: Four Chapters on the Concept of Sovereignty*, translated by George Schwab, xxxvii–lii. London and Chicago: University of Chicago Press, 1985.

Shakespeare, William. *As You Like It*. Edited by Barbara A. Mowat and Paul Werstine. New York and London: Washington Square, 2004.

Shakespeare, William. *Macbeth*. Edited by Burton Raffel. New Haven and London: Yale University Press, 2005.

Shakespeare, William. *Othello*. Edited by Burton Raffel. New Haven and London: Yale University Press, 2005.

Shakespeare, William. *The Tragedy of Hamlet, Prince of Denmark*. Edited by Burton Raffel. New Haven and London: Yale University Press, 2003.

Shakespeare, William. *Twelfth Night*. Edited by R. S. White. New York: St. Martin's Press, 1996.

Shayegan, M. Rahim. *Aspects of History and Epic in Ancient Iran: From Gaumāta to Wahnām*. Washington: Center for Hellenic Studies, 2012.

Shelley, Mary. *Frankenstein; or The Modern Prometheus*. Hertfordshire: Wordsworth Classics, 1992.

Shelley, Percy Bysshe. 'The Triumph of Life'. In *Shelley's Poetry and Prose*, edited by Neil Fraistat and Donald H. Reiman, 481–500. New York and London: Norton, 2002.

Sherwood, Yvonne and John D. Caputo. 'Otobiographies, or How a Torn and Disembodied Ear Hears a Promise of Death [A Prearranged Meeting between Yvonne Sherwood and John D. Caputo and the Book of Amos and Jacques Derrida]'. In *Derrida and Religion: Other Testaments*, edited by Yvonne Sherwood and Kevin Hart, 209–39. New York and Oxon: Routledge, 2005.

Singer, Peter. *Practical Ethics*. Cambridge: Cambridge University Press, 2011.

Singh, Rustam. 'Not This, Not That: Maurice Blanchot and Poststructuralism'. *Comparative and Continental Philosophy* 8, no. 1 (2016): 72–82.

Skeat, Walter W. *The Concise Etymological Dictionary of the English Language*. London: Clarendon Press, 1887.

Skidmore, J. 'Duties to Animals: The Failure of Kant's Moral Theory'. *Journal of Value Inquiry* 35, no. 4 (2001): 541–59.

Soanes, Catherine and Angus Stevenson, eds. *Oxford English Dictionary*. Oxford: Oxford University Press, 2006.

Sophocles. 'Antigone'. In *Antigone, The Women of Trachis, Philoctetes, Oedipus at Colonus*, edited and translated by Hugh Lloyd-Jones, 1–127. Cambridge: Loeb Classical Library with Harvard University Press, 1998.

Stone, Alison. 'Natality and Mortality: Rethinking Death with Cavarero'. *Continental Philosophy Review* 43, no. 3 (2010): 353–72.

Stone, Alison. 'The Relationality of Death'. In *On the Feminist Philosophy of Gillian Howie: Materialism and Mortality*, edited by Victoria Browne and Daniel Whistler, 165–80. London and New York: Bloomsbury Academic, 2016.

Stranges, Douglas, Alan Lucerna, James Espinosa, et al. 'A Lazarus Effect: A Case Report of Bupropion Overdose Mimicking Brain Death'. *World Journal of Emergency Medicine* 9, no. 1 (2018): 67–9.

Straub, Stephanie M. 'Introduction. From Capital Punishment to Abolitionism: Deconstructing the Death Penalty'. In *Deconstructing the Death Penalty: Derrida's Seminars and the New Abolitionism*, edited by Kelly Oliver and Stephanie M. Straub, 1–9. New York: Fordham University Press, 2018.

Strong, Tracy B. 'Foreword'. In Carl Schmitt, *Political Theology: Four Chapters on the Concept of Sovereignty*, translated by George Schwab, vii–xxxvi. London and Chicago: University of Chicago Press, 1985.

Su Rasmussen, Kim. 'Foucault's Genealogy of Racism'. In *Theory, Culture & Society* 28, no. 5 (2011): 34–51.

Svendson, Lars. *A Philosophy of Boredom*. Translated by John Irons. London: Reaktion Books, 2008.

Sweeney, Kevin W. 'Lying to the Murderer: Sartre's Use of Kant in "The Wall"'. *Mosaic* 18, no. 2 (1985): 1–16.

Tarrant, Harrold. 'Justice and Duty (II): Socrates in Prison – Introduction to *Crito*'. In Plato, *The Last Days of Socrates: Euthyphro, Apology, Crito, Phaedo*, translated by Hugh Tredennick and Harrold Tarrant, 71–5. London: Penguin Books, 1993.

Taylor, Mark C. 'Ghost Stories'. In Mark C. Taylor and Christian Dietrich Lammerts, *Grave Matters*, 7–43. London: Reaktion Books Ltd., 2002.

Terada, Rei. 'Review'. *SubStance* 30, no. 3 (2001): 132–136.

Thomas, Dylan. 'Do Not Go Gentle into that Good Nigh'. In *Collected Poems 1934–1952*, 148. London: J.M. Dent & Sons, 1957.

Thoreau, Henry David. *Walden: A Fully Annotated Edition*. Edited by Jeffrey S. Cramer. New Haven and London: Yale University Press, 2004.

Toker, Leon. *Nabokov: The Mystery of Literary Structures*. Ithaca and London: Cornell University Press, 2016.

Tolstoy, Leo. 'Master and Man'. In *The Death of Ivan Ilyich and Other Stories*, translated by Alymer Maude and J. D. Duff, 235–87. New York: Signet Classic, 2003.

Tolstoy, Leo. 'The Death of Ivan Ilyich'. In *The Death of Ivan Ilyich and Other Stories*, translated by Alymer Maude and J. D. Duff, 93–152. New York: Signet Classic, 2003.

Torok, Maria. 'The Illness of Mourning and the Fantasy of the Exquisite Corpse'. In Nicolas Abraham and Maria Torok, *The Shell and the Kernel: Renewals of Psychoanalysis*, vol. 1, edited and translated by Nicholas T. Rand, 107–24. Chicago and London: University of Chicago Press, 1994.

Tréguer, Pascal. '"A Horse That Was Foaled of an Acorn": Meaning and Origin'. In *Word Histories*, 5 October 2016, https://wordhistories.net/2016/10/05/horse-foaled-of-an-acorn/.

Tyson, Sarah. 'The Heart of the Other?' In *Deconstructing the Death Penalty: Derrida's Seminars and the New Abolitionism*, edited by Kelly Oliver and Stephanie M. Straub, 226–38. New York: Fordham University Press, 2018.

Verderame, Lorenzo. 'Means of Substitution. The Use of Figurines, Animals, and Human beings as Substitutes in Assyrian Rituals'. *Rivista degli Studi Orientali* 86, Supplemento no. 2 (2013): 300–23.

Vernant, Jean-Pierre. 'The Historical Moment of Tragedy in Greece'. In Jean-Pierre Vernant and Pierre Nidal-Naquet, *Myth and Tragedy in Ancient Greece*, 23–8. Cambridge: Zone Books, 1990.

von Clausewitz, Carl. *On War*. Edited by Howard Michael and Peter Paret. Princeton: Princeton University Press, 1984.

Walton, John H. 'The Imagery of the Substitute King Ritual in Isaiah's Fourth Servant Song'. *Journal of Biblical Literature* 122, no. 4 (2003): 734–43.

Webb, Jonathan. 'Male Faces "buttressed" against Punches by Evolution'. In *BBC News*, 9 June 2014, accessed 2 July 2022, http://www.bbc.co.uk/news/science-environment-27720617.

Wild, John. 'Introduction'. In Emmanuel Levinas, *Totality and Infinity*, translated by Alphonso Lingis, 11–20. Pittsburgh: Duquesne University Press, 2012.

Wilde, Oscar. *The Picture of Dorian Gray*. Hertfordshire: Wordsworth Classics, 1995.

Wills, David. *Killing Times: The Temporal Technology of the Death Penalty*. New York: Fordham University Press, 2019.

Wocke, Brandon. 'Derrida at Villette: (An)aesthetic of Space'. *University of Toronto Quarterly* 83, no. 3 (2014): 739–55.

Wolfe, Cary. 'Introduction'. In *Zoontologies: The Question of the Animal*, edited by Cary Wolfe, ix–xxiii. Minneapolis and London: Minnesota University Press, 2003.

Woolf, Virginia. *Orlando: A Biography*. London and New York: Penguin Books, 2000.

Young, Julian. *Schopenhauer*. London and New York: Routledge, 2005.

Index

acknowledgement 81, 87–9, 96
Adelsberg, Geoffrey 14, 43, 172 n.34
Agamben, Giorgio 178 n.11
  on the death penalty 41, 141–3
  homo sacer 5–8, 15, 54, 137–47, 150, 196 n.60, 196 n.63, 197 n.66
  on ontology 143–4
  whatever being 117, 144–50, 155
alterity/the other 29–30, 44, 46, 50–61, 74, 77, 83–8, 92–7, 101–11, 117–18, 126, 128, 155, 166 n.23, 175 n.72, 185 n.1, 185 n.2, 187 n.21
  of death 2, 20
  as infinity 92, 101–2, 107, 110, 114, 123, 130, 134
  of the sovereign 40
angel/angelic 50, 95, 106–7
animal, the 12, 27, 37–9, 45, 116, 142–3, 145, 149, 153, 155, 169 n.6, 169.n.8, 169 n.11, 170 n.13, 196 n.66. *See also* horses
anonymity/namelessness 14, 103, 110–15, 121–3, 126, 130–3, 138–9, 141, 149, 196 n.60, 198 n.85
Antigone 17, 66–81, 94, 133, 148–9, 178 n.23, 179 n.24, 179 n.31, 179 n.34, 181 n.50, 182 n.58, 182 n.61, 182 n.63
assembly 11, 35, 94, 116, 118, 121–3, 146, 155, 190 n.77, 191 n.83
autothanatography 18, 23, 27, 59, 107, 114, 127–32, 135, 145, 158

Baillie, Joanna 11
ban 8, 66, 81, 87, 133, 138–46, 154
Bataille, Georges 7, 109, 137, 189 n.63, 196 n.59, 198 n.86
Benjamin, Walter 41–2, 71, 138, 181 n.43
biopolitics 4–8, 67, 140–2, 160 n.17, 161 n.28, 163 n.59, 181 n.55

Blanchot, Maurice 42, 46, 49, 153–6
  on death 63–4, 116, 126, 129, 132–4, 147, 156
  and Derrida 20–1, 24–5, 153
  on the fragment 134–5, 150, 156
  and Heidegger/ontology 31, 129, 147, 150, 153–5
  The Instant of My Death 14, 18–35, 37, 79–80, 82, 91, 109, 113–15, 127
  on language 11–12, 129–32, 137
  and Levinas 112–15, 129–32, 134
  on literature 11–14, 20, 129–37, 156
  on the neuter 12, 34–5, 129–37, 141, 147, 150 (*see also* neutrality)
  on sovereignty 136–7, 145–6
Bottéro, Jean 1–3, 30, 159 n.1, 167 n.33
Bradley, Arthur 9, 16, 73–4, 155, 163 n.59, 199 n.95
Brooks, Peter 128, 185 n.91
Butler, Judith 59, 69, 71, 74, 131, 179 n.34, 187 n.37

Callus, Ivan 127, 135
clothes 88–90, 93, 104, 117, 184 n.82, 191 n.84
Cochetti, Stefano 54
Cohen, Richard A. 95–6, 101, 107, 186 n.9, 188 n.48
Comay, Rebecca 76–7, 90, 182 n.61, 182 n.64
community 30, 35, 42, 90, 94, 102, 142, 145–50, 155–6, 198 n.87
Critchley, Simon 112–15, 131, 147, 190 n.72, 191 n.81

death
  in abeyance 24, 29, 32–3, 46, 62–6, 107, 114, 121–2, 140, 150 (*see also* limbo; waiting)
  certainty of 40–4, 60–1, 66, 68, 82, 85–6, 90, 105–8

dying in-stead/exchange of 2, 7, 10, 30–3, 53–4, 59, 81–90, 99–100, 104–6
and dying with 25–6, 29–33, 54–7, 60, 79–81, 87–8, 99–100
human 37–8, 157
instant of 22, 24, 32–3, 49, 59, 62–8, 77, 86, 91–2, 98, 133–4 (*see also* the instant)
as *Jemeinigkeit*/mineness of 19–21, 26, 31–2, 44, 46–60, 88–97, 106–10, 115, 121–3, 127, 129–36, 141, 146, 151, 153
and language/literature 2–3, 8, 11–13, 15, 20, 23, 44, 49, 114, 126–36, 143, 147, 150, 155, 158
penalty/condemnation to 4, 7, 13–17, 38–44, 48–9, 60–1, 63–9, 73–84, 89–95, 98–100, 103, 113, 125–6, 141–3, 148, 154
and philosophy 10–11, 104, 113
and politics 1–10, 15–16, 30–3, 41, 51, 67–81, 83, 87, 94, 137–50, 155–7 (*see also* necropolitics; thanatopolitics)
relationality of 2, 10, 16–17, 41, 44, 46–60, 63–6, 68, 77–97, 102, 104–10, 115, 117, 121–3, 128, 135, 141, 153–8
surviving of 2, 24, 30–2, 51, 60, 71, 91, 99–100, 125–6 (*see also* living on)
and time/time of 2, 15, 20, 22–5, 29, 31–3, 41–4, 46, 49–50, 57, 60–6, 73–8, 80, 82, 85–6, 89–94, 96–8, 104–8, 113–15, 121–2, 133–4, 153–4
de Beauvoir, Simone 56, 107
decomposition 18, 93–4, 97–9, 115, 120, 123, 147, 155, 188 n.40. *See also* unbecoming
demon/demonic 53–4, 85, 90, 95, 106–7, 189 n.58
Derrida, Jacques 151, 154
on the *arrivant* 34, 110, 124
and Blanchot 20–35, 42, 46, 153, 155
chora 18, 113–14, 117–18, 126, 155, 194 n.25, 198 n.84
on death 11, 22–35, 44, 49–54, 58–9, 98, 136, 154

on the death penalty 16, 26–32, 40–2, 44, 48, 71, 74, 100, 105, 152–3
and Heidegger 46, 48, 50–3, 59, 153
and Kant 40
and Levinas 53
on literature 12, 23, 27, 49, 132, 135
on mourning 58
on responsibility 52–3, 57, 90
on sovereignty 12, 44, 116, 148
on subjectivity 70, 106, 110, 126, 127, 136, 146, 148–9, 156
Dickens, Charles 84, 86
A Tale of Two Cities 84–6, 88, 91, 95, 117
Dillon and Fletcher 20, 25, 33
Donne, John 44, 56, 89
Dostoevsky, Fyodor 22, 41, 60
The Idiot 60–1, 63
double/doubling 83–4, 87–8, 91, 94, 98, 117–18, 123, 141, 180 n.41, 191 n.85

Ebury, Katherine 16, 24, 154, 163 n.60, 168 n.39, 169 n.6
epilogue/epilogic 18, 59, 131–2, 149, 158
ethics 18, 53, 57–8, 68, 70, 84–5, 90, 95–8, 101–3, 105, 110, 112, 121, 188 n.40. *See also* Levinas, Emmanuel, on ethics
exception, state of 3–9, 14–15, 32–3, 42–3, 51, 72–3, 106, 126–7, 136–44, 155, 174 n.62
execution 27–9, 118, 125, 129, 140–4, 157
histories of 11, 13, 40, 165 n.11, 166 n.17, 183 n.71

finitude 44, 64–6, 85, 92, 114, 136, 153, 186 n.8, 200 n.17
Foucault, Michel 4–9, 14, 65, 104, 133, 144, 148, 162 n.45, 171 n.22, 181 n.55, 199 n.97
Freud, Sigmund 58, 153, 159 n.3, 191 n.81, 196 n.63, 199 n.3
Fynsk, Christopher 26

Greene, Graham 182 n.67
The Tenth Man 17, 82–3, 91, 99, 117–18

Hamlet 18, 29, 108
Hegel, G. W. F. 5, 22, 79–80, 91–4, 178 n.15, 180 n.37, 196 n.59, 198 n.89
  history 70, 75–9, 90–1, 129
  Kampf auf Leben und Tod 69–73, 77–9, 83, 85, 87, 103–4, 116, 141
  work/habit 70, 75–9, 93–4, 98, 104, 112, 127, 134, 147
Heidegger, Martin 17, 44–62, 74, 84, 91, 94, 96, 115–16, 128–9, 141, 143, 146, 149, 153–4, 173 n.59, 187 n.18, 193 n.13, 195 n.51, 199 n.98
  being-towards-death 31, 44–51, 54–7, 60–5, 94, 111, 119, 128–9, 141, 153
  on boredom/*Langweile* 63–6, 79, 89–91, 107, 122, 200 n.17
Herzog, Werner 163 n.57
horses 19, 25–7, 37–9, 79–80. *See also* animal, the
Howells, Christina 43, 140, 152
Hugo 49, 86, 123
  Last Day of a Condemned Man 14–17, 86–9, 91, 93, 117, 139
human, the 2, 13, 16–17, 27, 37–9, 44–5, 56, 60, 63, 69, 85–7, 95–6, 102–3, 108, 151–8, 173 n.46, 195 n.51
  human society, sociality 6–7, 18, 42–3, 69, 71, 74, 90, 96–7, 100–5, 107, 112, 121, 128–9, 140, 144, 155
  human thing 4, 18, 69, 98–9, 103, 105, 109–10, 115–20, 123, 126–37, 140–50, 153, 155–8 (*see also* living dead; the thing)

immortality 31, 44, 48, 50–1, 62, 107–11, 114, 116, 120–1, 141, 153, 180 n.41, 190 n.74
indifference/passivity 10, 35, 71, 79, 133–4, 144–50, 155–6, 168 n.49, 200 n.10. *See also* resistance
instant, the 20–7, 32–3, 49, 59–60, 62–9, 77, 80, 86, 90–2, 94, 99, 107, 112–13, 122, 127, 132–4, 146, 154, 182 n.67
interruption 8–9, 24, 32–3, 44, 63, 66, 80–2, 90, 92, 96, 104–8, 134, 147, 154–5, 200 n.17

justice 13, 22, 31–4, 42, 76, 84, 96–7, 100, 102–3, 187 n.21

Kafka, Franz 14, 129, 156–8
Kamuf, Peggy 14–16, 28, 44, 156, 172 n.35
Kant, Immanuel 38–40, 42, 56, 60, 68, 100, 116, 142–3, 189 n.62
Kojève, Alexandre 70–5, 78, 98, 182 n.64

Lacan, Jacques 67–9, 97, 116, 159 n.3, 178 n.23, 179 n.34
language 8, 10, 12, 53, 57, 101–3, 123, 126, 128–32, 137, 141, 147, 156
law 13, 15, 31, 33, 38–9, 41–3, 66–7, 69, 82–3, 100, 103, 116, 134, 136–40, 144, 147–8, 163 n.57, 171 n.26, 171 n.27, 172 n.36, 179 n.35, 199 n.96
Lazarus 106, 125, 174 n.61
Levinas, Emmanuel 18, 95
  and Blanchot 34, 112–14, 129–34
  on death 53, 95–7, 107–9, 113, 123, 129–34, 153, 177 n.102
  and Derrida 53, 174 n.63
  on ethics 34–5, 53, 68, 81, 84, 95–7, 100–5, 110, 117, 121, 126, 146, 155 (*see also* ethics)
  and Heidegger 88, 111–12, 115, 173 n.59
  il y a 104, 110–23, 126–7, 130–1, 155
  on literature 12, 108
  on time 91, 94, 96–7, 108
limbo 63–6, 87, 91, 106, 122, 133, 142, 144, 154–5, 200 n.17. *See also* death, in abeyance; waiting
literature
  and death 2–3, 8, 10–12, 20, 37, 113, 129–36, 150, 158
  of the death penalty, academic 16, 152
  of the death penalty, fiction 14–15, 24, 35, 118, 152–4, 157–8
  of the death penalty, non-fiction 13–14
  and the death penalty 15, 17, 44, 49, 60, 104–5, 107, 113, 128, 135, 143, 150

living corpse/living dead   4, 7–10, 12, 15–17, 49, 67–9, 71–84, 86–7, 90, 93–4, 97–100, 104–5, 108, 111–13, 116–18, 120–1, 126, 128, 133, 135–6, 140–1, 144, 148, 151–4, 157, 179 n.31. *See also* human, the, human thing
living on   10, 29–31, 33, 46, 51, 54, 63–4, 68–9, 71, 79–82, 90, 93, 98–100, 105, 108–9, 121–3, 145, 154

Macbeth   27–8, 37, 167 n.30, 188 n.54
Malabou, Catherine   89–93, 98, 185 n.109
Mbembe, Achille   3–9, 14, 67, 71, 98
Morisi, Ève   14–16, 86, 154, 184 n.78, 192 n.95
Morson, Gary Saul   131–2
mortality   6, 18, 52–7, 76, 85, 90–2, 96, 102, 107, 114, 119–20, 122, 153
Murray, Stuart J.   8–9

Nabokov, Vladimir   118, 173 n.46
  Invitation to a Beheading   18, 110, 118–23, 126, 133, 145
Nancy, Jean Luc   74, 127, 159 n.3, 181 n.48
Narcissus/Narcissism   47–8, 54–5, 60–2, 64, 86, 90, 94, 96, 102, 112, 115, 173 n.59
necropolis   94, 102, 105–7, 109–10, 112–13, 121–4, 127–30, 140, 144, 147–8, 155
necropolitics   3–8, 147
neutrality   10, 12, 18, 34–5, 115, 129–37, 141, 146–9, 155, 194 n.24. *See also* Blanchot, Maurice, on the neuter

Oliver, Kelly   16, 66, 151, 193 n.1
ontology
  of death   2, 10, 24, 31, 44–56, 73–80, 86, 90, 93–9, 123, 132–4
  of the human self   9, 16–17, 93–4, 102, 121, 128, 132–4, 143–4, 150, 154 *See also* human, the, human thing
  limits of being, nonbeing/being without being   9, 18, 59, 65, 76–8, 86, 93–4, 103–4, 108–16, 119–23, 127–35, 143–4, 146–7, 153–5, 158, 189 n.63 *See also* limbo

Pattison, George   55–61
philosophy
  and death   10–11, 60, 103, 113
  and the death penalty   17, 48, 143
  and language/literature   11–12, 15, 113
Plato   10–11, 41, 45, 113, 118, 120–1
postsovereign   9, 16–18, 33, 35, 93, 124, 126, 136, 144–5, 149–50
psychoanalysis/psychology   13, 15, 17, 56, 58, 153–4, 163 n.57
punishment   3–4, 13, 39–40, 43, 49, 60, 78, 87, 100, 155, 172 n.34, 199 n.95, 200 n.17

race/racism   13–14, 163 n.59, 163 n.60
recognition   71–3, 75, 81, 87–9, 96, 118–19
religion   1–2, 13, 52, 58, 95–6, 101–2, 106–7, 133, 168 n.39, 174 n.62. *See also* theology
resistance   5, 8, 10, 18, 33, 77–9, 114, 146–7, 155–6, 181 n.54. *See also* indifference/passivity
revolution
  of the death penalty   89–92, 129, 141
  French   3–4, 17, 76–8, 84–7, 90–1, 96, 182 n.64, 183 n.69

sacrifice   14, 30, 46, 52–4, 68, 82–5, 90, 100–1, 137, 142–3, 196 n.59, 200 n.17
Sartre, Jean-Paul   57, 89, 97, 104, 109, 186 n.14
  'The Wall'   18, 98–100, 103–4, 109–10, 117, 123
Schmitt, Carl   3, 5–6, 8, 41, 67, 106, 137, 148–9, 174 n.62, 199 n.92
Schopenhauer, Arthur   39, 116, 176 n.94
sex   59, 117
Singh, Rustam   130, 134
sovereignty   1–10, 14–17, 38–44, 66–84, 87–9, 100, 106, 117, 133, 136–51
  and language/literature   12–16, 44, 136–7, 141, 143

limits of 7–10, 14–17, 24, 32–3, 62, 66–83, 89, 93, 105–6, 123–6, 133, 136–50, 154–5
Stone, Alison 55–61, 80, 131, 175 n.80
subjectivity 2, 57, 61–2, 66, 78–9, 82, 86–97, 101–4, 107–8, 110, 112–17, 121, 126–30, 133, 136–7, 147–9, 151, 153–4, 179 n.23, 185 n.95, 185 n.109, 196 n.59, 198 n.85
substitute king 1–3, 7, 18, 29–30, 38, 41, 73, 100, 137, 159 n.1, 167 n.33, 184 n.82

thanatopolitics 7–10, 24, 31, 51, 67, 73, 94, 105, 124, 140–1
theology 41–2, 45, 48, 50–4, 114, 146, 168 n.39, 174 n.62, 176 n.98, 185 n.95, 188 n.44. *See also* religion
thing, the 4, 18, 34, 38–40, 46, 70, 73, 79, 110–11, 115–16, 118, 120–3, 126, 129–37, 140–50, 155–6, 197 n.73, 200 n.17. *See also* human, the, human thing
third, the 32, 34, 38, 40–1, 44, 80–97, 101–6, 109–13, 119, 130–3, 141, 155, 157, 172 n.36, 185 n.95
Tolstoy, Leo 60

tragedy 68–70, 78, 103, 107–8, 115, 123, 133, 147–8, 156, 180 n.40
transgression 3, 7, 34, 67–9, 72, 74–5, 78–81, 87, 89, 140, 179 n.35, 198 n.85

unbecoming 97–9, 103, 105, 107, 108, 112–15, 135, 156. *See also* decomposition
unexperienced experience 22–4, 29–30, 60–2, 65, 71, 73, 80, 85–6, 98, 103, 112, 114–15, 133, 140, 154, 196 n.59
unworking 9, 11–12, 92, 127, 134, 146–8, 158

voice/polyphony 8, 18, 61, 126–8, 130–5, 147, 194 n.22

waiting 29, 34, 61–6, 80–1, 89, 100, 107. *See also* death, in abeyance; limbo
war 3, 5–7, 25, 27–8, 31–2, 54, 78–9, 82, 98
Wills, David 16, 65, 162 n.54, 164 n.60, 200 n.17

www.ingramcontent.com/pod-product-compliance
Lightning Source LLC
Chambersburg PA
CBHW071835300426
44116CB00009B/1547